✳

✳

✳

Books by H. Allen Smith

*A
Short
History
of
Fingers*

*

*

*

*

A
Short
History
of
Fingers

(AND OTHER STATE PAPERS)

****

H. Allen Smith

ILLUSTRATED BY LEO HERSHFIELD

Little, Brown and Company · Boston · Toronto

"A Short History of Fingers" and "Avery the Sinner" ("Luggageless Love") originally appeared in *Playboy*.

"The Water Pistol Caper" and "The Achievement of H. T. Wensel" originally appeared in "The Phoenix Nest," *Saturday Review*.

Portions of this volume first appeared in *The Reader's Digest*.

Published simultaneously in Canada
by Little, Brown & Company (Canada) Limited

PRINTED IN THE UNITED STATES OF AMERICA

This book is for (in the order of their appearance):

Donnell Van Noppen, III
Allen Van Noppen
Eric Dean Smith
David Smith
Mark Van Noppen
David Van Noppen
and
Sara Smith

✳

✳

✳

Contents

A
Short
History
of
Fingers

✱

✱

✱

✱

*

*

*

Public Notice

ON A SHELF across the room from my desk is a fat book of 1,577 pages called *Twentieth Century Authors: A Biographical Dictionary.* Beside it stands its first supplement, which runs to 1,123 pages. Often when I am prowling through those 2,700 pages, studying the life stories of the peculiar people who compose our fiction and history and plays and poetry, I encounter a person who is identified as a "miscellaneous writer." For a long time I was unable to puzzle out the precise meaning of that designation, but now I know the answer. I've discovered, in putting this book together, that I am a miscellaneous writer. Why? Because I'll tackle anything.

Most of the articles and stories contained herein have appeared in American magazines. *Miscellaneous* American magazines, ranging all the way from *Playboy* to *The Saturday Review* to the *Reader's Digest.* I wrote for the old *Saturday Evening Post* and I write for the new *Saturday Evening Post.* As a miscellaneous writer for these miscellaneous periodicals, I usually cast myself in the role of domestic philosopher, dedicated to the task of solving the problems that beset the average American in his search for equilibrium and intelligence in his day-by-day existence. I can do it, too. Yet it seems that the more of these problems I get settled, the more arise to confront me. Now at the end of my fifty-fifth year I find the human race being tortured by greater dilemmas than ever before in its history.

Fetridge's Law is causing some difficulty. Fools are scaling mountains in ever-increasing numbers. Flagrant discourtesy on our highways has achieved frightening proportions. Small Carolina boys are running amuck with water pistols at the ready. Heaven, it has been discovered, is somewhat hotter than Hell. People are not paying adequate attention to their marvelous fingers. They ignore their fingers and indulge in outbursts of unreasonable anger over such trivial matters as milk bottles, the Tahitian hula and low-numbered license plates. Woolgatherers are stumbling around the streets, confusing the issue and confusing one another. Flat feet have suddenly become desirable (but not in a sexual sense). Antiquarians are having trouble finding an apt name for the woofinwhiffle. Housewives and chambermaids defy all logic when they hang a roll of toilet paper on the wall. Gourmets are misbehaving. I tell you, *these* are the times that try men's souls.

Thus, just a few of the grave matters examined in this book. A few days ago I got a letter from a man in New York City who had paid money for my last book and then read it. He advised me that he was now willing to lay out more money, this time for a coil of rope, which he would gladly send me if I would use it to hang myself. Immediately. His is somewhat typical of the glowing fan mail I receive in a steady flow. I enjoy such little expressions of appreciation; they are all that keep me going. Under such gentle encouragement I drive ever onward, helping the race, helping humanity.

I confess to violating one of the basic rules prescribed for a book of this kind. The average author of magazine articles and short stories who puts a clutch of them together to make a book does the job by the stacking process and never touches his typewriter. He takes the magazine tear sheets and stacks them together, haphazardly and higgledy-piggledy, with no regard for organization, no attempt to correct anachronisms, or restore material cut out by magazine editors, or smooth out dumbhead sentences that slipped by in the original version. Three or four of these chapters have never been published anywhere. The others, for the most part, have been revised, amended, lengthened or shortened, refined, enriched, and henrymillered up a trifle. Good substantial vulgarisms have been reinstated. In this connection I would like to inform the reader, if he doesn't already know it, that I glory in vulgarity. The word itself comes from the Latin and has to do with The People. I write for The People, not The Shidepokes. And The People are vulgar, whether they know it or not.

Let us proceed, then, with . . .

*

*

*

1. Fetridge's Law Explained

OUR NOBEL Prize novelist John Steinbeck wrote not long ago of a transcontinental motor trip he undertook for the purpose of getting reacquainted with his native land. On a lonely road in Oregon he took down with car trouble and, describing his plight, he said: ". . . that ancient law went into effect which says that when you need towns they are very far apart." Somewhat later a critic remarked that Mr. Steinbeck had been a victim of Fetridge's Law.

This is not so. In the case of Mr. Steinbeck and the far-apart towns, Gumperson's Law was in operation. Gumperson's Law says that the vacant parking spaces are always on the other side of the street; that you can throw a stubbed-out cigarette from a car window and start a raging forest fire, whereas it'll take an hour and a half to get a blaze going in a fireplace loaded with dry wood and sloshed with kerosene; that grass seed planted in rich soil, fertilized and kept moist, will not grow, although a few seeds may blow onto the blacktop driveway, settle into a crack, and there take root and flourish. That is the law of Dr. Gumperson. It is a pseudoscientific statute that is in no way related to Parkinson's Law, which deals largely with personnel matters in the corporate world, or to Murphy's Law, known to missile men, which says that if anything can possibly go wrong, it will.

Gumperson's Law is related, however, to Fetridge's Law in the same way that the law concerning vehicular homicide is related to the statute covering first-degree murder. Mr.

Steinbeck's dilemma on the Oregon highway was a demonstration of Gumperson's Law at work. Fetridge's Law takes over at a later point. Suppose Mr. Steinbeck's vehicle developed a rattle, an unnerving, unending noise similar to a ratamacue on the drums. He is unable to locate this rattle himself, but it grows into a great botheration, and he plugs along the Oregon highway mile after mile until eventually he does come to a town, and a garage, and he turns in at the garage and instantly the rattle stops. The garage mechanic takes the car around the block and there is no rattle. He drives it outside the town and runs it over a bumpy country road. Not a whisper of that rattle. This is perhaps the most common form of perverse behavior resulting from the operation of Fetridge's Law. It is so reliable that whenever I get a rattle in my car I simply drive rapidly to the garage, turn in, back around, pause briefly so the car can sense the presence of a skilled mechanic, and then drive home — my difficulty is cleared up without my ever speaking to the garage people.

Gumperson's Law, first codified by the magazine *Changing Times*, has been wordily defined this way: the contradictory of a welcome probability will assert itself whenever such an eventuality is likely to be most frustrating or, in other words, the outcome of a given desired probability will be inverse to the degree of desirability. Fetridge's Law, in simple language, states that important things that are supposed to happen do not happen, especially when people are looking or, conversely, things that are supposed to *not* happen do happen, especially when people are looking. Thus a dog that will jump over a stick a thousand times a day for his owner will not jump over a stick when a neighbor is called in to watch; and a baby that will say "Dada" in the presence of its proud parents will, when friends are summoned, either clam up or screech like a jaybird.

Fetridge's Law takes its name from a radio engineer named Claude Fetridge, once in the employ of the National Broadcasting Company. This Mr. Fetridge, back in 1936, thought up the idea of broadcasting the flight of the famous swallows from Mission San Juan Capistrano in Southern California. As is well known, the swallows depart from the mission each year on October 23rd, which is St. John's Day, and return to the mission on March 19th, St. Joseph's Day. Claude Fetridge conceived the idea of broadcasting the whirr and flutter of eager wings of the departing swallows on October 23rd. NBC went to considerable effort and expense to set up its equipment and transport its crew to the mission. And with the entire nation waiting anxiously for this soul-stirring, mystical event, it was discovered that the swallows, out of sheer orneriness or because the devil had got to them, had taken their departure a day ahead of schedule. Thus did a flock of passerine birds of the family hirundinidae, eager to moult, lend a sort of immortality to a man named Claude Fetridge.

Television sets, of course, are often subject to the workings of Fetridge's Law. If a friend of mine tells me he is going to appear on a television show and asks me to watch it, I groan inwardly, knowing this is going to cost me money. The moment his show comes on the air my picture tube blows. Jackie Gleason was in my living room one evening and wanted to inspect a show he had taped a few days earlier. I flicked the switch and the sound went *zing, gugg, vump* and lightning flashed and the screen went dark, all of which I knew would happen. Another time, my set will begin flickering and flopping over and the screen will snow up or acquire the look of an old school tie. I turn it off and call the repair man. He travels three miles to my house and turns the set on and the picture emerges bright and clear, the contrast exactly right, a better picture than I've ever had before. It's that way always and forever, days without end.

For three years in a row my wife and I closed our house, which stands in the north intemperate zone, and sailed away to spend the winter months in warmer climes. Each time we returned our neighbors taunted us with the news that the winter had been wide open and warm, with very little snow.

So for the fourth winter we decided to stay home. From late November until March it was one long uninterrupted blizzard, the worst winter our neighborhood had experienced in thirty years. Fetridge's Law was at work in the field of meteorology.

I have a friend in Connecticut who put in a seven-

thousand-dollar swimming pool and then found it was impossible to use it after dusk because of mosquitoes swarming out of the nearby woods. He had a screened-in gazebo built and furnished it with electric lights and comfortable furniture and a little bar and a refrigerator. The moment the last nail was driven and the last basket chair set in its place, the mosquitoes disappeared from the premises and not a single one has been sighted since. Fetridge in action.

An attractive woman neighbor of mine is accustomed to driving her husband to the railroad station each morning. On rare occasions she has been late getting her backfield in motion, and hasn't had time to get dressed. These times she has thrown a coat over her nightgown and, wearing bedroom slippers, headed for the depot. Fetridge's Law always seems to give her trouble. Once she clashed fenders with another car on the highway and had to go to the police station in her night shift. Twice she has had motor trouble in the depot plaza requiring that she leave her car in robe and slippers and pin curlers. The last I heard she was considering sleeping in her street clothes.

There are thirty-two points to the compass, meaning that there are thirty-two directions in which a spoon can squirt grapefruit, yet a professor of chemistry named Louis Sattler has found that the juice almost invariably flies straight to the human eye. Professor Sattler is skipping around the fringes of the area in which Fetridge's Law prevails. He observes that buttered bread always falls to the floor with the buttered side down, that if you put on a freshly pressed suit it will surely rain, and that if you start to light your pipe with your last match, a stiff wind will spring up.

Fetridge's Law operates fiercely in the realm of dentistry. In my own case I have often noted that whenever I develop a raging toothache it is a Sunday and the dentists are all on the golf course. Not long ago my toothache hung on through the weekend and Monday morning it was still throbbing and pulsating like a diesel locomotive. I called my dentist and proclaimed an emergency and drove to his office and going up the stairway the ache suddenly vanished altogether. By the time I got into his chair I was confused and embarrassed and unable to tell him with certainty which tooth it was that had been killing me. The X-ray showed no shady spots, though it would have shown several if he had pointed the thing at my brain. Claude Fetridge's Law clearly has its good points. It can exasperate, but it can also cure a toothache.

*

*

*

2. *The Bright Side of Pessimism*

MEMBERS OF my family tell me that when I was a boy I had uncombed reddish hair and freckles, went barefooted all summer, and usually wore faded corduroy knickerbockers and a frayed blue shirt (known then, even among boys, as a waist). I must have presented just such a charming picture on that warm day when I saw my first shell game in a downtown park in Decatur, Illinois.

The fast-talking grifter was shifting the walnut shells around with eye-dazzling rapidity and then challenging the adult yokels to pick the shell with the pea beneath it. I had never seen a shell game in operation before. I knew nothing about the evil ways of the world and yet something caused me to pipe up in a shrill adolescent voice: "Maybe it ain't under none ubbem!" (That is the way I talked when I was a kid; that is the way I still talk).

A silence fell on the proceedings and the yentzer glared at me a long time and then delivered a loud public denunciation of me. "Ladies and genmun," he said, "this here boy you see before you, this here miserable little boy, he is gonna grow up to be a pessimist. He is already a pessimist and he will grow up to be a worse one. And if you didn't already know it, ladies and genmun, there is nothing on earth as low-down as a pessimist." I feel sure that nobody in that audience knew what a pessimist was. Certainly I did not. I can remember that when the pitchman first began directing his eloquence against me I felt a momentary glow, a warm sense of importance, but pretty soon I was cringing beneath his bitter tongue-lashing (you see the pea really *wasn't* under none ubbem) and I crept away from the scene, for the people were beginning to glare at me as if I were an anarchist with a bomb in my waist.

This experience remained strong in my memory and eventually I looked up the word pessimist to find out what I was. I do know that since that time I have been a pessimist in almost everything I do. For years I believed that the shell game man was responsible for my condition — that I was a pessimist because he had called me one at a time when I was impressionable. But now I know better. I don't necessarily want to be a pessimist; I never sat down and decided that I would be one. I'm pessimistic by nature; I believe that true cynicism and skepticism and pessimism are characteristics that are not studied and deliberate — they are bred deep in the bone. The person possessing them cannot help himself; it is the same as being a Socialist or a Barnburner or a Zen Buddhist or the Life of the Party.

The dictionary definition of pessimism which fits me best is: "The tendency to expect misfortune or the worst outcome in any circumstances; practice of looking on the dark side of things." It is as if the dictionary people were writing my biography.

I contend that I lead a much more sensible life, because of my pessimism, than I would otherwise. I even make so bold as to say that I lead a more sensible life than my optimistic neighbors. I am always and forever anticipating misfortune and disaster, large and small. I am continually amused by people who have "premonitions" about airplanes crashing with themselves or their loved ones aboard. We read in the newspapers that a man who was killed in a crash told his friends or his family before take-off that he had a strong premonition of tragedy. Or, one of his friends or a member of his family had the premonition. Even the newspapers hint that there is something truly supernatural about these affairs. But I know better. I'm quite sure in my own mind that there is no extrasensory perception involved. *Every goddamn time I climb into a plane I murmur a sad and silent farewell to the world.* And I'm sure that there are many others like me. I feel quite positive that *this is it.* That this is the time I get it. And I have the same sensations each time I take friends or relatives to the airport and put them on a plane. I give each of them a final lingering look, knowing deep inside of me that it is the last time I'll see them alive.

What's good about this attitude? Why, you can't imagine how superbly elated I feel when they arrive safely at their destination. And as for me — I feel absolutely ecstatic when I make it.

To a somewhat lesser degree the same emotions are present when I start on an automobile trip. I prepare for every emergency that the human mind can possibly anticipate, even though I know that such precautions will never save me. I have flares that will guide rescue workers to the wreck of my car in the canyon, and rope for getting out of inaccessible gullies; I carry knives and a hatchet and a first-aid kit big enough for the U.S. Marine units in the Iwo Jima landings. Even with all this I have a strong feeling that I am on my final expedition and I usually give my house a last affectionate look just before driving away from it. I must confess that I am not at all logical about my automobile premonitions; if I'm making only a short trip, say downtown to the beer store, I don't contemplate anything more serious than a concussion and perhaps a broken leg; if I'm driving merely to the corner, I figure on just a few minor cuts.

I live in the country three miles from the nearest firehouse. I always knew that some day my house would catch on fire. I always figured that it would burn to the ground and burn me and my family with it. In my anticipatory, pessimistic thinking I was certain that when the dire moment came I would panic. Occasionally I would speculate on just how it would happen. How would it start? Would the roof take fire from

the chimney? Would the nearby woods burn and throw flaming embers onto my house and set it afire? Would the electrical wiring be responsible? And what would I do when the fire was discovered? Would I faint dead away, or throw a fit, or just start running in a westerly direction? One thing I knew: my behavior in the crisis would be so shameful that I would stand embarrassed before the world. That is, if I survived. Which I wouldn't.

And so one December morning it happened. The thermometer stood at ten above zero and a high wind was blowing. The house caught fire from a defective oil burner. My family still talks proudly of how I behaved. I was noble, almost heroic. I took charge. I did everything exactly as it should have been done, and in the proper sequence. I telephoned for the fire department. I quickly instructed my family in what to do for safety's sake. I got the cars out of the garage where the fire was centered and I had a garden hose hooked up and a stream playing on the flames before the first fire truck arrived. I'm inclined to think that my pessimism was responsible for my exemplary behavior during the emergency. If I had never once thought of the possibility of fire, if I had never considered ways and means of coping with it, *then* I think I'd have been helpless when it came.

My pessimism extends into my business. I write books and magazine articles. Whenever I finish the long rough job of writing a book I sit and shudder a while, thinking of the horrible things the critics will say about it, thinking of how book buyers will ignore it from coast to coast. Thus, when I do get nasty reviews they don't bother me — I expected them; if I happen to get some praise it comes as a surprise and makes me happy. And if the book is a flop in sales, okay — I knew all along that it would be. On the other hand if it should sell well and make me a lot of money, my pleasure is almost beyond describing. I've written scores of magazine articles and short stories and each time I finish one of them I read it over and arrive at the conclusion that no editor could possibly be so stupid as to buy it. When an editor does, I'm the happiest man in forty square miles.

I can give you a concrete example of how my pessimism works in my favor in the business world. One summer afternoon my agent telephoned me and told me to get a firm grip on something solid and then he said, "Mike Todd has agreed to buy the movie rights to your novel for . . . hold on now! . . . *one hundred thousand dollars.*"

"That's nice," I said. This was at a time when a hundred thousand dollars was almost top price for the movie rights to a book. "Listen," I said. "I'm watching a hot ball game and the Giants have the bases loaded. Let me call you back later for the details."

My agent still tells people about my casual manner, my almost total lack of response, my excitement over a baseball game in the face of such splendid news. Actually, it was my devout pessimism at work. The sum of a hundred thousand dollars was, and still is, almost astronomical to my mind, yet I knew what it meant. At the same time I didn't believe a word of it. My mind told me that nothing on earth could ever happen that would fetch me a hundred thousand dollars all in a lump. So I went back to my ball game and put Mike Todd and his money out of my mind.

Later on I had a meeting with Todd, and a contract was drawn and signed by him, and then I signed it in my agent's office. It was placed in an envelope and mailed and the next step, on the following day, would be the delivery to me of the hundred thousand. It was never delivered. The following morning, perhaps an hour before that envelope arrived in Mike Todd's office, somebody went to court and forced him into bankruptcy. I never got a penny out of him. But it was all right. I had known all along that I wouldn't.

James Branch Cabell once uttered an interesting definition of pessimism: "The optimist proclaims that we live in the best of all possible worlds; and the pessimist fears this is true." And somebody else said: "A pessimist is one who feels bad when he feels good for fear he'll feel worse when he feels better."

These definitions jibe with my own philosophy, in a way. I seldom suffer the awful disappointments that are the lot of most people. An optimist refuses to let himself dwell on tragedies to come. A pessimist thinks of them all the time. Let us consider a tragedy that may seem trivial to people who are not dog owners. Almost from the moment I acquired my dog I knew that the time would come when he would die — probably on my order. I often thought of that eventuality, and felt sad about it, but I knew it had to happen and when it came it wasn't nearly as rough as it has been with some of my neighbors. I had prepared myself for it; I had, in effect, lived through the death of my dog many times before it happened.

My pessimism covers almost every phase of my day-to-day life. If I should make a bet on a horse or a ball game I have no hope whatever of winning — it is just as if I had taken the money and thrown it to the winds; and if I do win I am delirious with joy. If I get a pimple or some sort of minor interior ache I race for the doctor's office, knowing in advance what his diagnosis will be: malignant. These and countless other pessimistic judgments and conclusions make me, in the long run, a happy and contented man.

The true pessimist has great material to work with nowadays. I have reference to The Bomb. I can't truthfully say that I'm ready for it, though I know for certain that it is on the way. Optimistic people scoff at me and exclaim, "Why, don't be ridiculous, nobody is going to drop The Bomb!" And my answer to them is: "Somebody did. Twice."

In common with most of my fellow citizens I am doing nothing about it. Sometimes I try to think of a way to escape, but my mind always returns to the shrewd Australian who figured out, well in advance, the course that World War II would take, and then chose a spot for himself where reason and logic told him no shot would ever be heard: the island of Guadalcanal.

Being convinced that The Bomb will fall, I decided for a while that I would go to Mexico and take up residence in one of that country's mountain-girt valleys. I felt that in some place like Taxco I would escape the fiery blast and that if the fallout got me, it would be comparatively gentle, maybe like twilight sleep. Then my pessimism asserted itself. I knew that if I got into a Mexican valley, one of those tremendous rockets would leap from its pad at Cape Canaveral and, instead of following its prescribed course out over the Atlantic, it would somehow twist itself around, arc into Mexico and land right on my adobe hacienda.

I can't win but I have a lot of fun losing. And when I realize that many other people, who anticipate only eventualities that are pleasant and healthful, spend much of their time groaning and whining about the unpredictable cruelty of fate, then I feel good; I get to feeling downright optimistic about my pessimism.

*

*

*

3. A Short History of Fingers

FINGERS ARE good for you.

They play a tremendous part in your day-by-day existence and if you didn't have them, life would be infinitely more difficult.

If man were born without fingers Nature would probably compensate by putting additional vigor into the toes and making them larger and much longer than they are now. (Shoes would have to be bigger and would cost more, and God knows they cost enough as it is). Many little acts and duties which we perform today with our fingers would then be performed with our toes. If you would appreciate the full importance of such a state of affairs, please try to visualize Winston Churchill giving the "V" for Victory sign with his toes. Or a teen-ager standing beside the highway, big-toeing a ride.

Fortunately our race has had fingers as far back as we can trace history. It is obvious that if earliest man had been without fingers the whole pageant of civilization would have been of a different cast and color. Assuming that Eve could grab hold of things only by using her toes, she would have had to stand on her head in order to pluck that apple, and I doubt that she'd have gone to all the bother. And what of the Netherlands? I think it probable that there would be no Holland today. That little boy who held his finger in the dike — he couldn't very well have done the job with his nose. Think, too, of that man in the circus who could turn himself upside down and stand on his index finger. If he had no fingers at all, how could he make a living? What else could he stand on?

Anatomists and medical men have their own names for the fingers, beginning with *pollex* (for the thumb) and continuing through *index, medius, annulary,* and *minimus.* The gloriously fingered man in the street is familiar with only one of these terms: *index.* The digit which we call the index finger was originally known among the Anglo-Saxons as the *towcher.* The Anglo-Saxons were notorious for their bad spelling ("Sumer is icumen in, Lhude sing, cuccu!") and the word they spelled *towcher* means, simply, *toucher.* The towcher was the finger used in touching. It was always called the towcher in towns and cities where, presumably, a lot of touching was done. Out in the rural districts the towcher had another name: the *scite-finger.* This word actually means "trigger-finger" and we can only assume that country people were more inclined to shoot something than to touch something.

On the other hand the ancients who lived across the channel on the Continent believed that the index finger was just about the worst finger a person could possibly use for touching. It was poisonous, they said, and if it were used to touch a wound, that wound would never heal. It was loaded with toxins, hence they always kept it well away from their soup.

The middle finger doesn't seem to have any history at all. Nature apparently just stuck it in there to keep the others apart. In mythology the middle finger is mentioned somewhat vaguely in connection with Saturn. Since Saturn was the god of agriculture, perhaps this finger served as the world's first dibble. A dibble is a pointed instrument for poking holes in the ground preliminary to planting. This is pure speculation on my part and the Dibble Theory probably wouldn't hold up in court. I don't think I'd ever use my middle finger as a dibble. Still, it appears to be the largest of the fingers and there ought to be *some* employment for it.

Biographical material is also wanting on the little finger. We do know that the Anglo-Saxons called it the *ear-finger* because it was the most easily introduced into the ear. When I was a boy in the Midwest a common thing was to see a grownup stick his little finger in his ear, with the rest of the hand held at jawbone level, other fingers folded, and then waggle the hand vigorously up and down. An uncle of mine told me that this maneuver relieved the pressure on the brain. I have never had occasion to employ it.

The opposable thumb is, of course, a great source of wonder to anthropologists who consider it a more revolutionary development than the wheel, the printing press, or the plumber's snake. I think the story of the opposable thumb is quite dramatic (Tennessee Williams could make a fine play about it) and I don't want to belittle it at all, yet my own favorite among the fingers is the *leche-man*. The *leche-man* is the ring finger. *Leche* is the way the Anglo-Saxons spelled "leech" and a leech was a doctor and so it came about in the olden days that this finger was known also as the *medical* finger. The Greeks and Romans believed that it contained a special nerve that ran out of the finger itself, up the arm, across the chest and into the heart. So they, the Greeks and Romans, used that finger for stirring things. If the brew they were stirring contained anything in the way of poison, a warning was transmitted along that special nerve, straight to the heart. They must have believed strongly in this theory. If you doubt it, just try to stir something with your ring finger; it would be easier and more graceful to use your elbow. Still, the theory of the medical finger survives to this day in parts of England, where the inhabitants are careful to use that finger in applying salves or medical ointments to the body. Moreover, they use the same finger exclusively when they want to scratch an irritated part. I have seen a cultured Englishman remove his bowler hat and scratch his scalp with his medical finger. It looks silly but it is just as natural for him to do it that way as it is for him to retain his fork in his left hand throughout a meal. He isn't really conscious of what he is doing, of the fact that he is taking antiseptic precautions against mange, ringworm and other scalp disorders.

Now, why do we moderns call this particular digit the ring finger? The expression derives from those same Greeks and Romans. They reasoned that if this finger contained the super-nerve leading straight to the heart, then this finger was the proper place to install a wedding ring. The theory got fouled up a bit when it was translated from Latin into English. In seventeenth-century England we find one Henry Swinburne, an ecclesiastical lawyer, writing a book about romance and matrimony in which he said: "The finger on which this ring is to be worn is the fourth finger of the left hand, next unto the little finger; because there is a vein of blood which passeth from that fourth finger into the heart called *vena amoris*, or love's vein." So, it became a vein of blood rather than a super-nerve. Why quibble?

Sad to relate, the Greeks, the Romans and Henry Swinburne were all in error. In modern days experiments have been undertaken to determine the degree of sensitiveness of each of the fingers. These experiments show that the index finger is the most sensitive of the lot, the middle finger ranks next, then the thumb, after that the little finger and, finally, the ring finger. And George Stimpson has written: "The fourth digit on the human hand is the least mobile, the least sensitive and the least used of all the digits." In other words, the ring finger is a real stupid digit. Like some of our leading television performers, it lacks talent and it lacks personality but somehow it gets along.

Down through the centuries the fingers have been of inestimable importance in every known kind of pursuit except, possibly, grape pressing, the mile run and the stamping out of forest fires. There was a time back in the Middle Ages and earlier when most people used their fingers instead of paper and pencil whenever they wanted to tackle a problem in arithmetic. I don't mean the simple counting processes which we ourselves employ, such as counting forward on our fingers to determine what day of the month next Tuesday will be, or counting backward on our fingers after hearing the gladsome tidings that a new baby has been born. The ancients went much further than that in their finger calculations. They refused, for example, to memorize the multiplication table on the simple and sensible grounds that it was impossible to do so; they learned, instead, to multiply with their fingers. The way they did it, according to the usually reliable *Encyclopaedia Britannica,* is as follows:

To multiply 8 by 6, turn down $8 - 5$ fingers on one hand and $6 - 5$ on the other. There are then 3 turned down and 2 standing on one hand and 1 turned down and 4 standing on the other. Add the fingers down $(3 + 1 = 4)$ and multiply those standing $(2 \times 4 = 8)$, and the result is 4 tens, 8 units, or 48; that is, in terms of mathematics, $ab = [(a - 5) + (b - 5)] \, 10 + (10 - a) \, (10 - b)$. Numerous variants of the plan were in use, some having been brought to Europe from the Arab schools.

I would like to see some of those variants. I would like to have a whole bunch of variants brought from the Arab schools, because I can't get any right answers with the variant given above. I worked on it until my wrists got tired, and then had to give it up.

The most effective way of demonstrating the value of fingers, as I've said, is to visualize a world in which there are none.

Stop right now and hold up a handful of fingers and examine them closely. Pretty crazy looking, aren't they? If you could manage to detach one of them and lay it on the coffee table, it would look even sillier. You'd likely burst out laughing. If you did, you would be doing that finger and all its fellows a gross disservice.

If man didn't have any fingers he would not, of course, know that there ever were any such things as fingers. In such a world, suppose you went to your doctor and he felt your pulse with his toes; you would consider it to be quite the normal thing, even if you had to get down on the floor to make it more convenient for him. In other words you would be accustomed to an existence without fingers, just as a dog is, and it wouldn't bother you. You might observe a group of Italian men playing the game of *morra*, shooting out their toes and crying *"Nove!"* and *"Uno!"* and *"Quattro!"* You wouldn't even smile. Your garage mechanic would use his foot to flip open the hood of your car, then thrust his leg inside and begin tinkering with your carburetor, and you wouldn't give him a second glance. Your dentist would . . . but let's pass that.

As I've already suggested, Nature has a habit of compensating for our physical deficiencies. If we had no fingers our bodies would be organized quite differently from the way they are now. I think it probable that we would have an opposable big toe so that we could handle tools with our feet. No — we wouldn't "handle" the tools, we would "footle" them. We'd be able to stand on one leg for long periods, like the yellow-crowned night heron and the marbled godwit, and thus be able to play baseball, throwing and catching with the loose foot. But the changes in body function would be far more extensive than these examples. We would develop universal joints in our knees and hips in order that we might, with ease, bring our toes into position for such duties as shaving, extracting cinders from the eye, feeding ourselves, applying lipstick and hailing cabs. The custom of tipping the hat would be abandoned; too many men would fall down while doing it.

I've already mentioned the likelihood of our shoes being bigger. On further consideration I think it probable that our shoes would be more like gloves in order that our toes would have greater play. With our feet encased in ordinary shoes, we would be unable to cross our toes when passing a graveyard, to snap our toes at a dilatory waiter, to crack our knuckles as a means of finding out who dearly loves us, or to put the whammy on an enemy.

The absence of fingers would be a boon to our teeth. They would grow bigger and stronger so that we could use them for unscrewing caps off pickle jars, changing electrical fuse plugs, picking gooseberries (strawberries would be picked with the toes), and squeezing toothpaste . . . hold it! Let's face up to this problem — the business of the teeth. I somehow don't cotton to the idea of brushing my teeth with my toes. It wouldn't have to be done that way. We could have fixed, stationary brushes, fasten our mouths over them, and agitate our heads. I tell you, the human brain can solve *any* problem.

The nose, too, would likely be different — longer and more rigid at the tip — so that it could be employed in dialing telephone numbers, operating pop-up toasters, manipulating the thermostat and turning the pages of a book (William Randolph Hearst had fingers but he preferred placing newspapers on the floor and turning the pages with his bare toes. Great men *do* things).

Since we are visualizing a world without fingers, what would we have on the ends of our arms in their place? The best scientific opinion available at this moment seems to think we would have knobs in place of hands. This sounds unpleasant, I know, but knobs have their points. I mean their uses. You wouldn't be able to button your shirt with knobs, but you could mash potatoes. You could do all kinds of work ordinarily performed with a ball peen hammer, and think what a cinch it would be to pound flour into swiss steak.

If we had knobs instead of fingers the world of music would be vitally affected. I can't see how anyone would be able to play a violin effectively, or a harp or a guitar or a six-hole flute. Of necessity our symphony orchestras would go in heavily for xylophones, marimbas, kettledrums, possibly harmonicas, and people would still be able to blow into a jug. Yes, I think we'd get along fine with knobs, even though something delicately beautiful would go out of romance, or at least out of romantic writing. Somehow it doesn't sound soul-inspiring to say, "He ran his knobs through her glorious golden hair."

In the Fiji Islands there are certain savages, or there used to be, who cut off their fingers as a sign of mourning after the death of their chief. A noble gesture but, like many noble gestures, a foolish one. We should not only hang onto our fingers; we should cherish them, and protect them against sprains, dislocations, fractures, felons, warts and all the other ills to which finger-flesh is heir. We should honor them by taking notice of them historically; so far as I know this is the first history of fingers ever undertaken; so far as Gibbon was concerned, there wasn't a single finger in the entire Roman Empire, and Toynbee ignores fingers altogether. We really need our fingers in so many areas of modern life. Without fingers to snap, today's singers of popular songs would go slack-jawed and mute. And finally, I think it's clear that we've got to have something to rub over the lettering of other people's stationery so we can tell if it's engraved or merely printed.

*

*

*

4. *Commencement Address . . . Undelivered*

THE GREATEST commencement address ever delivered, in my opinion, was a brief oration by the late Mayor Edward Joseph Kelly of Chicago before a high school graduating class. Mayor Kelly stood up and surveyed that sea of bright and eager young faces (eager to get it the hell over with) and then spoke:

"Boys and girls, remember that when you go out into the world you will find that money won't buy happiness, money won't buy respect, money won't buy honor. Confederate money, that is."

That might be just a trifle short for a graduation ceremony, although the most important element in a commencement address ought to be brevity.

I'm somehow reminded of the story Damon Runyon used to tell about the dying gambler whose son sat at his side and listened to his father's parting advice, which went as follows:

"Son, as you go around and about this world, some day you will come upon a man who will lay down in front of you a deck of cards with the seal unbroken and offer to bet you he can make the jack of spades jump out of that deck and squirt cider in your ear. Son, do not bet that man, because just as sure as you do you're going to get an ear full of cider."

That single anecdote would make a suitable baccalaureate sermon. I wish I had devised it, as I wish I had composed Mayor Kelly's speech. They both seem to contain more sapience and horse sense than any of the mephitic and meaningless vaporings that, I understand, have been emanating each Junetime from human gasbags in all quarters of the land. I hear that these gasbags number twenty thousand but I refuse to believe it; it is my guess that they number less than twenty thousand, say, nineteen thousand eight hundred and seventy-five.

Still, it happens that I have written a short talk which I think would be effective if delivered before a graduating class. It is longer than Mayor Kelly's masterpiece and the dying gambler's exhortation. It is a trifle more on the serious side but I think it punches across its moral point just as effectively as the oration on Confederate money and the sermon on the cider-squirting jack of spades.

I tell a tale that is factual, of a character who truly lived. When I face my audience of graduating students, I intend to counsel them on the need to Live With A Flourish. I shall tell them that no matter what their station in life, no matter if they live in hovels and sleep on straw, they should never let their lives become drab. And I shall tell them of a man who exemplified the art of Living With A Flourish better than any other person I've ever heard about. His name was Dr. Hobie Archibald Sloat.

The story of Dr. Hobie Archibald Sloat was given to me years ago by Norris Goff, who was the Abner of the old and long-mourned (by me at least) radio show, "Lum & Abner." Dr. Sloat lived in Norris Goff's hometown in Arkansas when Norris was a boy. Many citizens of that town sometimes searched their memories in an effort to recall when Dr. Sloat had done an honest day's work. All testimony was negative save that of an old man who remembered that Hobie Sloat, when he was in his twenties, had trotted half the length of the main street in furious and unrelenting pursuit of a runaway horse which he didn't catch. For want of a more caustic word, he was strictly a bum; yet he lived flamboyantly, and With A Flourish.

He bestowed the title of "Doctor" on himself because he believed it gave a certain additional rhythm and flow to the name Hobie Archibald Sloat. He was not a doctor of anything; he would not have known how to get rid of a pimple short of shooting it off with a forty-five. He was content to go through life in either of two positions: sitting down or lying down. His wife took in washing and did some sewing and mending, and Dr. Sloat saw no reason why he should go out and shorten his life by employment. "I don't intend to be beholdum to nobody," he once explained, and when his listeners gave signs of not understanding such high-flown language, he simplified it, this way: "Nobody is ever gonna be a boss over Dr. Hobie Archibald Sloat if I can he'p it. I was not made to be bossed over." He refused to pick up and deliver the laundry for his wife and it was necessary for her customers to fetch their own "warsh" and then come and get it.

For the reason that customers were coming to the Sloat house in an almost steady procession, Dr. Sloat chose to put on a front — to give the establishment some style and character. So he installed himself as a sort of office manager. Somewhere he acquired a cutaway coat and with it a gates-ajar collar which he wore without a shirt. More important than his apparel, however, was his office equipment. He had a roll-top desk in the middle of the front room of the house and piled on this desk, in disorderly confusion, were fifty or sixty rubber stamps.

It was young Norris Goff's duty to call once a week for the family laundry. He'd walk into the "office" and up to Dr. Sloat's desk. The Doctor would look at him over the rims of his glasses and then he'd seize hold of his intercom — a schoolhouse recess bell — and give it a few hearty swings. Then he'd turn his head slightly and bellow: "Oh, Maw! Norris Goff wooshes his warsh!"

After Mrs. Sloat had brought in the Goff laundry from the Processing Rooms at the rear of the house, Dr. Sloat would set to work figuring out the charges. His calculations (he always called it ciphering) were Dead Sea algebraic and vaguely related to Euclid's incommensurable magnitudes. He'd loll out his tongue as he scratched away, or he'd talk to himself something in this manner:

"Now, lemmy see now. Times four thousand three hunnerd an' eighty-five, put down eight and carry the two, long-divided by fifty-three, plus four cents fer darnin' up a hole in a sock, eekals half of . . ."

Having arrived at a final figure that seemed reasonable, he'd take a sheet of ruled paper and begin writing on it with pen and ink and with a certain Spencerian grace. When he was finished his document would read something like this:

On this second day of August, year of our Blessed Lord nineteen hundred and twenty-two anno domino, came into the presence of the undersigned one Norris Goff, being sound of mind, wind and limb, hereafter the party of the first part. Undersigned conveys and quit-claims all and singular appurtenances, appendages, advowsons, privileges, advantages, and butts and bounds of whatsoever name or description, in fee simple and in consideration of the sum of forty-five cents, one piller-case full of washing to same by authority of the power vested in me by the Commonwealth of Arkansas, done and did until death do us part go and sin no more.

During the composition of this document Dr. Sloat would stop now and then to consult a ragged and faded law book, for it was his custom to make certain changes in the legal terminology from time to time. Having completed it he would sign it with a flourish, as if it were a treaty doing away with all war, terrestrial and interplanetary, for all time to come. Then he would turn to Norris and put him through an oath-taking which involved a hand on the Bible, the Pledge to the Flag, and a few phrases out of Lincoln's Gettysburg Address. On completion of this ordeal, Norris would sign. And now it was time for the ceremonial of the rubber stamps.

Dr. Hobie Archibald Sloat would drag out his stamp-pad and begin whamming away at the document, front and back. His rubber stamps had been acquired over a long period of years and some of his customers, who traveled to far places, often brought him new ones. None of them had any bearing on the laundry business. Dr. Sloat would reach out and grab them up indiscriminately, so that Norris Goff's quit-claim advowsons might bear such exciting endorsements as:

FOR DEPOSIT
WORMSER'S FEED STORE

APPROVED
COMMISSIONER FOR INDIAN AFFAIRS

MILFORD SPEERS
NOTARY PUBLIC
MY COMMISSION EXPIRES
MAY 10, 1882

PLEASE HAND TO GATE MAN
SELLS-FLOTO CIRCUS

EDWARD SHEEHAN
PARLOR ENTERTAINER
RATES ON REQUEST

So there, my young friends, you have a man of perhaps limited talents but one who had imagination, one who had the knack of making life exciting for himself and for many of the people who came in contact with him. Dr. Hobie Archibald Sloat knew how to Live With A Flourish. He had fun. I'm quite sure that he had more fun than . . . well, than his wife.

*

*

*

5. On Mountain Clambering

A FEW YEARS AGO, in another book, I delivered a scathing and devastating attack on bullfights, bullfighters, believers in bullfighting and writers about bullfighting. As the whole world knows, bullfighting ceased almost immediately, everywhere. I think it is time now that I turn my big guns on mountain climbing.

Sometimes of an autumn evening I love to sit by the fire and reflect on the vast wisdom that prevails all over the world. Occasionally my thoughts dwell on Mr. Charley Macey of Crowborough in England who, not so long ago, added another glossy leaf to his crown of laurel. Mr. Macey, in the presence of friends and well-wishers, mounted a pogo stick in a Crowborough pub. Ninety-five minutes later he set his throbbing feet on the floor after having bounced up and down twelve thousand times — an achievement no other human being could claim.

Charley Macey was not unknown to glory before he set the world's record for bouncing on a pogo stick. Some years ago he played golf for sixteen consecutive hours while wearing a heavy steel helmet. On another occasion he spent three hours and fifty-five minutes walking backwards, during which time he traversed sixteen miles. And just prior to his pogo stick adventure, he kept a yo-yo whirling steadily for one hour while walking six miles.

The trans-Atlantic cables have reported that Mr. Macey is seeking new worlds to conquer and has been toying with the idea of rolling a hoop a greater distance than any hoop has ever been rolled before. I think he has reached the point in his career where he needs something a little more spectacular than that. In my opinion Mr. Charley Macey is ready to climb a mountain. He has demonstrated that he has both grit and stamina, plus a keen sense of balance, and he seems to be qualified mentally.

Mountain climbing has been attracting wide public attention in recent years because of the "conquest" of Mount Everest and Annapurna as well as that of several lesser peaks. Books written by and about mountaineers have ascended easily to the summit of the best-seller lists. Motion pictures of men climbing mountains have been saluted with roseate prose by the critics. One of the men who made it to the top of Everest lectured to big audiences in the United States and was received at the White House and decorated by the President. Meanwhile the Sherpa workhorse, Tenzing, who went with him to the summit, was rewarded with an electric refrigerator, possibly to remind him of the fact that he almost froze to death.

Years ago there was an Indian in South Dakota named Asa Sweetcorn, a man with an acute need for whisky and a disinclination to work with his hands in order to get it. One day he sat down and figured out an easy way to acquire drinking money. That is, *he* thought it was easy. He would wander around the countryside and make bets that he could ram his head through the wall of a barn. Without a hat on. During a single afternoon he stove six separate portholes in a barn. They say he staggered a little afterward.

I mention the career of Asa Sweetcorn for the reason that there were some people in South Dakota who contended that he should have been restrained — not the people whose barns were being riddled by his head, but people who thought Asa was somehow breaching the moral code as well as the barns. It is my contention that a man should have the liberty to ram his head through a barn wall as often as he wants, whether for pleasure or for money. And I contend that a man should have the liberty to climb the highest mountain whenever he chooses. My complaint is against that portion of the public which receives and embraces the mountain climber as a great benefactor of mankind, a hero to compare with Horatius who held the bridge.

The responsibility for the public's distorted view of the mountain climber rests, I think, with the critics who approach a kind of daffy delirium in their commentaries on the books and the movies.

It might be expected that a mountain-man like Justice William O. Douglas (a good man when he's got his courtin' robes on) would say of the Everest book: "This book . . . will lift the hearts of men as long as there are mountains. . . . Some of us would give our lives to stand with Hillary and Tenzing on Everest . . . no moment of life is more exquisite."

Or that James Ramsey Ullman, himself a climber, should say of the same volume: ". . . the book of triumph and fulfillment . . . one of the fine moments in human history."

But even the stay-at-home groundling critics joined in the mad chorus, crying: ". . . the knot of brave and gifted men . . . are in a sense the advance guard of humanity as a whole. Every one has an interest and a stake in their success . . . Rational or not, the urge that drove these men is the one which has made it possible for our species to survive."

There have been reams of such drivel and nowhere, to my knowledge, a single sharply dissenting note. Yet if you'll take a little time to question the people around you, this very day, you will probably find that a majority look upon mountain climbers as fools and fatheads. You will find that most of the people you know agree with everything I am saying.

The critics, or commentators, recognize the persistence of the main question: Why? But they usually say it doesn't matter why — it's still noble and inspiring and thrilling to the hearts of all men.

I have heard and read all sorts of psychological explanations of the inner drive which sends these men up the mountains, including the theory that it is an expression of the death wish. The Annapurna man, Maurice Herzog, has been described as "a mountain climber by religion," and his own report of his sensations on reaching the summit certainly sounds like a form of religious frenzy. Monsieur Herzog is the one who had most of his fingers and toes frozen off and who came within an inch of going irretrievably mad. The last I heard he was getting ready to do it again. I'm reminded of Mark Twain's comment after reading a graphic account of Edward Whymper's misadventures in the Alps. Whymper fell something over two hundred feet, bouncing from rock to rock, ending up unconscious with blood spurting from twenty cuts. "His wounds," observed Mark Twain, "kept him abed some days. Then he got up and climbed the mountain again. That is the way with a true Alp-climber; the more fun he has, the more he wants."

Among the attempts to explain motivation is that of the mountaineer Emile Javelle, who wrote: ". . . for it is a thrilling thought that through all the incalculable ages in which these rocks have stood proudly raising their naked strength into the sky, no man, till this moment, has ever reached them, no eye has seen what you are seeing, that your voice is the first to break the silence which has lasted from the beginning of the world. . . . The human race has ceased to have any significance, it has disappeared."

That last sentence suggests to me that someone is suffering from cirrhosis of the head, but the first part is understandable: a reflection of the desire to do something that has never been done by any other person before. Unquestionably a fine sense of exhilaration goes with doing a thing for the first time in history. I can remember back to the early 1930s when an advertising agency asked the late O. O. McIntyre to write them something that had never been written before in the history of the world. Mr. McIntyre complied by writing: "Hootnanny on the hickey." Possibly the finest thing he ever wrote.

I myself have a substantial and glorious "first" to my credit. When the history of television is written my name will be included, if only in a footnote. Fifteen years ago I was on a television program originating in a New York studio and down in Virginia a frend named Ira L. Smith set up a camera in his living room and took a picture of my head as it appeared on his screen. He sent me prints of this picture. A short time afterward I appeared on one of Arthur Godfrey's early television shows. I alerted Ira Smith in Virginia to have his camera set up again. Then when the Godfrey show was on the air, I held up a print of the picture Ira Smith had taken before. And I announced to the public that it was now viewing a genuine television first. It was the first time that a man sitting down in Virginia had ever taken a picture of a man sitting up in New York while the picture of the man up in New York was being held in the hand of the same man, sitting once again up in New York so that the picture of the picture could be taken by the man sitting down in Virginia. The very first time it ever happened! I still get a glow from thinking about it and sometimes boast about it although I usually have trouble stating it accurately. I believe it to be as great an achievement as Mr. Charley Macey's twelve thousand bounces on the pogo stick, and as great and as sensible as the achievements of the men who mounted Annapurna and Everest. And it didn't wear me out.

As far as the "conquerors" of the great mountain peaks are concerned, how can they be sure that they were the first men to reach the top? Some of the people who live in the neighborhood of the Himalayas are a strange lot, as queer as some of the people we have in the United States. I think it entirely possible that certain of their ancestors, a hundred years ago, or five hundred, or five thousand years ago, made their way to the top of Everest or of K^2, possibly for religious reasons. What did Tenzing do when he achieved the summit in 1953? He dug a little hole and put some candy in it as an offering to the Buddhist gods he believes make their home up there. It is a historical fact that Guatama Buddha was born beside the Nepalese Himalayas and acquired his first followers there. According to legend he was conceived in a golden palace high in the Himalayas in the sixth century before Christ. I won't bet money on it but I suspect that in later years a few of the Buddhists went up to the top of Everest to pay their respects to the gods. Let's keep in mind that these people lived close by the lands where other people drove nails into their heads just to demonstrate their devotion.

Something of a spiritual nature sends the modern climber up these mountains. One man said he achieved "a feeling of release and mystic union." Release from what? His toes? Mystic union with what? Well, they can't put it in words. We know, however, that in those altitudes a human being grows real lightheaded and giddy, as if he had recently downed a tankard of scopolamine. Sometimes he doesn't quite know what he is doing, or why he is up there, and kaleidoscopic visions dance before his eyes. He doesn't give them long to dance. He doesn't linger at the destination he has been busting his butt to reach. He arrives at the goal, glances around, snaps a few quick pictures before his fingers drop off, waves a flag, buries some gumdrops for the gods, and then high-tails it out of there — to receive the hysterical plaudits of his native land plus the cheers of people all over the world who agree with him that mountain climbing is an intelligent form of endeavor.

I'm informed that upwards of a thousand human beings have lost their lives trying to climb mountains in the last few years. They are falling off mountains in Asia and in Europe and in South America and in our own land. It is my opinion that all of the climbers could save themselves a lot of effort and a lot of expense and a lot of toes if they'd stay at home and risk their lives in the presence of their families. Let them climb to the top of a tall silo and then jump off, into the pigpen. And if they ask me why they should do such a seemingly ridiculous thing, I'll reply: "Because the pigpen is there." Even though jumping off a silo hurts at the end, it must be enormously thrilling in transit. And if they must deal with mountains, I'd recommend that they approach Mount Everest from a practical angle. Let them take some picks and shovels and chop the whole thing down and throw it away, and then plant some corn. That would be a thing worth doing.

Some people say that the eternal fascination of the horrible and the dangerous attracts these men to the high peaks, and that this is true in a lesser degree in the sport of skiing.

Recently I saw a photograph taken in a big ski lodge some-where in New England. More than half the people loung-ing around the big room had their legs and arms in plaster casts or slings and some had bandages around their heads. The text that accompanied the picture warned that these maimed and mutilated citizens were not to be pitied. Their plaster casts and their bandages were emblems of honor. They gloried in and flaunted the compound fractures that were achieved while wearing a pair of skis. I'm glad their philosophical attitude was explained because it evoked a splendid vision in my mind. A man on skis swishes along at ninety miles an hour and whams into a tree. Splat! He ricochets into a snowbank where he lies upside down with broken arms and shattered legs and mashed face, and when the rescuers, laughing like crazy, come racing up he spits out a few teeth and gasps, "Man, this is livin'!"

Yet skiing is a sensible form of outdoor activity when com-pared with mountain climbing. It's just that the emphasis is in the wrong place. If there were something on top of those mountains worth getting at, if there were something on the summit of Everest that would improve the lot of man, I'd recommend that we take a helicopter and go get it. One re-cent British expedition carried a ladder up Everest. The

Americans who got near the crest of K² had a metal A-frame for hoisting supplies from crag to crag. Old-time mountain climbers, especially in sporting England, scoffed at the use of oxygen and ladders and pulleys and said these modern climbers were going soft. Is there to be a prescribed limit to the amount and type of equipment allowable on these expeditions? What's wrong with taking along a smallish helicopter, just as a sort of good-luck piece? When Mark Twain was organizing his expedition to the top of the Matterhorn he made out a list of his requirements, a great long list which included a wagonload of forty-foot ladders, umbrellas for everyone, mattresses, crutches, a surgeon, a barber, a pastry cook, two thousand cigars, a barrel of pies, and sufficient dynamite and nitroglycerin to blow down anything that got in the way.

The climbers bestow lovely names on their mountains. Yerupaja in South America is known affectionately as "The Butcher." An American boy got his toes frozen off on it a few years ago, and they no longer keep count of the dead. K² in the Himalayas is "The Savage Mountain." One American was killed there and another lost a toe and a half not long ago. They don't bother with the necrology any more — it's too big a job. They are all killers, even the Alpine peaks where the traffic is so heavy in the summer that climbers have to climb over each other to get to the top. The normal score for the Alps alone has risen to one hundred and twenty-five climbers killed each season. When Whymper "conquered" the Matterhorn in 1865 — a feat that seems puny to the present breed of mountaineers — four of the seven members of his party were killed. Who conquered what? Queen Victoria knew the answer. That astute lady asked her Ministers if such antics shouldn't be forbidden.

I would enjoy feeling admiration for mountain climbers, but it's not in me — they are only playing a variation of the childhood game of Who-Can-Lean-The-Farthest-Out-The-Window-Without-Falling. I'd like to be able to clap them heartily on the back and say, "Well done, old boy!" I'll still clap them on the back, but candor will compel me to say, "Meaning no offense, old boy, but you've got fragments of granite in your head."

I think that it is quite possible to have humility and noble thoughts and a sense of profound wonder while sitting at home in front of a fire. I think that it's possible to get in tune with the infinite and still keep your toes. And I think that among all the people I've questioned on the subject of mountain climbing, the best response came from my wife.

"I don't get it," she said. "It's hard enough and dangerous enough nowadays to get along on flat ground."

*

*

*

6. A Friend in Las Vegas

In the developing folklore of contemporary America there is a story about a newlywed couple holding hands late in the evening on the front stoop of their home. Down the street a cat manages to claw the lid off a large garbage can. The lid hits the pavement with a crash and a clatter, the garbage can falls over, the cat lets out a few frightening shrieks and yowls, and the young woman says softly to the young man, "Oh, darling, our song!"

There must be fogey blood in me because I enjoy that story. I enjoy it because I think that much of the stuff that passes for popular music today is somewhat less melodic than the grunting of hogs in flytime. I happen to hold membership in a generation which grew up on sweet music and a sweet singer named Gene Austin.

Along with almost every other boy and girl of my time I romanced and courted to the music of his records. Those were the days when we cranked up the machine between numbers, and if we ran out of needles we used a straight pin, and if we ran out of anything else to say, we said, "You tell 'em, I stutter."

I've known Gene Austin for thirty-five years. I first met him in Tulsa in the summer of 1927, when he was at the peak of his celebrity. I was a young reporter just barely sapient enough to pour lemonade out of a boot, while he was a national hero of sorts — a young man who was feted and cheered and given the keys to the city wherever he went.

There in Tulsa I talked my city editor into letting me interview him, and then approached the assignment with fear and trembling. "Gene Austin!" I kept saying to myself. "I'm going to interview Gene Austin! In person!" I'm telling you, he was that big in 1927. Yet within two minutes after I had walked into his hotel room he had put me at my ease. He was, if anything, country-er than I was. He not only asked me to hang around with him all afternoon but took me to dinner and then let me go backstage with him at the Orpheum and stand in the wings while he sang his songs.

In subsequent years I knew him in Denver, in New York, in Hollywood and in Las Vegas. He went into a long period of eclipse but then, just a few years ago, the voice of Gene Austin was again being heard in the land. It was a voice out of a seemingly ancient past, vibrant with nostalgia, and all of us who knew it so well in the middle and late twenties somehow achieved a sort of vicarious rejuvenation from listening to it again.

Gene is now in his early sixties. He could easily pass for ten years less than his actual age. I had lost track of him, though I knew he had become a permanent resident of Las Vegas. And then about five years ago things began to happen. Someone in Hollywood started talking about producing a movie to be called *The Gene Austin Story*. Back East the television crowd, remembering, went on the alert. The people at RCA-Victor, remembering, dug into their files and came up with the startling fact that Gene Austin was probably the biggest star that they or any other recording company ever had. What was even more interesting to the Victor people was the report they got from California that Gene Austin was a better singer now than he was when he made "My Blue Heaven" his theme song. They sent out a hurry call for the biggest money-maker they ever hired.

So Gene headed for New York to fill some new recording dates, to appear on a television show in which a somewhat hopped-up version of his life story was told, and to cut up some touches with his old friends. When I heard he was in New York I went looking for him and found him in an apartment hotel near Central Park. With him were his wife, Lou, and his mynah bird, Jack. As I walked into the apartment the bird said, "My God, why doesn't somebody tell me these things?" A few minutes later he whistled an old familiar refrain and then — I swear it! — he sang the words, "When whippoorwills call, and evening is nigh . . ." After that he asked another question: "Why don't we sell this damn bird?"

There was a portable fold-away electric piano in one corner of the room, gimmicked up with earphones so Gene could write his songs in the middle of the night if he felt the urge. On the piano was a foot-high reproduction of the RCA-Victor dog and beneath it a golden plaque citing Gene's achievements in the recording business. And as for old Gene himself, he was the same easygoing, soft-talking guy I'd known for so many years.

He is a lineal descendant of a woman famous in the history of the American West — Sacajawea, the Shoshone Indian girl who accompanied the Lewis and Clark Expedition from North Dakota to the Pacific Coast and back in 1805-1806. Known as the "Bird Woman" and celebrated for her courage, her resourcefulness and her good humor, she was Gene's great-great-great-grandmother.

He was born Eugene Lucas, in Gainesville, Texas. His parents were divorced when he was three and his mother married an itinerant blacksmith named Jim Austin. "My old man," says Gene, referring to Jim Austin, "was quite a horseshoer in his better days. He worked around the trotting tracks, used to shoe Dan Patch regularly, but he had a hankerin' for that ole whisky bottle, and the good times didn't last, and we found ourselves in Louisiana, roamin' around the lumber country. The old man shoed the mules at the sawmills and I think you might say we could have qualified as poor folks."

Gene was seven or eight when they moved into a house in the little town of Yellow Pine, Louisiana. The previous occupants had left behind an old beat-up piano of Civil War vintage, and Gene began fooling around with it.

"There was a little colored gal," he remembers, "used to come around and do some work for us when we could afford it. I knew she used to sneak into the colored church on weekdays and play the little organ they had out there. So one day I told her I'd give her two bits if she'd show me how to play a song called 'Hard Times.' She did it, and that's the first piece of music I ever learned."

The family settled shortly afterward in the larger town of Minden and the old piano was toted along, despite the protests of Jim Austin. He didn't like it because it produced music, and he had no use for music of any nature or description. "Music," said Jim, "is jest fer ladies."

"What little music I knew," says Gene, "I learned from the colored folks. I used to wander out to the quarters at night and snoop around and listen to them playin' their guitars and their pianos and singin'. Minden was one of those towns where the only music the white folks knew was church music — hymns. Oh, once in a while some white gal would get up at a church supper and sing a soprano solo, somethin' like "The Little Dickeybird Is Climbin' Up My Garden Wall, Tra-la, Tra-lee." I didn't go much for that type of jazz; I liked the way the colored folks sang and I liked their songs, especially their blues songs."

When he was fifteen Gene ran away from home, hoboed around the South for a while, joined a circus and learned to play "When You Wore a Tulip" on the steam calliope, and when he was sixteen joined the Army. During the early part of World War I he was assigned to guard duty on the New Orleans docks. "I almost hate to tell you this," he says, "because you hear it from so many singers and musicians, but it's a God's honest fact that when I was off duty

I spent many an evenin' playin' piano in New Orleans sportin' houses."

Eventually he found himself in a New Jersey Army camp, where he was put to work in the hayfields. One day he learned that they were rounding up twenty men to fill out a contingent for shipping overseas. So Gene said to himself, "What'm I doin' here? Balin' hay from mornin' to night. Hell, they got hay to bale back home in Looze-ee-anna." He put down his tools and fell in with the group of twenty and soon found himself in France.

One evening an Army dentist heard Gene playing the piano and singing a blues song. "This guy came over and talked to me," Gene relates, "and said he liked music, and he needed an assistant, so I became a dental mechanic. Along came the Armistice and this dentist told me he wanted to stay in Europe and practice dentistry. For some reason he wanted to settle in Lithuania — he said that every tooth in Lithuania had a cavity in it. He wanted me to study dentistry and be his partner, and we'd get dirty rich in Lithuania. I was agreeable, but I had to get an education, so we came back to the States. He opened a dental office in Baltimore and I enrolled in dental school. He had a lot of patients, but they weren't paying their bills, so one day I said as a gag that I'd better switch over and study law so I could collect the bills. Somehow that crack put the notion into my head to become a lawyer, so I entered the University of Maryland Law School."

In the evenings after school Gene began playing and singing occasionally in small clubs in and around Baltimore. Other times he was accompanist for various acts in the local vaudeville houses. He drifted away from dentistry and then he drifted away from the law. Wanderlust, always a strong element in his makeup, led him to sign on as an entertainer aboard a ship headed for the Orient. Within a few days someone decided he wasn't very entertaining and, anyway, they were short a fireman in the black gang. He shoveled coal over and back and when he came home he met a fellow named Roy Bergere.

Bergere liked Gene's singing and talked him into teaming up in a vaudeville act featuring blues numbers. They toured the East and Midwest without setting the country on fire, but they were improving all the time, and finally they wound up in New York. They were still playing club dates and small vaudeville houses when Roy Bergere got married and headed west to try to crash the movies. Out of their association came one song which they wrote together: "How Come You Do Me Like You Do?"

Gene went it alone and got a job singing in the Club Mah-Jongg, which was run by Lou Clayton. Out of that engagement one episode sticks in his mind to this day. Clayton came to Gene one day and told him that the club needed a good trio. "There are three guys over at some little club," said Clayton, "and I hear good reports about them. Drop over there tonight and have a look, and let me know what you think." Gene had the look, came back and told Clayton, "No good. They've got no class." The trio was called Harris, Jackson and Durante and before long Lou Clayton himself had supplanted Harris to begin one of the most memorable associations in all show business.

About this time Gene got married, the Club Mah-Jongg got padlocked by prohibition agents and Gene turned seriously to the business of writing songs. To sustain life he took a job with a music publisher as a song plugger. He was required to make the rounds of the recording studios, playing and singing the publisher's latest songs, trying to convince people that those songs were worthy of recording.

Nathaniel Shilkret was in charge of music at Victor and one day Gene told him about a new song he had written, called "When My Sugar Walks Down the Street." Shilkret listened to it and decided it was zingy enough for records. He recommended, however, that Gene not try it solo. Gene as a singer was an unknown quantity and the high command wouldn't push his record. Shilkret suggested that they bring in a name singer to do the number with Gene. Aileen Stanley, already a prominent star, was chosen and the record was cut. Gene remembers that he had very little singing to do on that first record. Miss Stanley would sing, "When my sugar walks down the street, all the little birdies go . . ." and Gene would chime in with, "Tweet-tweet-tweet."

Soon thereafter he sang his first recorded number alone — something titled "The Only, Only One" — and Victor gave him a one-year contract under which he would be paid a hundred dollars for each song he did. Next he recorded "Yes Sir, That's My Baby," which made a minor stir, and after that, "Yearning." This was the record that made Gene Austin, and though it sold and sold and kept on selling, his financial take from it remained a flat and feeble one hundred dollars.

Dealers began clamoring for more of this boy's songs, but Victor couldn't find him. He had become unhappy about his contract and had gone off on a vaudeville tour. Victor sent a man to California to beg him to hurry back and make more records. But Gene still didn't like that contract. He wanted the customary royalty arrangements, and he wanted the privilege of choosing his own songs. He got both.

"The most important element in the success of a record," says Gene, "is the song, not the singer. I got an old sayin', 'Hit songs don't care who sings 'em.' "

His first royalty check under his new contract was for ninety-six thousand dollars. He decided it was time to go back and preen himself before the home folks in Louisiana. On his first day at home in Minden, after the big reception at the depot, he was out in the barn with his stepfather.

Old Jim Austin, the music hater, said, "Gene, I hear tell that these here people that sings makes as much jack as a hunnerd, hunnerd 'n' fifty dollars a week. I figger that's all newspaper talk. It is, ain't it?"

"Sometimes it is," said Gene, pulling the ninety-six-thousand-dollar check from his pocket, "and sometimes it ain't. This is what I got for about three months of singin'."

Old Jim Austin's eyes popped when he read the figure on the check. He was about to say something when Gene's mother called him from the kitchen door. Some folks had dropped in and wanted to see him and wanted him to sing a few songs for them. Gene went in and greeted the people and sat down at the old square piano and began singing. Suddenly he sensed an alien presence in the room. Out of the corner of his eye he saw Old Jim Austin, head cocked to one side, forefinger alongside his nose, listening intently.

"I think," says Gene, "that his head was a-bobbin' to the beat; just a trifle, mind you, but a-bobbin' just the same."

Gene bought a comfortable house for his parents and headed back for New York and the making of more records. He resumed his prowling for songs and one day came up with an item called "My Blue Heaven," by George Whiting and Walter Donaldson. This number had been languishing in the files for seven or eight years and hadn't even been copyrighted. Something about it appealed to Gene and he took it along to his next recording session. He knew his own mind about it, but he wasn't sure how the Victor people would react, so he put it last on the day's agenda. By the time they got to "My Blue Heaven" the orchestra leader announced that time had run out and the band was finished for the day.

"I grabbed an old guy with a cello," Gene recalls, "and talked him into standing by. Then I grabbed a song plugger who could play pretty fair piano. And the third fellow I got was an agent who could whistle — bird calls and that sort of thing. I made the record with those three." In the intervening years Gene has cut fourteen successive versions of "My Blue Heaven" and these records have had an aggregate sale of more than seven million copies.

When I first knew him in Tulsa and Denver, Gene had no inkling of the fact that he and the whole country were riding for a heavy fall. I remember the day in Denver when he was to make a personal appearance in a music store on Champa Street, autographing records for all comers. The entire block was decorated with banners bearing his name in letters four feet high, and traffic had to be blocked off an hour before his arrival.

Several factors combined to thrust Gene into comparative obscurity within the next few years. Radio changed from a hobby to a habit, and then came the depression. People put their phonographs in the attic; they no longer had the seventy-five cents that a record cost and, anyway, they could get their music for nothing on the radio. Another factor, less important, was Gene's affinity for the ole black bottle. He did a lot of drinking in the wild bootleg days and occasionally he got into trouble with the law. It should be remembered, however, that he and the century were in their twenties at the same time, and both he and the century were suffering from severe growing pains. Moreover, it should be kept in mind that Gene was a boy up from the piney woods, a boy who had never had anything; that money was piling in faster than he and all his pals could spend it, and all he had to do to get that money was to appear once each month or so and sing a few songs into a ridiculous recording horn. He played and he played hard in those years. He had half a dozen fancy cars, a mansion on the Jersey shore, a seventy-foot yacht named *My Blue Heaven,* and a host of Good Time Charlies to keep him company. I suspect he was actually a little happy about it when the bottom fell out of things. He disappeared into the West and he remained in obscurity, so far as the national consciousness was concerned, for almost a quarter of a century.

What was he doing in all those years? Surprisingly enough he was making money. And he was still singing. He teamed up with Ken Murray to inaugurate the musical show *Blackouts* which ran for seven solid years in a Hollywood theater. Gene knew a good deal about the economics of night-club operation, so he spent several years as an entrepreneur. He'd shop around Los Angeles until he found a club that was tottering. He'd buy it for peanuts, move in, change its name to "Gene Austin's Blue Heaven," and build it into a profitable business. For example, he bought one club for thirteen hundred dollars and in six months sold it for thirty-six thousand dollars. He performed this operation with three or four different clubs, and in each case he was the floor show, the attraction that fetched in the customers. A little rinkey-tink piano would be wheeled onto the dance floor. Gene would bounce out, settle himself, and then spend an hour or two singing the old favorites, always finishing with "My Blue Heaven." There were plenty of customers (myself among them) who wanted to hear him sing those old songs again and his clubs were always crowded.

In between times he was involved in other musical shows, in motion pictures, in writing songs and in night-club appearances around the country. Once in the 1930s a wealthy auto manufacturer in Ohio heard that Gene Austin was in town. He telephoned Gene, said he had been an Austin fan for years, and then made a proposal. "I'm having a party at my home tonight," he said, "and I'll give you a thousand dollars if you'll come out and sing six songs."

Said Gene, "I'm on my way."

When he arrived at the mansion the auto manufacturer met him at the door and escorted him quickly through a crowd of people and into a library where there was a piano. He closed and locked the door, nodded toward the piano and said, "Okay, start off with 'Melancholy Baby.'"

Gene was perplexed. "But the party's out yonder," he protested.

"The hell with the party," said the host. "I want you to sing just for me."

Gene had many such private engagements, especially back in the twenties when the millionaires of Long Island and Westchester would summon him to their parties and pay him fabulous sums for singing a few numbers.

"Those were usually tough assignments," Gene remembers. "I was the first of the crooners, and some of the men were pretty nasty about it, making loud cracks about me, suggesting that I was sorta ladylike. In those days almost every party I went to ended in a fight, and for the same reason. I'd listen to the cracks and then I'd say, 'Okay, brother, come on outside and we'll see who's ee-femminit.' I'm not much inclined to brag, but the truth is I flattened many a Yale-type cooky pusher in those days."

Gene has been married four times. He has three grandchildren by a daughter who lives in Kansas City. His other daughter, Charlotte Austin, is a stunning brunette beauty who acts in the movies. His present wife, Lou, is a bright and attractive girl out of Springfield, Missouri. She knew Gene Austin's records when she was a teen-ager, and loved them. About twelve years ago she was living in St. Louis when she read in the newspapers that Gene Austin was singing at the Park Plaza Hotel. That night she was at a ringside table with a friend. When Gene finished his act he wandered down into the audience. He stopped at Lou's table and asked her if there was any special number she would like to hear.

"Oh yes," she said. "I remember a long time ago, the first Gene Austin record I ever heard, and it became my favorite."

"Which one was that?"

"I Wish I Had Died in My Cradle, Before I Grew Up to Love You."

"Great day!" exclaimed Gene. "I forgot that one ninety years ago." But he went back to the piano and noodled around, and it came back to him. When he had finished singing it, he sat for a moment in thought. What kind of a dame would choose a corn-popper like that out of all the songs I've sung? He decided it was a question worth investigating, and returned to her table . . . and so they were wed.

In recent years the Austin home has been a fifty-foot

trailer called, naturally, the Blue Heaven. Gene has it based permanently in Las Vegas, with a second trailer serving as studio and office alongside it. He and Lou do a lot of traveling, for he's still in demand in the supper clubs from Key West to Alaska.

Five years ago when Gene was in New York and there was talk of a Big Comeback for him, I decided to try to help matters along by writing a magazine article about him. I turned out a fairly long piece (which was substantially this piece you have been reading) and then sat down and read it through and decided it wouldn't work. There is an axiom in my trade which says that a writer is usually the worst judge of his own product; if he thinks a piece of his work is good it probably smells to middle heaven, whereas, if he judges it to be a malodorous botch, it is very likely a masterpiece. I point to my Gene Austin article to demonstrate the point. I said to myself, after I finished writing it, "Well, I did the best I could. It was a labor of love, an attempt to help an old friend. Nobody will buy it, nobody will publish it. Maybe, because it's show biz, I'll just trim it down and see if Abel Green would like to have it for *Variety*." Still, I felt that I should go through the motions so I handed the manuscript over to my agent. Two days later he notified me that the *Saturday Evening Post* had grabbed it up and was paying me the biggest dough I'd ever had from a magazine for a single piece.

After the article was published in the *Post*, Gene was called upon for various guest appearances on radio and television and one evening he was interviewed on the air by the incomparable Jinx Falkenburg. Miss Falkenburg was famous for her naïveté, her artless simplicity, whenever she was grappling with the seamier side of life, and this night she was stroking par.

"Is it really true," she asked Gene, "that you once were a piano player in the sporting houses of New Orleans?"

"Well . . ." said Gene, a drawling smile in his voice. But

Miss Falkenburg, herself once a figure in the sports world, plunged right ahead, and it was obvious that she had no idea of the nature of a sporting house. She suggested that it might have been difficult playing piano in such a place. "All that noise," she said. Gene hemmed and hawed around a bit and finally she asked him if there were lots of sporting houses in New Orleans in those days and Gene brought down the house by answering, "Oh, yes. The Spalding people were opening new ones all over the country."

All of these interviewers asked Gene how it felt to be making a big comeback and he answered each of them the same way: "I'm not makin' any comeback. I ain't been away." This was a normal response for anyone in show business. A performer will withstand thumbscrews and the Chinese water torture before he'll ever admit that he has been in eclipse.

In 1962 Gene came home from a successful singing engagement in Alaska to run for the Democratic nomination for Governor of Nevada. The main plank in his platform was that he could do anything his opponent could do and he could also sing. He said, too, that he would be able to give the state one hell of a fine First Lady. It is my impression that he didn't win.

When he was sixty years old he drove down from Vegas to Hollywood and spent a couple of days making a long-playing stereo record which was released under the title, "Gene Austin's Great Hits." On this record he sang "My Blue Heaven," "Lonesome Road," "Melancholy Baby," "Bye Bye Blackbird," "Ramona," "Sleepy Time Gal," "Jeannine," "I Can't Give You Anything But Love," "Someday Sweetheart," "Girl of My Dreams," "Weary River," and "How Am I to Know?" All songs that were closely associated with his name in the days of yore. I speak as a confirmed Gene Austin fan but I also speak with absolute sincerity when I say that he never in all his years sang as well as he does on that record.

And so it was that all of us who belonged to his generation

were happy that he was back. Red Barber was happy, and so was John Crosby, and Richard Watts, and Sherman Fairchild, and R. W. Woodruff of Coca-Cola, and Harry S. Truman, and Alfred Vanderbilt. All of these people have remained steadfast Gene Austin fans down through the years — and there was one other.

Jimmy Byrnes, of South Carolina, once told Gene: "I never heard F.D.R. play but one record, and he played that one a lot. It was Gene Austin singing 'Lonesome Road.'"

That, of course, made Gene feel real good, for he not only sang it. He wrote it.

*

*

*

7. A Gourmet Society Meets

WESTCHESTER COUNTY, where I have made my home for the last twenty years, lies to the immediate north of New York City and is famous for, above all else, its atmosphere of luxury and wealth. A national magazine, considering the county in a long article recently, described it in this subtitle: "Money, property and an impeccable background form the social trinity of New York's fanciest suburban area."

In the light of all this it may be understood why I was nervous when an invitation came for me to be a guest at the monthly convocation of the Westchester Gourmet Society. It seemed to me that if any one region in the land could produce a gourmet group of class and tone and super-gentility, that region would be Westchester.

I am, quite frankly, of plebian origins and I subsisted on navy beans until I was maybe fifteen years old. My whole adult life has been rough and raffish in general outline. I am not comfortable wearing dinner clothes at splendid feeds, even when they are given by my good friend Joan Crawford, who is ornately and majestically democratic.

"We meet once each month," said William G. Carlson, Esq., president of the Westchester Gourmet Society, "and I would like for you to be my personal guest at our August excursion."

"Excursion?" I repeated.

"We will be going up the Hudson on a yacht," he said.

Just like that. It was too big a thing for me to reject on the grounds of social ineptitude. The date was a month and a half away, and so I said I'd be happy to come. I had known Mr. Carlson for years, as the proprietor of a good country restaurant a few miles from my house. He was a bluff, hearty, outgoing sort of man and I felt that if I were under his wing I would be able to cope with any problems of gourmet etiquette that might arise. Still, I was inclined to tighten up whenever I contemplated cruising the Hudson in all that splendid company. I thought of Westchester Rockefellers and Reids and Loebs and Lewisohns and Wainwrights and Lawrences and as for the yacht, well, it would surely be as big and as elegant as the *Honey Fitz.*

Twice before in my life, in the role of reporter, I had been to meetings of gourmet societies, once in New York City and once in Beverly Hills. I had a good idea of how they are organized. Each member is an amateur chef in his own right (unless he happens to be a big-name professional chef). Each member comes prepared to step up to the stove and demonstrate his particular esculent nonesuch. There would be rules about smoking, and no preprandial cocktails. I had a feeling that here in posh Westchester there might even be more rigid patterns of conduct, when it came to epicurean ceremonials, than in other centers of high living.

The question came into my mind: why had they invited me? Could it be that I have acquired a reputation as a gourmet? Or, rather, as an amateur chef concerned with exotic preparations? If this were so, then I was sailing under spurious colors. I do quite a bit of cooking but to be honest about it, I'm still not able to tell thyme from basil and basil from oregano by sniffing at the jars. Yet, I felt that I must be prepared with *something* for the swells of Westchester.

I finally settled on the Roast Duck With Orange Glaze. Once I had come upon a description of this Lucullan extravaganza in one of the many cook books I keep around the house. I had, single-handed, using both hands, cooked a Roast Duck With Orange Glaze. It took me two days but I made it and, for the reason that I followed every step of the procedures faithfully, it turned out to be a beautiful production. Messy, and ruinous to napkins, but great. I decided that the Roast Duck With Orange Glaze should be my dish in the event they called upon me for an example of my peerless cuisine. I got out the cook book and memorized the recipe — down to the last single caraway seed. I memorized it and recited it to myself and then to my wife until I had it beyond chance of error.

Mr. Carlson had instructed me to be at the entrance to his restaurant at nine o'clock on a Monday morning. At my house I went over Roast Duck With Orange Glaze once again while putting on my conservatively handsome black linen suit, and selecting a gray silk tie of twill weave with just a hint of gloss to it.

I drove to Mr. Carlson's restaurant, timing myself to be just ten minutes late, and immediately got my first shock. I had dressed improperly. Lounging at the entrance to the restaurant were seven or eight men. They wore sports shirts and loafers and slacks and one of them had on a baseball cap. I pronounced a few swear words, softly but distinctly, and parked my car under a tree and walked over to the group. The first man I confronted was a man I knew. A plumber. The man who fixes my sinks and my toilets. He gave me a hearty greeting and I responded in kind, thinking bewildered thoughts. Well, hell, I said, why shouldn't a plumber be a gourmet? God knows they make enough per hour to eat as high off the hog as anybody else. No reason on earth why a plumber shouldn't be a trencherman of quality, a devotee of Brillat-Savarin and old Escoffier.

Then I recognized others in the group. One was co-owner of Ravetto's Restaurant up at Amawalk Reservoir, one was proprietor of my favorite stationery store, one was a contractor whose boys plow the snow off my driveway, and one was the printer who does my letterheads. I saw no Rockefellers, no Lewisohns, no Wainwrights.

Mr. Carlson came round the corner of the building with a big carton in his arms, which he now placed in the back of a station wagon. Another man brought another carton and soon we were all ready to travel. We climbed into four cars and headed for the Tappan Zee Bridge. We whisked merrily across the bridge and bore right to Nyack and made our way to the waterfront. Our four cars pulled up at a pier and I looked at the *Vagrant III*. The yacht.

It was a scow with a tin roof on it.

By this time I had shed my coat and tie, and a notion was beginning to knock around in my head: it could be that my original estimate of the Westchester Gourmet Society was tinged with error.

Mr. Carlson told me to get on board the *Vagrant III*, saying that he and the others would carry the supplies, the excellent comestibles, onto the vessel. Other autoloads of men were arriving at the pier and by now we had a complement of perhaps fifty gourmets. There was much jollity, much hearty backslapping and, considering the high-toned nature of the expedition, altogether too much crude language.

I climbed aboard and found that the yacht was really a sort of floating dance floor; the entire middle part of the scow consisted of open space with wooden benches along the sides. At the stern was a step-down into a small area which was the bar. A steady procession now moved toward this area, gourmets carrying boxes and cases, and I was surprised to note that the boxes and cases contained assorted whiskies, gins, vodkas and beers.

I must admit that a sense of frustration had taken possession of me. This wasn't at all what I had expected. And then almost without warning we had shoved away from the pier and *Vagrant III* turned upstream and there was a great deal of yelling and whooping in the stern section as the boxes were yanked apart and bottles opened.

By the time we were opposite the gray walls of Sing Sing the booze was flowing like Niagara. As we approached the Bear Mountain Bridge a big circle of kneeling gourmets formed amidships and the crap game started. Some of the men were drinking straight from the bottle. And the crap game looked like and sounded like a flashback to the era of Arnold Rothstein on Broadway. They were not playing for half-dollars.

I can't say that I was crushed by disappointment. But I was mystified and at last I went to a man I knew, a man who works in a local bank, and I asked him, "Where's all the gourmet food?" He indicated a doorway and said turn right and I'd find a whole cabin full of it. I found it. There were two trestle-tables stretched across the little room. White cloths had been draped over the food itself, so that I couldn't tell what it was. There wasn't another soul in sight. I lifted the cloth at one table and looked. Piles and piles of cold fried chicken. Nothing else. I went to the other table and lifted the cloth. Piles and piles of more fried chicken.

That was the *carte de cuisine* for the monthly meeting of the Westchester Gourmet Society.

I stood there and found myself grinning, and then I checked the contents of my wallet. I made my way back to the main arena. I got me a good strong drink and I entered the crap game.

We cruised to a spot just beyond West Point and then turned around and floated lazily back to Nyack. All the way up and all the way back we were traveling one of the most scenic river stretches in the whole wide world, yet nobody looked at the water, nobody glanced at the sylvan shore. By the time we arrived at the dock the *Vagrant III* could have passed as a shambles. The crap game was still in progress but most of the players had gone broke or decided that the pleasures of the bar were greater than the pleasures of the dice.

At Nyack four men had to be carried off. Half a dozen had to be led.

The Mount Kisco delegation, my own group, was in fair shape, although Mr. Carlson, the president of the Society, was engaged in a marathon oration which seemed to be about the glories of good fellowship and down with women.

For some strange reason it was midnight by the time I got home. My wife looked me over with a suspicious eye.

"Well," she said, "how did it go?"

"Beautiful," I said. "Bee-yootiful!"

"Did you give them the Roast Duck With Orange Glaze?"

"Indeed I did."

"How'd they like it?"

"They *loved* it!"

I suspect that I have qualified as an authentic Westchester gourmet.

＊

＊

＊

8. *The Water Pistol Caper*

THEY SAY THAT if you are a writer of fiction you must be very careful in the use of coincidence. "It is only in literature that coincidences seem unnatural," said Robert Lynd. I don't know which Robert Lynd said it — there seem to be several Robert Lynds — but one of them did. In any case, if I incorporated this little story into a novel or a short story, people would say it was unbelievable and call me a lousy writer, lacking in invention. But as a reporter, setting down bald truth, I have no hesitation in telling it.

In the town of Morganton, over near Asheville in North Carolina, there is a small boy whose identity I do not know but about whom I sometimes worry. I suspect that he has lately been given to sitting around the house, listless and moping, brooding in a vague way over the fact that Fate is a dirty dog. I know about this boy because I know a young man named David Parmelee who once lived in Morganton.

David Parmelee is a witty man and a brilliant conversationalist. He is a close friend of my daughter and her husband, who were until recently residents of Rockview Lane in Morganton. Not long ago, on a Sunday afternoon, Mr. Parmelee was making some social calls. He attended a cocktail party in the home of some friends and he was due a bit later at the home of my daughter. As he was preparing to leave the cocktail party he noticed a child's water pistol lying in a corner of the hallway. He thought that it would be fun when he got to my daughter's house to greet my young grandsons with a few vigorous bursts from the water pistol. He borrowed it and filled it with water and dropped it into his coat pocket.

So now we have young Mr. David Parmelee strolling blithely along a residential street in Morganton. The sky was cerulean blue, the patches of cirrus clouds were stunning in their beauty, the birds were singing in the mimosa trees and it was greenup time (Good God, boy, take it easy!)

Mr. Parmelee had not a worry in the world as he strolled along, and then a movement in the bushes caught his attention. From the corner of his eye he observed that a small boy was creeping toward him, a boy about six years old. And in each hand this boy had — of all things! — a black water pistol, held at the ready. The boy moved stealthily through the shrubbery, coming always closer to Mr. Parmelee, and Mr.

Parmelee pretended not to notice anything amiss. At last the boy arrived at a small open space just a few feet from the sidewalk, a suitable spot for ambuscade. He raised his pistols and took aim. And then . . . faster than Marshal Dillon ever did it, Mr. Parmelee whirled and drew and fired. Before that boy could ever pull the trigger a stream of water struck him full in the face. Of all the adults in the world who were walking abroad on that particular day, that unhappy boy had picked on the only one who had a water pistol in his coat pocket. Loaded.

*

*

*

9. The Big Blackout

FUTURE HISTORIANS must keep in mind that the spending of incredibly immense sums of money didn't enter into it at all. The generality of American citizens accepted this extravagance without a great deal of complaint, even though the money was coming from their own pockets. And so the government continued to accelerate its program of celestial science at the various launching pads scattered along the two ocean fronts. There were times when the rockets and missiles were banging off the pads so rapidly that the astronauts, already in orbit and looking earthward, bethought themselves of skyrockets and aerial bombs going up from a state fair grounds on the Fourth of July.

There were a few neurotic citizens who spoke of the possibility of self-inflicted disaster. Most of these dissidents lived within a hundred miles of the major launching stations. A retired native of Georgia, sitting out his hours of quiet desperation in the city of Orlando, fifty miles west of Cape Canaveral, sounded a typical note of alarm whenever he could get an audience.

"You watch'n see," he said. "One a these days one a them things is a-gonna flip ovah backwuhds and steada goin' ovah the ocean, it's a-gonna land rat smack dab in the middle a one a these towns down heah. Pussonly I hope it's Miamuh. But you watch'n see. It'll still be shootin' fyah outa its tail, and it'll go a-skitterin' aroun' like a skahrocket that zigs and zags back and fo'th in the street, only *this* skahrocket will be as big as that Singin' Tow-wuh down at Lake Wales — nilly as big as the Am-pyah State Buildin'. And it'll knock down evvything and set fyah to evvything and fry and frizzle a few thousand folks to death, and then maybe the gov'-ment'll get some sense in its haid. I said it befoah and I say it again, this country went plumb to the dawgs when it put that shidepokey peckerneck in the What House."

"Ay-yuh," said a retired druggist from Vermont.

There were quite a few eggheady people who adopted a Progress-*Can*-Be-Stopped attitude.

"How foolish can you get?" these people demanded. "Is there no end to the stupidity of mankind? We have not come within sixty million light years of solving the problems that harass us each day on our own sleazy, disorganized little planet. Look at us — two tremendous armed camps, ready to let fly at each other at the drop of a tin hat. We haven't even learned how to fly people safely from city to city. We haven't, in fact, learned to process their tickets and baggage in anything but an atmosphere of frenzy and clamorous madness. We aren't able to cope with juvenile delinquency and our finest public parks are more dangerous than the deepest jungles of Africa. Labor and management are as violently at war as they ever were in the past, and each side stands ready to pick up bludgeons and start shattering skulls. The population explosion, described by reputable scientists as a bigger threat to the world than all known diseases, is in turn described by reputable ecclesiastics as a pure fantasy, a figment of someone's imagination. Our highways and systems of traffic regulation become obsolete almost before they are opened to public travel. On every side people are clawing and clutching for dollars, cheating on their income taxes, loopholing their way through life. Think of what it might mean if all that missile money and rocket money were being put into the fight against cancer, and against those crippling diseases that affect so many of our children. So we shoot for the moon. If that is Progress, then we say Progress can be stopped, and should be stopped."

Let us remember that none of these carping movements had any more effect on the thinking of the general public than the stout declaration made by a woman in Southern California when she was stopped by a TV man who was conducting sidewalk interviews. Asked what she thought of the whole space program, she said:

"All them people ought to quit that fool stuff and go home and watch television like God intended we should."

This lady's statement was made in 1960 and recorded in the nation's press, and all over the country sensible people read it and smiled, or laughed outright. Even the clergy was amused. Nobody suspected that there was more than a grain of unconscious prophecy in that sidewalk interview.

The occasional complainings went all but unnoticed and the man-in-the-street seemed indifferent and uninformed about moon-shoots and other space delvings, save one. Considerable public interest was aroused when the Soviets playfully put a jeep into orbit, and even more when we countered by orbiting a jeep with a man at the wheel. Somehow the very idea of a jeep circling the earth tickled the public fancy and the greatest of the orbit-rubbering crowds turned out each time one of the vehicles passed across the continent — a tiny speck of light with four-wheel drive.

And then came that grim February day when the trouble began. People in the lower Mississippi Valley apparently were the first to notice it. Their television sets began to "act up crazylike" as they phrased it. Some sets developed an unnerving and incurable condition known as fast flopover. Others brought in nothing but snow. And still others acquired the look of old school necktie patterns. Soon the TV sets in other parts of the country began to jerk and flicker, to fade in and fade out. Television repair men were driven frantic by the piles of fix-orders in their shops, especially since they were unable to fix anything at all except by pulling the plug. The audio began to go haywire. Sound, whether of music or the human voice, was slightly garbled at first and then in a matter of weeks everything that came out of the speakers sounded like blah-blah-whee-whee-blub-blub-blub. The network people and the owners of individual stations and the ulcerated advertising executives were in a towering frenzy trying to find out what was causing the trouble. And while they sweated and roared, the lights and the noises faded away altogether, and television was dead.

Now the shrill voice of the people was heard in the land. The public began screaming for the government to get off its posterior and find out what was going on. It took a while — three and a half months from the time of the total blackout. Then a team of scientists in Chicago found the answer. They hurried to the White House and reported to the President. They told him that television reception had been nullified by the vast increase in rocket launchings plus the steady procession of orbiting objects moving across the outer sky. There were times, they pointed out, when great chunks of metal were sailing through space less than a mile apart. And rockets of varying sizes were crisscrossing back and forth in the heavens because everyone now, even El Salvador and Haiti and Luxembourg and Baja California, had launching pads in operation. All this celestial activity had created an atmospheric condition in which television waves were stifled and beaten into the ground.

The President had ample knowledge of the temper of the public; he could hear the rumblings and the roarings from every quarter of the country. He listened, grave of countenance, to the report of the Chicago group and then retired to think for an hour or so. After that he notified the scientists that their discovery would have to remain top secret. He had a vague premonition of what might happen if the public learned about it.

But it leaked out, as all secret matters affecting the well-being of the people have a way of leaking out. Somebody talked and Scotty Reston, III, listened and away it went like a white tornado sweeping across the nation.

Angry murmurings now increased in volume and became a shout.

"It's the missiles! It's the rockets! It's them damn jeeps and all that other scrap iron whirling around out there!"

Neighborhood meetings were summoned. Then town meetings, and these grew into great outdoor gatherings. Spellbinders were hired by the television industry to address these growing throngs and to keep them stirred up, though this was hardly necessary. The people were angry to the point of untrammeled fury, *to the very verge of revolution.*

"You idiots have killed TV!" they howled.

They shook their fists in the direction of Washington and cried:

"You have taken the joy out of our lives!"

"We're not able to see *Ben Casey* any more!"

"We haven't watched the *Untouchables* in six months!"

"We've almost forgotten who's in *Gunsmoke!*"

"We feel like as if Ed Sullivan was dead and buried!"

Mobs of unruly citizens began marching on Washington. Coxey's Army and the Bonus Marchers were as subcommittees alongside these furious throngs. Ball parks and amphitheaters were crowded with outraged citizens. And then under steady prodding from the television magnates, a program of protest backed by grave threatenings began to take form. It culminated in an ultimatum which was laid on the President's desk as four and a half million shouting citizens milled around in Pennsylvania Avenue.

The public's manifesto was clear and to the point, demanding:

That all rocket shoots, all space adventuring, all orbiting experiments, shall cease within one week from this date or:

1. *We will refuse to go to the polls on any election day hereafter.*

2. We will defy jury summonses.
3. We will refuse to send our children to any school or college.
4. We will not enter the employ of any manufacturer who uses steel in his product or products.
5. We will cash in all our government bonds at once.
6. We will refuse to pay one penny in income taxes, either federal or state.

That did it. The President and his advisors knew, from hurried but trustworthy surveys, that at least eighty-eight per cent of the people were in sympathy with the movement and would obey the terms of the decree, down to the last letter. The remaining twelve per cent — a group that we must always have with us if democracy is to survive — were listed under "Don't Know."

There was no alternative. In a sense it was a greater crisis than the War Between the States. Immediately, then, all the launching pads were closed down and the personnel dispersed. Stop orders went out to all plants producing missiles and rockets, or parts for missiles and rockets. Coded messages zipped into space telling all our astronauts to return to earth at once. Down came the jeep. Meanwhile the President got on the Telestar phone to Moscow and said, "We'd like to have you stop all space activity at once." The Kremlin responded, "Certainly. Whatever you say." And so, with the United States and Russia calling off their orbiting procedures, all the lesser nations followed suit.

Now the picture and the sound came back to television. *Candid Camera* returned, and Jack Paar, and baseball, and David Brinkley, and the Beverly Hillbillies. The people settled back in their chairs, fastened their eyes on their screens, and were contented once again. The images were clear and lovely on the screens in living room, lounge and ginmill.

The lonely stars twinkled in the night sky and the nation, and the world, were at peace.

CONFESSIONAL NOTE

From time to time accusations are made that I do not write my own stuff. It is usually stated that I stay drunk all the time and am unable to write an intelligible sentence. I have heard it said (sometimes in letters directed to me) that my wife writes my stuff, that my agent's daughter writes my stuff, that my son, a chemical engineer, is secretly a writer and writes my stuff, that my daughter, in between bearing me four grandsons, writes my stuff. So now I have a confession to make. The foregoing bit belongs to my daughter. She gave me the idea for it. And I was able to sober up long enough to get it on paper. Now my conscience is clear; I return to the bottle and hand my typewriter back to my wife.

*

*

*

10. *A Friend in Baltimore*

THE SUBSTITUTE cleaning woman tried to throw it away today. This is the second time it has happened. Our regular cleaning woman was halfway to the garbage can with it when I caught her and snatched it out of her hands. It is the only keepsake that I own, outside of a paperweight off the desk of Gene Fowler, and it is probably my most cherished possession; yet everybody who sees it in my office says, "Why in the world do you keep *that* old thing around here?" It probably cost, originally, ten cents or maybe as much as fifteen cents.

It is a gnarled, fire-scarred, twisted bit of metal called by some a "copy-spike" but known to its former owner, Henry L. Mencken, as his "copy-hook." Any newspaper city room contains a forest of such copy-hooks. This one was the first item released by the Mencken estate following his death in 1956. I inherited it.

It may be an ugly, misshapen thing, but for me it has a fascinating history and a sentimental significance. I knew Henry Mencken for thirty years and he was always a hero to me, and always kind to me, even when I was a dirty-shirt reporter with a residue of moisture behind my ears. I knew about his copy-hook, which stood on top of a bookcase in his workroom at the famous Baltimore address, 1524 Hollins Street, where he lived all but the first three years of his life and where he died in his sleep. I knew the story of that copy-hook and the reason he kept it always in view when he was working. It was an important symbol to him.

Its story goes back to a February morning in 1904 when Henry Mencken, at the age of twenty-four, was already city editor of the Baltimore *Herald*. On that wild and blustery morning the greatest fire in the city's history swept downtown Baltimore and before it had burned itself out, it had destroyed a square mile of the business district.

Mencken and his staff, forced to evacuate their own building, went to Washington and used newspaper facilities there to get out a four-page paper; then they traveled to Philadelphia, a hundred miles from Baltimore, and put together the *Herald* in that city for the next five weeks.

"It was brain-fagging and back-breaking," Mencken wrote years afterward, "but it was grand beyond compare — an adventure of the first chop, a razzle-dazzle superb and elegant, a circus in forty rings."

In the month following the fire the young city editor, destined to become one of America's greatest literary stylists and the nation's most flamboyantly acerb critic, made his way back to the blackened and gutted *Herald* building. Its frame was intact and Mencken managed to shinny up to the fifth floor where the city room had been. "It was easy to find the place where my desk had stood," he recalled, "though the desk itself was only a heap of white dust, for its hardware survived and so did the frame of the goose-neck light that had stood upon it. I also found my old copy-hook, twisted as if it had died in agony. . . ."

He described his adventures during the great fire, and his return to the *Herald* city room, in one of his autobiographical books, *Newspaper Days*, published just twenty years ago. Shortly after that I wrote to him and hinted that I would greatly enjoy having that old copy-hook some day. Promptly came his reply:

That copy-hook will become yours the day I am translated to bliss eternal. I have left orders that my carcass is to be stuffed and deposited in the National Museum at Washington. I had planned to ask the taxidermist to put the copy-hook in my hand, but that request is now canceled and you will get it in due course.

When he died I was so upset that a month passed before I remembered the bequest. I wrote to his brother, August, who is almost a carbon copy of Henry in physical structure and caustic manner of speech, and told him about the copy-hook.

Back came a letter from August, telling me that the executors of Henry's estate, the Mercantile Safe Deposit & Trust Company, had instructed him to let nothing go however small — that it would take about a year and a half to wind up the estate. August suggested, however, that if I would send along Henry's letter, the Mercantile Safe Deposit & Trust Company might unbend a bit. And so it did. Thus it came about that a solemn mandamus was issued by the Mercantile Safe Deposit & Trust Company releasing into my custody and ownership one crippled and fire-scarred copy-hook, relic of the Baltimore fire of 1904.

August Mencken now had trouble locating it. After about a week he wrote to me that he had found, in Henry's workroom, "a paper spike which is made up of a wire spike fixed to a small cast-iron base and which looks as if it had been through much worse things than the Baltimore fire." He wondered if this could be my inheritance. By return mail I informed him that it was indeed, and he, an amateur cabinetmaker, constructed a neat little crate to hold it and shipped it off to me.

It stands today on a shelf in my office, not far from a panel containing two photographs of its former owner — a Pinchot portrait he gave me off the parlor piano in 1935, and the last photograph taken of him before his death, sitting beside his famous woodpile in the backyard of the Hollins Street home.

There remains only the need to outline the symbolism of

the copy-hook. A few months after his death the CBS Radio Workshop did a fine half-hour program, written by Allan E. Sloane, dramatizing the fabulous career of H. L. Mencken — the copy-hook serving as a device through which the old and dying Mencken remembered the glorious time of his youth. Standing there in his workroom where he turned out such prodigious quantities of slam-bang, iconoclastic prose for so many years, it reminded him of "how full of steam and malicious animal magnetism I was when I was young."

But more to the point, the copy-hook was emblematic of a transition that came to him with the Baltimore fire; it was a sort of badge representing the time, the moment, when he reached maturity. He sometimes said that he had gone into the disaster a boy, "and it was the hot gas of youth that kept me going." When he came out of the adventure at last, "I was a settled and indeed almost a middle-aged man, spavined by responsibility and aching in every sinew."

For several years I spiked no single piece of paper on that copy-hook. But now it carries a piece of white cardboard on which is lettered the warning:

DON'T THROW THIS OUT!

It will stay with me as long as I live.

I first saw Henry Mencken plain on a spring afternoon in 1930. He was standing at the entrance to a Fifth Avenue office building, talking to another man, possibly Alfred Knopf, and I recognized him instantly. I had but lately come to New York from the West and I had looked at all the major sights, from the Statue of Liberty to the Chrysler tower — but this was the greatest scenic wonder of them all: H. L. Mencken in the flesh. As I've said, he was a hero to me then, as he remained all the rest of his life, and as he remains in fond memory today.

I was twenty-two years old that day I saw him on Fifth

Avenue. He looked then much the way he would look for many years to come — a short, stubby man of brisk movements, a squarish face dominated by a snub nose and remarkable china-blue eyes, hair parted in the middle and pasted down, and dressed like a Nebraska farmer on his way to church. For a few moments I toyed with the notion of walking boldly up to him and introducing myself. I even took a couple of steps toward him, but then my knees turned to jelly and I walked slowly away, filled with a strange sort of throaty embarrassment.

Within a couple of weeks, however, I had decided that he might be a human creature rather than a god, and so I arranged to do an interview with him at the Hotel Algonquin (where he always lived when he was in New York). When at last I sat in his presence I was astonished to find that *he* was interested in *me*. He asked me questions about my job and my family and where I came from and how it was in Denver and what I hoped to achieve in New York and so on. I came away from that first meeting convinced, against all reason, that I now possessed some sort of electric personality, some new dynamic quality, that could compel this greatest of living men to hang on my every word.

That was one of his glowing attributes: the easy ability to make every person he met feel that he, above all others, was the favorite person of Henry L. Mencken. He demonstrated this quality over and over during all the subsequent years I knew him. For a dozen or more years he made me believe that he preferred my company to that of almost anybody else on earth. "When are you coming to Baltimore?" he would write me. "I long to see you and sit with you and talk of literary whales and the power of prayer." Or, "What are you doing these days? I haven't heard from you in months. Fill me in." I could scarcely believe the evidence of my senses when he wrote me one day and asked *me* to autograph one of *my* books for *him*.

On those occasions when I did go to Baltimore to visit him

and listen to his marvelous talk, he would convince me that I was doing him a great favor. He would accompany me to the door, at the end of such a visit, and say, "For God's sake, don't stay away so long." What this sort of thing did for me is far beyond evaluation.

The day came when I found out that there were a thousand others who got the same treatment from him. A thousand others who believed that *they* were the chosen ones. A thousand others who were told that he missed their company, that he wanted them to visit him in Baltimore, that he itched to see them, that he was anxious about the projects they were working on. When I found out the truth I might very easily have been resentful, but I was not. The man's capacity to inspire affection was so great that I felt not a shred of chagrin.

I used to interview him so often that it became an office scandal. "Good God!" they'd exclaim at the United Press, "Here comes Smith with another Mencken interview!" Actually there was never any objection, for the reason that no Mencken interview could ever possibly be dull. Newspaper editors all over the country were always eager for more copy about the salty sage of Baltimore.

It often confused and irritated me that such a courteous and kindly man as Mencken should have such a fierce reputation. Back in 1912 he was writing a daily column in the Baltimore *Sun*, a column in which he first established himself as a spike-tailed monster spitting sulphur and cinders over the Maryland landscape. One day a *Sun* artist named McKee Barclay turned out a hideous caricature of "The Subconscious Mencken." The man he pictured was the Mencken visualized by the multitudes of good souls whom he outraged with his writings. The portrait was that of a mean, bulbous-nosed, white-mustached, malevolent old man — the most unpleasant looking character imaginable, with a puss so sour it would clabber spring water. As a joke Mencken occasionally would run this picture in connection with his column, and before long the portrait was being printed in other cities, and everywhere people assumed that it was a true likeness. I'm told that to this day there are people in Baltimore who believe Mencken actually looked like Barclay's fusty old curmudgeon.

Mencken often described the intent of his work as "stirring up the animals" and stir them up he did, with the consequence that he in turn was almost constantly under bitter attack. He was abused and reviled in print so much that he once gleefully put together a book containing the printable invective that had been fired at him (*Menckeniana: a Schimpflexicon*). He was called a dirty buzzard, a maggot, a ghoul of new-made graves, a polecat, a howling hyena, and "a cheap blatherskite of a pen-pusher." Clergymen and editors and politicians had at him alike. He was called "a disappointed, dishonest, distrustful, disgraceful, degraded, degenerate evolute of a species fifty-seven varieties lower than a turkey buzzard." A minister said that Mencken had "a dilated brain impregnated with ego, indigo and gangrene." And another said, "If he ever had a real idea, his skull would pop like a rotten pumpkin."

One reason his reputation suffered was the fact that he employed a stylistic device common to the American humorous writer, namely, gross exaggeration. During the period of his marriage to Sara Haardt when he lived in Cathedral Street, I was walking with him in that neighborhood and he poked a thumb toward one of Baltimore's landmarks — a statue of George Washington standing on a high pillar. "The first American gentleman," said Mencken, "and the last." He didn't really mean that there have been no American gentleman since the time of Washington. It was his way of saying that there is an acute shortage of gentlemen in America, that there are not nearly as many gentlemen in this country as there ought to be.

There remain, to this day, many people who for want of better information believe that Mencken was a gross and evil man, satanical and anti-social. Yet the plain truth is, Henry L. Mencken was one of the most polite and considerate gentlemen this country ever produced. He was a good man. He was a prime example of the philosopher who abominates the human race for its congenital and incurable foolishness, yet loves and respects individual members of that race. Mark Twain was of the same breed and it is worth noting that the writings of Mark Twain were largely responsible for Mencken's decision to become a writer rather than a tobacco merchant. It is further worth noting that he wrote blistering, bruising things about people and they hated him deeply until they met him, and then invariably they succumbed to his warmth and his personal charm.

He was famous for the amount of hard work he got through each day, hence time was valuable to him. Still, he gave of it freely to almost anyone who came along. He was a man who appeared to thrive and prosper by doing things for other people. He usually spent two afternoons of each week visiting people in hospitals. He was almost a landmark at Johns Hopkins Hospital in Baltimore. He would arrive bearing gifts — bottles of wine and boxes of candy and armloads of books — and the word would travel through the long corridors. Immediately there would be a sort of mass movement in his direction; doctors and internes and nurses hurried to greet him and when he entered the rooms of various patients they would follow along because they knew he always put on a good show, delivering mock lectures on medical topics, spouting the old-time religion in the accents of Billy Sunday, or simply littering the premises with quips and drolleries. If a top editor of the *Sun* were in hospital, Mencken would be at his bedside regularly; but he also visited the *Sun*'s Negro elevator operator, or his wife or his children, if they were sick.

This man so long regarded as the embodiment of churlish evil could evoke from those who knew him best such expressions as George Jean Nathan's, "He is above the malice and envy of little men." Or Alfred Knopf's, "The private man was . . . sentimental, generous, and unwavering — sometimes almost blind — in his devotion to people he liked." Or Jim Tully's, "His comrades for years have never known him to do a small thing." Or Walter Lippmann's, "He denounces life and makes you want to live."

Lippmann, incidentally, once described Mencken as "the most powerful personal influence on this whole generation of educated people." There is no estimating the number of younger writers who were not only influenced but given active aid by Mencken. He was a major factor in the careers of such literary whales as Sinclair Lewis, Theodore Dreiser, F. Scott Fitzgerald, James T. Farrell and James Branch Cabell. Yet there is many a lesser author or journalist obligated beyond measure to the Baltimore iconoclast. Thumbing through the thick reference work *Twentieth Century Authors*, mentioned in the introduction to this book, it is amazing to find so many writers who say such things as, "With the active assistance of H. L. Mencken . . ." and, "Then H. L. Mencken persuaded me to . . ." and, "At the urging of H. L. Mencken I wrote . . ." Speaking of Mencken's relations with younger writers, Gerald W. Johnson, the Baltimore historian and scholar, has remarked, "To say that he was generous, even lavish with sympathy and assistance for them is true enough, but not the whole truth; he also gave them the rarer gift of genuine admiration, and this to some who, as writers, did not deserve it."

Newspapermen idolized Mencken. At the political conventions and other major news-producing carnivals he was often a greater attraction than the main show, and he knew it, but he never held himself aloof from his fellow reporters, no matter how undistinguished they might be. As a magazine editor he never retained a manuscript longer than three days. He knew that most writers urgently needed money and he felt they were entitled to a quick decision on their work. He was equally and famously punctilious in his correspondence. It was his practice to answer every letter on the same day he received it. He never abused people by mail. Much of his incoming correspondence was scurrilous in the extreme, yet he answered the most abusive letters with politeness and tact. He had a delightful method of dealing with people who were in violent disagreement with him. He would write: "Dear sir (or madam): You may be right. Very truly yours, H. L. Mencken." He carried on a running dispute with Upton Sinclair for years, but the quarrel was over principles. Once Mencken wrote to Sinclair: "I find your note on my return from Europe. As always you are right — save in matters of politics, sociology, religion, finance, economics, literature and the exact sciences." They remained warm personal friends to the end.

Julian P. Boyd, former head of the Princeton University Library, considers Mencken to have been one of the great letter-writers of this or any other age, and Boyd once launched an ambitious project for the collection of Mencken letters. Before he resigned to edit the papers of Thomas Jefferson, he managed to gather up eleven thousand letters written by Mencken to about five hundred individuals. Boyd tells me that, even then, he had only scratched the surface — that there were many thousands of additional Mencken letters in the possession of people all over the globe.

Mencken himself has said that recognition came to him first in England and France, rather than in the United States, so it is not remarkable that a young Frenchman, Guy J. Forgue, collected and published in 1961 the only book of Mencken correspondence yet in print. It comprises something over four hundred letters dealing mainly with literary matters — four hundred out of a possible fifty thousand in existence.

Mencken has been called the American Swift, the American Voltaire, and "one of the great comic spirits of world literature." He was a man of almost wildly unorthodox views, yet he was not a forward-looking man. He was old-fashioned, bitterly opposed to many material things which we have come to associate with progress. He was reactionary in almost everything except affairs of health and matters of beauty. I have been told that he, more than anyone else, was responsible for the purification of Baltimore's water supply and the control of diphtheria, typhoid and intestinal sickness in his home city.

He was a train man, and refused to fly. He hated to use the telephone and instead wrote one-line notes to his Baltimore cronies, proposing meetings for lunch or dinner. It was his opinion that the telephone was a contrivance designed specifically for bores, and he avoided it as much as possible.

He rode trolley cars and taxis. "Back in 1918," he once told me, "I owned an automobile. One morning I drove it up in front of the *Sun* building and stopped at the curb. A cop came up and said, 'Hey, you can't stop here.' I said, 'The hell I can't.' He said, 'The hell you can!' So I said, 'Why the hell can't I?' And he said, 'We got new rules. We got a parking law.' Well, I looked at him a minute and then I said, 'Nuts to that,' and got in the car and drove it around the corner and sold it and invested the proceeds in booze. I've never owned a car since that day."

A few years ago I went back to Baltimore to prowl his old haunts and talk to some of his old friends and visit with his brother August. I went to lunch with Philip M. Wagner, editor of the *Sun*. Wagner's hobby is winegrowing and he is an authority on American winemaking. He had a tank of his own vintage in his car and we delivered it to Haussner's, a famous Baltimore restaurant. In the car Wagner mentioned the fact that Henry Mencken was largely responsible for his interest in wines and the growing of grapes. And at Haussner's he remarked that the restaurant had been no more than a lunch counter until Henry Mencken started whooping for it.

Later I dined with Robert P. Harriss, a columnist who was

once associated with Mencken at the *Sun*. For some years Harriss was the editor of a successful Maryland magazine called *Gardens, Houses and People*. "The magazine's success," he said, "was due mainly to suggestions that Henry gave me."

The next day I was at the home of Gerald Johnson. "I was just a smalltown newspaperman in North Carolina," he said, "when a man named H. L. Mencken got in touch with me about something I had written. We carried on a correspondence for a while and then he recommended me for a job as editorial writer on the *Sun*. So here I am."

I went to a famous restaurant operated by an Italian woman. She said that Henry Mencken had been responsible for her success. When she first opened he came in and told her that she should take down the big *Spaghetti* sign out front, that she should de-emphasize spaghetti and go in for more esoteric Italian dishes; otherwise the public would regard her place as just another spaghetti joint. He gave her other suggestions, she followed his advice, and she prospered. And so it went: he influenced every life he touched, often profoundly.

He was inconsistent in many directions. He scoffed at joiners, yet for forty years he was the moving spirit behind the Saturday Night Club, an organization of amateur musicians and beer-drinkers (he was a pianist). And toward the end of his life he joined the sedate Maryland Club because, he said, he had grown tired of saloons and wanted a quiet and dignified place to entertain visiting whales. He ridiculed churches, yet he was married in one by his own arrangement. He spoke of religion as pure superstition, yet he hung horseshoes around his house and refused to do a lick of work on any Friday the thirteenth. Of the many contradictions between his writings and his personal life George Jean Nathan once said, "Consistency is unimportant. Mencken and I both used to believe in Santa Claus and the wisdom of the President of the United States, but the passing years have changed all that." My own way of excusing him is to quote the lines of Walt Whitman: "Do I contradict myself? Very well, then, I contradict myself; (I am large — I contain multitudes)."

Mencken was a confirmed agnostic, as his father was before him. Yet in his later years, according to Edgar Kemler, he undertook to copper his bet and rehearsed himself for his first day in Heaven just in case he should wake up and find himself there. He pictured himself arriving before the judgment seat, surrounded by the Twelve Apostles, and in this setting he planned to say, simply, "Gentlemen, I was wrong."

During that stay in Baltimore I made my way, to be sure, out to the Hollins Street house, remembering other visits there. I recalled the time he complained about the deterioration of the neighborhood, speaking of an influx of "morons from Appalachia," and yet I knew that toward his neighbors, toward these Appalachian "morons," he was the friendliest man in all of West Baltimore.

August Mencken greeted me at the white stoop. When Henry had his stroke in 1948, August, an engineer, retired and devoted his every hour to his older brother's comfort and well-being. He waited on Henry hand and foot, read to him, escorted him to the movies, carried breakfast to his third-floor bedroom, and sat for long hours talking with him in the back garden or "on The Cement" in front of the house. The Cement was a concrete slab at the inner edge of the sidewalk, almost as common an institution in Baltimore as the white stoop. August did all these things happily for Henry, because Harry, as he was known to the family, was also a great hero to him.

August and I sat all afternoon in the garden. It is ninety feet long from the back of the house to the alley gate, and twenty feet wide, and within this narrow enclosure Henry Mencken spent not only the happy days of his childhood, but he dozed and puttered about here during the last eight years of his life when he was no longer able to read or write. On the west side of the garden is the famous eight-foot brick wall which he built back in the 1920s. Set into the wall are various decorative tiles, the Mencken family coat of arms, and a mask of Beethoven. At the back of the garden, next to the alley, stands a small square wooden structure — the stable that was built for the Shetland pony which the Mencken boys had when they were children. Henry kept this stable painted in vivid colors, inside and out, right up to the time of his death. In front of the stable stands the woodpile, a stack of old lumber daubed with red and yellow and blue paint so that from a distance it has the look of an abstraction. One day the Mencken lawyer was due for a visit and Henry, all his life something of a prankster, said to August, "When he gets here I am going to be busy painting the woodpile. You let me know what he says." The lawyer arrived and stepped into the garden and there sat old Henry, daubing away at the lumber. "Well," said the lawyer, "after seeing this, I don't think I'll have much trouble getting the both of you put away."

On the east side of the garden is a white wooden fence and I noticed that a step had been attached to its base. August explained it. Next door, in the garden beyond the wooden fence, lives a boy called Butch. When Butch was four years old it was his habit to call out, "mencken! mencken!" Whereupon Henry would climb up and pop his head above the wall and talk to the child. Butch had no idea what a "mencken" might be, but he knew the word would almost always fetch that head, and it was a friendly head and it had some hands that sometimes supplied candy and toys, and so Butch continued calling out the magic word "mencken!" until his parents found out about it and taught him to call out "*mister* mencken!" Even as August and I sat talking about it I heard the voice, crying "mister mencken!" We both mounted the fence and there was Butch, now seven or eight years old, and August told him he was making a sailboat for him and it would be ready in a few days.

Henry had little time for pets. Yet he loved the family dog, Tessie, now buried in that back garden, and he once had a pet turtle which he named Mrs. Mary Baker Eddy. August told how one lazy afternoon Henry was sitting in the garden, half asleep, when a squirrel came over the wall and climbed up his leg and perched on his shoulder. He grew fond of the animal and could summon him by whistling and he had August go out and buy a large bag of roasted peanuts. The squirrel became a steady visitor, always sitting on Henry's shoulder. On chilly days the brothers would take chairs out and sit on The Cement where the sun would strike them. Henry loved to watch the children coming from school and he'd try to talk to them about their lives and their friends and their lessons. The children had no realization that they were talking to a famous man; to them he was just an old geezer sitting in the sun, wanting to be friendly but succeeding only in being a trifle boresome. The squirrel would come from the little park across the street to get his peanuts, and all was peace and contentment until the animal disappeared. A week or two went by with no sign of him and then Henry insisted that they cross to the park and search for him. "He may be sick," said the man who was the scourge of the twenties. They went over and found the tree where the squirrel lived, and they scattered peanuts around it. Now the squirrel started crossing the street to visit his friend again. Then came an afternoon when Henry and August were sitting out front; they saw the squirrel come out of the park and start loping across Hollins Street. Suddenly an automobile swished by, killed the squirrel, and went on without slackening speed. Henry was livid with rage. He cried out against the driver of the car, insisting that the man had hit the squirrel deliberately, calling him a murderer and worse, howling that the gallows would be too good for such a villain.

"He got madder at that man," said August, "than he ever got at the Anti-Saloon League."

We sat in the garden and then we prowled through the big old house, spending some time in Henry's office which August has kept just as it was when torrents of inflammatory prose were pouring out of it — literally millions of words and never a dull sentence in the entire output. It was a great and exciting and stimulating day for me, there in the surroundings where Henry Mencken spent almost his whole life, down to the night he died in his sleep in the little bedroom on the top floor. I thought about some of the things he had said or written, things that seemed to me to crystallize the ideas and beliefs he had been expounding all his life. A reporter once called him "the man who hates everything" and Henry protested, saying that he was quite favorably inclined toward some things in life. "I am strongly in favor of common sense, common honesty and common decency," he said. On another occasion he summed up his personal creed: "I believe that it is better to tell the truth than to lie. I believe that it is better to be free than to be a slave. And I believe that it is better to know than to be ignorant."

Finally, I thought of that gay yet poignant epitaph he once composed for himself: "If, after I depart this vale, you ever remember me and have thought to please my ghost, forgive some sinner and wink your eye at a homely girl."

Any man possessed of the sense and sensibility implicit in those lines . . . well, that man is qualified to be a hero. I have only one loud complaint to make against him. There are, in existence, seven volumes of autobiographical writings, concerned with his life as an author, an editor, and a newspaperman. Those seven manuscripts are tightly sealed in wooden boxes and stored in the vaults of the Baker Library at Dartmouth. By Mencken's own orders, those boxes are not to be opened by anyone until the year 1991. I feel quite certain that I will not be around then, and I'm pretty sore about it. Dartmouth College is straight north from where I live, about a five-hour drive. I could get there in five hours, arriving late in the night. That Baker Library can't be *too* big. Ten sticks of dynamite ought to do the job.

*

*

*

11. *A Wink at a Homely Girl*

I'M NOT CERTAIN that all of the events narrated in the next few pages actually took place. As I grow older I have a tendency to dream elaborately, and my dreams seem to be more tightly plotted than in my earlier harum-scarum days. This much I know to be fact: I was *in* Baltimore and I spent some time at 1524 Hollins Street and when I said goodbye to August Mencken, I decided I would walk back downtown to my hotel — a longish walk but one that Henry L. Mencken took scores and hundreds of times. I wanted to savor the fine experience I had just been through and . . .

I was coming into the downtown area when my mind wandered to that famous epitaph:

If, after I depart this vale, you ever remember me and have thought to please my ghost, forgive some sinner and wink your eye at a homely girl.

I spoke it over several times to myself, and each time it seemed to grow more meaningful and more poignant. And then I decided to follow the solicitation contained within it. If I would remember him and have thought to please his ghost — which I sure as hell did — I should forgive some sinner. I cast about in my mind for one and thought of a magazine editor who had recently turned down a beautifully written and howlingly funny article I had sent in. He had rejected it on preposterous grounds, saying that it was "not quite suitable for our purposes," and his rejection of it was certainly a sin of the first magnitude. So, walking along Baltimore Street I forgave him, and wiped out the black mark that stood against his name, and proclaimed him my friend for life, provided he didn't do it again.

By this time I was approaching Eutaw Street and I thought of the second injunction — "wink your eye at a homely girl." Immediately I began examining the features of every female coming toward me, and just before I reached Howard Street I had the one I wanted. She was homely enough; she was short and squat and her head and face had the contours of the head and face of a camel. As she came toward me I noticed that she was frowning and that while her face had that dromedary look, there appeared to be a deep sadness and hurt showing in it. I judged her to be a lonely and sorrowing person, shy and withdrawn, with an innate sweetness of character, and I made up my mind quickly. The instant her glance turned upon me, at a distance of maybe ten feet, I gave her a great big wink.

She stopped, and stood for a moment looking at me, an expression of mystification spreading over her countenance. In that brief moment I felt that I (or Henry Mencken) had succeeded — that we had brought a feeling of warmth and happiness to this homely girl.

Then something hit me.

That miserable female came at me without warning, swinging a pocketbook that was studded with heavy Mexican silver and that must have contained, in addition to the usual complement of woman-tools and accessories, one or two paving stones.

While this lethal instrument was thumping and clattering against my unprotected head, its wielder was shrieking like a wounded yak. And almost at once a policeman materialized out of the Baltimorean summer ectoplasm. He flung his arms around me, gripping me in a bear hug, and he held me thus while he cried out to the woman to cease and desist both her assault and her yelling.

"He tried to mo-lest me!" she howled. "Right square in plain daylight, he tried to mo-lest me!"

I managed a token struggle and loudly proclaimed that I had done nothing of the kind. The cop now had a firm hold on the collar of my jacket, and swung me around to get a look at my face. He didn't seem to like what he saw.

"When you bums ever gonna learn?" he demanded. "I had my way, I'd bust your head apart. You just open your mouth one time and I'll do 'er." He gave me a couple of hearty jerks that caused my cervical vertebrae to snap and crackle. "Now," he ordered, "you come along quiet if you wanna stay all in one piece. And you better come, too, Miss."

He walked us to the Central Police Station and jounced me up in front of a desk where a lieutenant sat writing in a big book. The man at the desk looked up questioningly and my captor said, "Mopery."

I knew the word. It is familiar around newspaper offices as identifying a specific felony: exposing oneself before a blind man on a public highway. (I have since learned that Baltimore police borrowed it from the jargon of reporters and then corrupted its meaning, applying it to the activities of all concupiscent mashers.) So now I had an inspiration. In my years as a newspaperman there had always been a certain fraternal feeling between cops and reporters, even though on the surface it often appeared that they were enemies. I spoke up.

"Listen, Mac," I said, addressing the lieutenant, "I happen to be a . . ."

"What was that you called me?" demanded the officer.

"Why," I said, "I called you Mac. That's what we always

call policemen in New York. It's a sort of affectionate form of . . ."

"Oh, so you're from New York!" said the lieutenant. He was not trying very hard to be pleasant. "You're from New York and you call police officers 'Mac' and you come down here to a *decent* town, a *clean* town, a *respectable* town, and go around the streets mo-lesting our women. Well, let me tell *you* something . . ."

The camel-headed girl had been edging forward and now she left her launching pad again. "Broad daylight!" she howled, swinging the pocketbook menacingly. "Right on the main street, in broad daylight! They'd orta put 'im in the gas chamber and turn on the spigots!"

"You're lucky," said the lieutenant, capturing some of her spirit. "You're lucky that the citizens don't roust theirselves up and wrap a rope around your obbaseen neck and string you up." He turned his gaze to the arresting officer. "Gimme th' details, Fenster."

"I heard her yellin' at Baltimer and Howard," said Fenster, "and I come bustin' around the corner, and he was grabbin' at her, and . . ."

"I was NOT grabbin' at her," I almost shouted. "Listen to me a minute. I'm a former newspaperman, twenty years in the business. You guys know better than to think that . . ."

"Well, well, *well!*" interrupted the desk man, smirking. "Whadda ya know, Fenster! We got us a newspaperman. Listen you. You ever on the *Sun?*"

"No," I said, "but I know . . ."

"You sure are runnin' in luck," he said. "If you was ever connected with the *Sun* in any way, shape or form, I might step down there personly and flatten your stoopid nose. But here in Baltimer we believe in justice and fair play, even tords dee-generates and sex mannyacks from New York. I will treat you like any other creep of your kind. You can put up collateral of fifty-one dollars and forty-five cents, or you can go to jail. Wait a minute. Maybe Magistrate Flodder is still around the building. Maybe we can get you all nicely convicted and incarcecrated in a jail cell right away."

"I want a hearing immediately if I can get it," I said. You may depend on it, I wanted to get this thing over as soon as possible. I knew that if I could get out of the hands of these boobs, these idiots, these Menckenian morons, and tell my story to an intelligent member of the judiciary, I would be able to straighten things out.

Five minutes later I stood before Magistrate Flodder, a grim-looking little man with a sunburst of reddish hair and a nose that resembled a ripe persimmon. Fenster, the arresting officer, told his story, including the frightful falsehood that I was grabbing at the hideous bitch. She in turn testified that her name was Hilda Gruntwood and that she lived somewhere out on Pratt Street (which I thought entirely appropriate considering the dimensions of her stern). By this time, too, she had embellished her story to include additional crimes on my part. "First, yonner," she said, "he wunk at me. Then he twisted his mouth around like in a sorta leer, very indecent. Then he begun grabbin' at me. Natchilly I tried to defend myself, and I . . ."

"That's enough," said the magistrate gruffly. He turned to me. "What have you got to say for yourself?" he demanded.

"I have an explanation," I said, "which I'm sure your honor will understand. I am a writer. For nearly thirty years I was a friend of one of the greatest men ever produced by the city of Baltimore — the late H. L. Mencken. I came down here to . . ."

"What's that?" broke in Magistrate Flodder. "Who? Who did you say?"

"H. L. Mencken. Henry L. Mencken."

The brow between the ripe persimmon and the sunburst of hair crinkled for a moment. "Oh, Mencken," he finally said, as if to himself. "Newspaper fella. Wrote a column. Against everything. Commie, if I remember aright."

"Your honor," I said, thoroughly outraged by this glaring display of ignorance, "H. L. Mencken was a very famous writer and philosopher, known all over the world."

"What's that got to do with you mo-lesting this lady?"

"Mr. Mencken," I said, trying to speak impressively, "once wrote an epitaph for himself in which he suggested that . . . well, he suggested that if his friends wanted to honor him after his death, they should wink at a homely girl. And as a friend of Mr. Mencken I was merely . . ."

Something hit me.

"Now he calls me homely!" shrieked Miss Hilda Grunt-wood, raining more blows on my head with her eight-pound pocketbook. Officer Fenster managed to drag her off of me but not before additional knots had been raised.

When order had been restored the magistrate looked down at me with a sardonic expression. "I heard you," he said. "In my time I have listened to some dillies, but this beats anything yet. You got a nerve coming in here with a story as phony as that. I'd ought to send you to jail for six months, but I'd much prefer to get you clean out of Maryland. I'm going to find you guilty, and fine you fifty dollars, and I hereby order Officer Fenster to escort you to the Pennsylvania Station and put you on a train for New York. And I'd recommend that you don't come within a hundred miles of Baltimer as long as you live."

Happily, I had the money to pay the fine. Then, under escort, I got my bag at the hotel and Officer Fenster drove me to Pennsylvania Station. As I've suggested, the whole episode is a little vague and dreamlike, but it seems to me that as we stood on the station platform, two thoughts entered my battered head. First, that newspapermen are not as popular with the police and the judiciary as they were in my day. And second, that H. L. Mencken was not an altogether credible writer when he dealt with matters of sentiment.

The only pleasant moment of the entire afternoon came just as the train was pulling in from Washington. Officer

Fenster suddenly grinned at me in a friendly way and then said, "Off the record, pal, I gotta say I don't admire your taste. We got a lot better'n *that* in Baltimer." And he *wunk* at me.

*

*

*

12. The Old Order Changeth

IN THE FINE CITY of Palo Alto not long ago I was a guest in the home of a local dentist and during the evening the subject of electric toothbrushes came up. With all the wisdom of my years, and thinking to make a hit with the host, I said, "Pretty silly business, don't you think?" And he replied, "Oh, no. Not at all. I have two of them in our bathroom." He then went on to explain that dentistry now recognizes one large fact: it is not so important to brush the teeth — the big, essential thing is to massage the gums. And electric toothbrushes are ideal for the job.

This was shattering news to me. I have wasted my entire life brushing my teeth — I mean the white part. I taught my children to do the same. I always told them to go brush their teeth. I didn't say to them, "You kids go brush your gums now."

In recent years I have been hit with a concatenation of such disturbances: the willful annihilation of long-held beliefs, many of which, in my personal Arcadia, border on the sacred. This steady assault on custom is beginning to stale my infinite variety. Not long ago I read a statement by a scientist who said that moths actually *enjoy* the odor of cedar wood, and that a cedar chest is of no special value for storing clothes. We've got three of them. At about the same time word reached me that mice don't care much for cheese. Experiments were undertaken in Milwaukee to determine which type of bait would trap the most mice. Guess what finished in first place. Lemon gumdrops. The mice would walk right past the cheese to get at those gumdrops, and this was quite disheartening to me; in my lifetime I have probably used up ninety-five pounds of sharp cheddar baiting mousetraps.

This sort of thing is difficult for me to take because I am, more than most of my fellows, a creature of habit; my kinfolks say that I was *born* set in my ways. It still horrifies me, for example, to see an open tin can of food standing in the refrigerator. My mother always got the food out of the can just as fast as she could move, once the top was off. She said that if she were to let it stand just a few minutes, it would turn into a death-dealing poison.

I have been a milk drinker for as long as I can remember. I consume as much as two quarts a day. It has always pleased me to hear knowledgeable people say: "Milk is the one perfect food — it's got everything." I drank it because I liked it. The health part was secondary, but I was happy to have it. I've always attributed my excellent digestive system, my cast-iron stomach, to this steady intake of milk. Now the good Doctor Alvarez (syndicated) and many of his compatriots advise me that milk is all right for some people, if taken in temperate dosages, but it might kill you. Something to do with cholesterol. The way I get the message from these doctors, some people shouldn't even *look* at milk.

Let me mention, too, another of my favorite foods — sweet corn. If there is one culinary fact that I have believed with all my heart, it is that sweet corn should be rushed from the stalk to the pot or the grill. I used to grow sweet corn and in season I ate it every day. I picked the ears from the stalk and I *ran* from the garden to the stove where the water was already boiling briskly. *I could have tripped and killed myself doing this, many times.* And then I found out that I had been wrong. The cookery experts advise us today that it is perfectly all right to *saunter* from garden to pot, that, in fact, sweet corn does not begin to starch up for hours after picking, and there is no need to hurry.

These same cooking experts have had me angry for quite a while in another direction. I don't understand why, but they decided one day that the old words, the tried-and-true terminology of the kitchen, were outmoded. They tried to do away with mashed potatoes. Mashed potatoes became *whipped* potatoes. *Fried* became a dirty word and was succeeded by the high-toned *sauteed.* Just recently I was reading a recipe which called for the use of "wooden picks" and bedogged if they didn't turn out to be toothpicks. And the semantic crime of the century, in my opinion, was the abolition of the hard-boiled egg. This one I have not been able to swallow. It is utterly impossible for me, at my time of life, to call a hard-boiled egg a hard-*cooked* egg. So far as I can determine, every cooking expert in the land has gone over to the hard-*cooked* school of usage. Why? Could it be that they don't boil them? I don't know anyone who in ordinary conversation actually says, "I've got to go hard-cook some eggs for the picnic." But I suppose that somewhere in the country there are impressionable young people who have been converted to this kind of talk. I, however, could no more refer to an egg as hard-cooked than I could call Mike Hammer a hard-cooked detective. I grieve over *The Ballad of Yukon Jake,* that splendid bit of poetastery by Edward E. Paramore, Jr., which I used to recite with great feeling, and which contains the immortal lines:

> *Oh, tough as steak was*
> *Yukon Jake —*
> *Hardboiled as a picnic egg.*

Just fancy how that would look under the new dispensation.

There are so many other continuing assaults upon the cherished beliefs of yesteryear. When I first heard that birds do not sing because they are happy, I refused to believe it. Now, more and more experts are assuring us that birdsong is bellicose and threatening in nature, in short, full of meanness. The singing bird is advising other birds that he has staked out an area as his own domain, and that other birds had best stay away from that territory on pain of getting their heads pecked off. Nothing to do with good feeling, nothing to do with the love of one bird for another bird. This information has made me good and sore. Not because it will tend to kill off a lot of famous poetry — I don't care at all about that. I live surrounded by thousands of birds and I've enjoyed their singing for twenty years, believing it to be sweet and filled with warmth and friendliness. Just recently a bird burst into song in our flowering cherry tree, and I yelled at it, "Shut your big warlike mouth, you quarrelsome bastard!" I don't like to have sounds of belligerency rollicking around my property.

Lord-a-mercy, the man-hours I have spent baking in the sun to improve my health and enhance my good looks! And now the dermatologists tell me to stay in the shade, that sunshine is responsible for skin cancers and that sunshine causes the skin to age and wrinkle before its time. I can remember back to the fuss which the English call the Fourteen War, and how the draft worked in this country, and how the most common excuse for physical rejection — or so it seemed, anyway — was flat feet. I have had flattish feet all my life, and because of them I have felt inferior, and now I find that flat feet are splendid things to have; it is said that many of our nation's finest athletes have arches fallen so low that they scrape furrows in the ground.

The doctors came out a few months ago with the pronouncement that it is not necessary at all to warm the baby's bottle. Great leaping balls of fire! When I think back to those shivering, middle-of-the-night gropings and fumblings in the kitchen, warming up the damned milk, I could spit square in the eye of Aesculapius, and also old Hippocrates, and possibly Benjamin McLane Spock.

They tell us now that the worst thing in the world for

snakebite is a stout slug of whisky. We know that it isn't necessary to ram the kids full of spinach, as it was when *my* kids were little. Over in the neighboring town of Armonk on New Year's Eve the cops set up a coffee station, and invite all party-goers to stop in and tank up on coffee and thus avoid death and disaster on the highway. I hate to tell Chief Hergenhan that he's living in a fool's paradise. They've finished some experiments out at the University of Indiana, and established the fact that if you load up the system with caffeine, it'll take you much longer to throw off the effects of strong drink. (Please, Papa, come home with me now, the clock in the belfry strikes one; don't drink any more of that bad old coffee!)

By this time everybody knows that the beautiful blue Danube is actually a dirty brown, and that lightning frequently strikes twice in the same place. There is a bronze statue of William Penn on top of the Philadelphia City Hall and the lightning belts away at the old Quaker all year round; it is my own theory that the lightning keeps coming back to Philadelphia because it is looking for Ben Franklin's kite.

A few months ago we acquired a new ironing board. A real tricky one. You press a lever and the legs fly out in all directions, like something in an old Buster Keaton comedy. But it's not really an ironing board. The label said distinctly that it is an "ironing table." I refuse to go near it for two reasons: I don't like that change of name; and I'm afraid of it — it could get those legs to going and throw me to the floor and thump me to death.

My friends tell me that they have hideous frustrations, but it fair crushes me to hear, as I have heard recently, that charcoal doesn't give a charcoal flavor to steaks or chickens or anything else. It is now asserted that a combination of fire and outdoor oxygen is the element that imparts the so-called charcoal savor to the meat; charcoal itself has nothing to do with it. Keeeee-ryst in the Andes! Since the end of World

War II I have burned up the equivalent of California's red-wood forests in charcoal, and I might just as well have been burning old rags.

They used to say that the best food for the brain was fish, that celery was good for the nerves, that if you ate cucumbers and ice cream together you'd get cholera morbus. All gone out the window now. You ask for it and you'll probably be able to get a cucumber sundae at Howard Johnson's.

I still say call the undertaker (not the mortician). I say washrag and not washcloth. The nation's barbers, in convention assembled, once voted to call themselves chirotonsors, but it didn't work, and for this I'm glad. At the butcher's I ask for "one of those little hams," refusing to call them picnic butts. A picnic butt to me is a girl you get along well with at an outing in the woods.

There is, too, the matter of the healthy liver. During my life I suppose I have heard it said ten thousand times during a bumpy, jostling ride: "Good for th' liver." I've heard it said, and I've said it myself. I've said it on flat-wheel trolley cars and in jeeps and on horseback and along washboard roads and even in a small plane bumping along above the Mediterranean Sea. So now what? A year ago in Hawaii some of us were riding over a volcanic area in a jeep and as we herky-jerked along I remarked, "Good for th' liver." A handsome girl named Jeri Bostwick, who works for the Sheraton hotels, spoke up. "Sorry," she said, "but that's a fallacy. During the war out here the Army conducted a series of experiments to test out whether bumpy rides are good for the liver. For months they sent their boys over the bumps in their jeeps. In the end they found out that bumpy riding is the worst thing in the world for the human liver, next to cirrhosis."

That nearly put me down, except that there was a worse one coming and the Army — the very Army I keep going with my tax dollars — was responsible again. I happen to be a person who perspires a lot. I also happen to be a person who goes around saying that I happen to be a person who perspires a lot. Everybody who hears me say it responds with, "Not as much as *I* do." Or, "You've never seen sweat till you've seen me sweat it." I have been, for a long time, a believer in the efficacy of salt tablets. In common with millions of other Americans, I have believed that in hot weather we sweat away so much body salt that our health is endangered, and that the condition can be quickly rectified by taking salt tablets. Now I have read in a reputable journal that during a large part of World War II the Army experimented with whole regiments of men and in the end arrived at a firm conclusion: salt tablets don't help one bit in hot weather or any other weather. The only possible good they could do a person is to make him thirsty — what he really needs is to replace a lot of water in his body.

I have in my house a bottle of salt tablets. Bottle! It's more like a jug! I don't know what on earth I'm going to do with all those tablets. They are really too small to put out for the deer to lick in the wintertime. I thought for a while that I might be able to use them in cooking. At a family conference I suggested that I might drop them into the delicious stews that I make, but my wife said *nyet*. They were a medicine, she said, and she has no intention of eating a beef stew that has medicine in it.

I may secretly mash up a few of those tablets and scatter them on the next batch of hard-cooked eggs. I certainly don't want to waste anything.

*

*

*

13. Avery Shoots a Rabbit

IN A BOOK CALLED *Let the Crabgrass Grow* I wrote extensively about My Neighbor Avery, a man of infinite wisdom who tackles every practical problem that comes along and invariably flubs the dub. A great man, Avery, a true original, and I have had a lot of mail from people over the country who have said they would love to meet him. For this book I have a few more things to tell about him.

I'm sometimes surprised at his sanguinary disposition. Occasionally we get up a small bet on a fight, and watch it on television together, and when the leather starts flying Avery sits there and howls for blood. Several times I have heard him say that the way to solve the problem of juvenile delinquents is to take them all over to Sing Sing and fry them in the chair. And the keystone of his international policy has been, for years, a frequently stated conviction that we should not wait for the Soviets to strike; we should, right this very minute, let go with every nuclear weapon we have and wipe them off the face of the earth. Once I said to him, "Women and children and authors, too?" And he replied, "Women and children and especially authors."

This is the same Avery who shot the rabbit.

He keeps a small vegetable garden which flourishes in the odd-numbered years. By this I mean that he'll have a prosperous garden in 1963 and a miserable one in 1964, and in 1965 he'll have a good one again, and so on. The explanation for this is slightly technical. His plot is only about thirty by twenty feet and he believes in diversified farming. He plants one row of radishes, one row of onions, one of lettuce, one of beets, one of string beans and so on until he fills out the plot. This system leaves him with leftover seed, so he carefully stores the packets away for use the following year. He plants this old seed the next spring, and precious little comes up, so the year after that he buys new seed and once

again has a splendid crop. It is a form of stubbornness I don't understand, as is his stubbornness in refusing to put a small fence around his vegetables.

"A fence," he insists, "spoils the looks of a garden."

Naturally he has trouble with rabbits and woodchucks and coons and even an occasional deer. This past year he thought he had found a way to fix that situation without surrendering his principles. He bought a .22 rifle and vowed that he'd rid the whole northern half of the county of rabbits and woodchucks before he was finished.

His garden is about a hundred feet from his kitchen door and one afternoon in July he glanced out the window and saw a rabbit. It was sitting quietly on the grass, a few feet from the edge of the garden, and it seemed to be staring at the lettuce.

Avery is a big man but now he moved quickly, uttering curses in a cautious voice and knocking over a kitchen chair as he rushed to the closet to get his rifle. His hands were shaking as he loaded the gun. Once it was ready he crept to the door, carefully opened the screen a couple of inches and poked the barrel of the gun through. The rabbit didn't move. Avery drew a deep breath to steady himself, took quick aim and pulled the trigger. The rabbit jumped, went over on its side, and lay still.

The accuracy of the shot both startled and pleased Avery. A harsh, triumphant noise came from his throat and his face was shining as he pushed open the screen door and glared out toward the fallen enemy.

"That'll learn ya!" he exclaimed aloud. Then gun in hand he walked down the slope to inspect his kill.

The rabbit was lying on its side, panting hard.

"Oh," said Avery, "so you're tough, huh? I'll fix that."

He started to raise the rifle and then he saw the rabbit's eye. It was a big, soft, brown eye and it was staring up at Avery. There was no hatred in it, but it was saying something to him, that eye. It was saying, "Why did you have to do this to me? You have hurt me terribly. Please do something for me." A lump began to form in Avery's throat and he quickly looked away to escape that softly accusing eye.

Then suddenly he gave way to panic. The gun slipped from his grasp and fell to the ground and he turned and hurried back up the slope and into the house.

Sara was in the living room when he burst in on her.

"What's that you shot at?" she asked.

"My God," he said, "he's *staring* at me."

Sara thought for a moment that he had been hitting the kitchen bottle and she looked at him a long moment before speaking.

"Who's staring at you?" she finally asked.

"The rabbit. It's awful. We've got to do something."

"You mean it's not dead?"

"It's lying out there on the grass," said Avery, "and its heart's beating a mile a minute, and it just . . . well, it just stared at me."

"Well," said Sara, "don't stand there. Go on out and hit it in the head."

"Hit it in the head?" Avery repeated, pronouncing the words slowly. "Hit it in the head . . . with what?"

"With a rock, with a stick, anything," said Sara. "No need to let it suffer."

Avery turned slowly and walked back toward the kitchen. The lump was still in his throat and he was having difficulty keeping his body from trembling. He was thinking, "What kind of a woman have I been living with all these years? Sit there cold as a stone and tell me to go out and hit it in the head."

But he knew he had to do it. He went out the door and glanced toward the rabbit, saw it was still there, and quickly averted his face. He went to the garage and looked around for a likely weapon. He picked up an old rusty jack handle and studied it and then decided it was too heavy, too formidable, too cruel. He went out and walked along the driveway and finally found a rock about the size of a grapefruit. Clutching it in his right hand he started walking back toward the rabbit but midway he stopped and looked again at the rock. It would never do. He would be too close; he wouldn't be able to hold it in his hand and hit the rabbit. He'd have to get a stick, or else go back for the jack handle. He walked out to the tool shed and rummaged around and finally came up with an old broomstick. He held it in his right hand and whipped it up and down a couple of times and the very act seemed to sicken him. He decided it was too long, so he got out the saw and cut about two feet off of it. Then he stood in thought for a few moments. Maybe there was another way out. He could take the rabbit down to Doc Grossman, the vet, and find out how seriously it was wounded. He could tell Doc it was sort of a pet rabbit and he'd shot it by mistake. No, that would look silly. It wasn't silly, but it would look silly.

"What on earth's the matter with me?" Avery asked himself. "I'm acting like a woman. Come on, old man, let's get the job over and done with."

Squaring his shoulders he marched out of the tool shed and made his way across the stretch of lawn. It was a short walk but his resolution was flagging before it had ended. Maybe, he thought, it would be dead by this time. He hoped so. Oh, how he hoped so. But it wasn't dead. It hadn't moved. It was still panting. Avery stood over it without looking at it. He raised the broomstick above his shoulder and then he looked down so he could deliver the blow straight and true. The rabbit's soft brown eye was again fixed on him. Pleading. And now it was saying more to him. It was saying, "I know you did this frightful thing to me, but I forgive you. You didn't realize how much it would hurt me. I forgive you for it, but please don't hurt me any more."

Avery dropped the broomstick, turned away quickly and then trudged slowly back to the house. He went inside and once again faced Sara.

"Well . . . ?" she said, looking up from her magazine.

"I'm going to call the police," he said.

"The police? What for?"

"Let them kill it. I can't do it."

"Have you gone out of your mind?" Sara demanded.

"No, I've not gone out of my mind. That poor little thing is lying out there staring up at me. I can't bring myself to hit it. I'll call the police. That's what they're for."

"You'll do no such thing," said Sara, putting down her magazine. "Good God! It'd be all over Chappaqua. Newt Avery called the police to kill a dying rabbit. You march right out there and whack that rabbit on the head and get it over with."

"I told you," said Avery slowly, "that I can't do it."

"What a big baby," she said. She got up and walked briskly out of the room and he heard the kitchen door slam. He followed along and watched her from the window. She marched across the lawn, reached the rabbit, gave it barely a glance, and picked up the broomstick. Avery turned his head away and then left the window. He was heading back for the living room when his eye fell on the big cocktail shaker. He picked it up.

"Manhattans," he said. "I guess I'll make it full of Manhattans."

He was well along with the job by the time Sara returned.

*

*

*

14. Avery at the Wheel

AVERY IS A RETIRED BUSINESSMAN, grew up in New England, acquired an education in the Ivy League, and comes as near to being a gentleman as is safe nowadays. He always gets to his feet when a lady walks into the room, he asks permission to pick up fried chicken with his fingers, and he shines his shoes even on days when he isn't going anywhere. In the normal pursuits of life he is extremely considerate of the feelings of all living creatures, as we have seen in his adventure with the rabbit.

I must mention, too, that Avery has strong feelings about the way people behave on our highways.

"Sometimes," he once told me, "on a Sunday morning I take my car out on the highways and just drive around, enjoying myself. That is the best time for driving — between 9 and 12 on Sunday mornings when all the reckless and irresponsible people are in church."

One day he told me he had figured out a way to escape from the eternal grind of sitting in front of his television set. He and his wife were going to drive down to Virginia to see the Natural Bridge in three dimensions. I asked him if he had room in his car to take along my new tape recorder and deliver it to my daughter who was then living in Virginia. Of course he had. He's such a thorough gentleman that, if necessary, he'd have left his wife Sara home in order to make room for it.

It is a new type of tape recorder which I devised one evening when I was fooling around in the tool shed, trying to escape from the eternal grind of sitting in front of my television set. It operates by atomic energy. There is a small compartment on one side of the machine. Crushed uranium is poured into this tank, a few drops of sodium sassatate are added to set up fission and the recorder will run for thirty-four hundred hours, give or take ten minutes.

I wanted the machine delivered to my daughter so that she could record the voice of my fledgling grandson; I wanted him to be the first human ever to speak into an atomic recorder. So I funneled in a batch of uranium, added the sassatate, and set the safety valve so the thing wouldn't explode and blow the north temperate zone across the Equator. I did not tell Avery the exact nature of the contrivance, knowing that he has a morbid fear of three things, namely; spiders, thunderstorms and nuclear fission.

When the time came for his departure, I simply stowed the machine on the back seat of his car. It didn't explode during the journey, but something else happened to it. Avery drove down to the Tappan Zee Bridge, crossed the Hudson and headed for the northern terminus of the Garden State Parkway. This led him to the Jersey Turnpike and as he was approaching the turnpike tollgate he came into proximity with something of an electronic character — perhaps a truckload of electric eyes — and my machine, stashed back there on the rear cushion, turned itself on. It ran steadily for fifty-five minutes and I have transcribed the sounds that were recorded in that period. The transcription follows:

(*Hum of motor. Car slows, then stops. Sound of window being wheeled down.*)

AVERY: How much?

MAN'S VOICE: Pay thuther end.

AVERY: Thank you very much, sir. Nice day.

(*Motor speeds up, settles into steady hum.*)

AVERY (*speaking in normal tone*): Get over, you jerk. (*Then, yelling out window*) Get over, you insufferable jerk!

(*Tempo of motor hum increases slightly.*)

MRS. AVERY: Don't you think you're going a little fast, dear?

(*No answer, except for perceptible speeding up of motor.*)

AVERY (*hums portions of "Indian Love Call" over steady throb of motor, then excitedly*): Holy Christ! Look at that lunatic! Weaving in and out. Dumb cops let a jerk like that get away with it. Wouldn't do it if I was a cop. Send the son of a bitch to the pen for fifty years. (*Increases his speed.*) Lemmy get up there, see his license, see where the bum's from. Ontario. I thought so. Shouldn't have allowed him across the border. Watch me take 'im! (*Hum of motor becomes a high whine, Avery yells*): Ya Canuck baboon! Come down here to a civilized country, try to show off!"

MRS. AVERY: Newt! Watch it! (*Sound of brakes applied.*)

AVERY: Jesus H. Presentable Christ! Get a load of *this* bird! *Dawdling!* Twenty miles an hour. Cops oughta get a howitzer and blow the bastard off the road. Build a superhighway so a man can make some time, and these yahoos take over with their beat-up jalopies and . . .

MRS. AVERY: You nearly took his fender off. If you'd been watching the road instead of that Ontario car . . .

AVERY: Kindly quit telling me how to drive this car. I've got everything under control. *Everything.* No danger of *me* hitting anybody. It's these maniacs they give driving licenses to, probly can't read or write. (*Yells out window.*) Get off the road, you dumb farmer!

MRS. AVERY: Why don't you close your window?

AVERY: Shut up! (*Steady hum of motor.*) Sorry I yelled at you like that, dear. How about getting out that road map?

MRS. AVERY: Where is it?

AVERY: Where *is* it? *Where is it?* Why, it's over there in the middle of Newark Airport! I glued it under the rear axle before we left! Where do you think it is? Home in the icebox?

MRS. AVERY: I suppose it's in here. (*Sound of glove compartment being opened.*) What do you want it for?

AVERY: Here, let me have it. Wanna have it handy.

MRS. AVERY: Woops! Look out!

AVERY (*unintelligible exclamation, slight screech of tires*): Whad I tell you? Look at 'er. Woman driver. Depend on it every time. Good God, look at that idiot go! I'm doing sixty-five and look at the way she passed me. She must be doing eighty-five. And where's the cops? Where's the great heroic cops? I'll tell you where they are. Turning their faces the other way. She's probly the wife of some politician. (*Motor speeds up.*) Well, I'm no dope. I'm not gonna have any homicidal female maniac up in front of *me*. (*Motor whines like a distant sawmill.*)

MRS. AVERY: Newt!

AVERY: Show that bigshot bitch a thing or two!

MRS. AVERY: I think you'd better stop at the next filling station.

AVERY (*no response to this suggestion, then begins speaking in monotone*): Okay. Get over. Get . . . over. Get over in the slow lane, boxcar. Look at the size of that monster. Big as the Empire State Building. Must have sixteen wheels chewin' up the pavement. Shouldn't be allowed on *any* highway. So what happens? They give that ape the right to drive and he squats himself down in the high-speed lane and stays there. The guinea bastard!

MRS. AVERY: You're doing sixty-five. You don't need to pass him.

AVERY (*beginning to blow short blasts on his horn*): Move over, you illiterate fathead! (*Long steady blasts on horn.*) Okay, so you wanna be passed on the right. I'll show ya. (*Roar of motor increases, Avery howls out window.*) Ya big dumb cluck! Why don't you learn the rules of the road, *ya no-good son of a bitch!*

DISTANT VOICE: Pull up, you blankety-blank-blank-blank, and I'll knock yer goddamn head off!

AVERY (*screaming*): You and who else, ya miserable louse!

MRS. AVERY: Watch him! He's trying to cut you off!

AVERY (*with a surging roar of speed*): For two cents I'd stop and give that bum a lesson in manners. Beat his stupid brains out.

MRS. AVERY: Don't be ridiculous, Newt. I saw him. He'd *kill* you.

AVERY: Whose side you on, anyway? Just for that crack I'll . . . no, I want to make Richmond . . . if I wasn't trying to keep on schedule I'd show you what I'd do to him. The pipsqueak.

(*Steady hum of motor for several minutes.*)

MRS. AVERY: Newt! I told you to stop at the next place.

AVERY: So what?

MRS. AVERY: You just passed one.

AVERY (*nonchalantly*): Didn't notice it. I have a habit of keeping my eyes on the road. There's another one up ahead a few miles.

MRS. AVERY: A *few* miles. More like forty miles.

AVERY: Anyway, I wanna make time, get along down the road.

MRS. AVERY (*firmly*): Newton Avery, I'm not going through this thing again with you. When I want to stop, I want to stop.

AVERY: Women! You want to get to Richmond tonight, or stop at every filling station on the road and get there next September? Oh, oh! (*Quick diminution of motor sound.*)

MRS. AVERY (*alarmed*): What is it?

AVERY: Wiseguy cop. Lurkin' back there behind that truck. (*Motor has settled into a low hum.*) Thinks I don't see him. Dirty little sneak. Tryin' to creep up on me like a bloodthirsty Indian. Corrupt as anybody in Washington. Flash a five-spot at him and he'd kiss my butt. Thinks he's such a wiseguy with that fancy uniform. Probly never got through grade school. Ignorant son of a bitch. Belongs in a coal mine instead of out here creepin' up on decent law-abiding citizens. (*Sound of siren approaching.*)

MRS. AVERY: He's waving at you.

AVERY: At *me*? What the devil's he waving at *me* for? What on earth have *I* done?

(*Motor slows, car moves off highway and stops, sound of motorcycle engine.*)

AVERY: Don't you say a word. Let me handle this.

COP (*amiably*): You in some kind of a hurry?

AVERY (*nervously*): Well, as a matter of fact, officer, my wife here has suddenly started having strange pains around her heart, I thought I'd try to rush her along to the next town, have a doctor look her over.

COP: Your driving license and registration.

AVERY: Certainly. Certainly, officer. Yes, *sir*. Right here. Here they are. Everything in order.

COP: Thank you.

AVERY: By the way, officer, did you happen to notice that green convertible go past me a mile or so back there? Damn fool must have been doing ninety.

COP: I'm not interested in green convertibles. I'm interested in (*pause*) light blue sedans that go seventy.

AVERY: Seventy! Did you say *seventy*, officer? Why, officer, I don't think I've ever driven seventy in my life. Scare me to death to go seventy. I don't even think this old heap of mine would *do* seventy. If it did, then the speedometer is sure haywire. That must be it. I was just remarking to my wife, just a moment before you came alongside, that I was holding 'er right on sixty so we'd make it to Richmond in time for early dinner. Didn't I, dear?

MRS. AVERY: Didn't you what?

COP: Just a minute, now. Did your schedule for getting to Richmond include stopping off so your wife could see a doctor about her heart trouble?

AVERY: Oh. Oh, sure. Yes. That's the reason I . . .

COP: How long you been driving?

AVERY: How long? How long have I been driving? Let me see, now. Thirty-five . . . no, thirty-eight years. Thirty-eight solid years, officer, and if there's one thing I keep telling people, keep lecturing people, it's that the traffic laws are important, more important really than any other laws we got, they ought to be observed. People don't observe traffic laws, then we got chaos. Utter chaos. And when we get chaos, then the Communists take over. That's what they want us to do, the Reds, get chaos. Like I was saying only last week to . . . why, it was your very own Governor, at that little party in the Waldorf, I said . . .

COP: Oh, you know the Governor?

AVERY: Know him! *Know* him? Fraternity brother of mine. Had a little reunion last week in the Waldorf and, come to think of it, he says, "Newt, you ever get in any jams in Jersey, just give me a ring." But I don't hold with that sort of . . . he's a great fellow and all, but I don't think a man should take advantage of a . . .

COP: I must say you're way ahead of me. I've never met the Governor. Don't know him. But one thing I do know. He's been on vacation in the West Indies for the last two weeks.

AVERY: It couldn't be. It simply *couldn't* be.

COP: It was, and it is. Now, how fast did you say you were going?

AVERY: I *thought* I was holding 'er right on sixty.

COP: Well, my clock said you were going seventy. A little over seventy. Now, would you want me to have to ride sixty miles all the way back to the shop and have them check my clock and find out if it's on the fritz?

AVERY (*grown suddenly humble*): Oh, no. Course not. I don't want to argue with you, officer. Look, I'm sorry. Maybe I was going a little above the limit. I apologize. I won't do it again. I promise you.

COP: That's better. (*Long pause.*) You go ahead now, but keep that speed down to sixty. I'll be keeping an eye on you.

AVERY: You can depend on it. And thank you, sir, thank you very much.

(*Sound of motorcycle starting, sound of car motor, resumption of journey.*)

AVERY: Outbluff 'em. That's the system. They're all a bunch

of bluffers. I felt like telling that twerp that I was driving a car before he was born. Lecturing a man of my standing as if I were some little schoolkid. The insolent bastard!

MRS. AVERY (*sighs audibly, begins humming portions of "Indian Love Call," then*): If you don't find a filling station or something in the next few minutes . . .

AVERY (*yelling out window*): Get over! Get in the right lane, you dumb rube!

MRS. AVERY: There. Up ahead there. See it? It's a restaurant.

AVERY: I saw it. I saw it. For God sake, you think I'm blind?

(*Motor slows, car stops, sound of doors opening.*)

AVERY (*conjugal politeness in his voice now*): Hurry it up now, dear. Want to make Richmond before six.

GAS PUMPER: Fill 'er up?

AVERY (*cheerfully*): Right to the top, son.

GAS PUMPER: Havin' a good trip?

AVERY: Oh, just average.

GAS PUMPER: Traffic's kinda light.

AVERY: Yeh. Nothing on the road but morons. Weaving around, driving ninety miles an hour, all drunk or acting like they're drunk. Cops oughta clear 'em all off the highway.

GAS PUMPER: You said it.

At this point the recording mechanism on the back seat stopped. Perhaps an electrical impulse from the gasoline pumps did it. There was very little time left on the tape for my grandson. And his performance was not what I had anticipated. I had forgotten that he was less than a year old, and not saying much. After the voice of the gas pumper was heard remarking, "You said it," there was a rumbling, crackling interlude of about fifteen seconds, and then the voice of my grandson saying:

"Wah. Waah. Waaah. Waaaaaaaaaaaaaaaah!"

Not much to keep and play back in later years. Nevertheless, I think I'll preserve it, just as a sort of curiosity.

*

*

*

15. Avery the Sinner

YOU ARE A WRITER (said Avery) and I remember when I was
in college and had a brief go at English Lit., and somewhere it
said that the best writing is the kind where it points a moral,
so now I got one for you.

Sometimes (Avery went on) a man finds himself in a situation where he wants to register at a nice hotel with a lady
who is not related to him in any way and the trouble is, they
got no baggage. I have reference, of course, to a floozie.

To a lot of men this is a very embarrassing situation. It
always was with me. That is, I mean, well, I don't mean to
say it happened to me very often but, oh, say, maybe two or
three or maybe four times. And every time it was the same.
I'd get up to that hotel desk with this babe alongside me
and the clerk giving me a fish-eye stare and I'd start to stam-
mer and stutter, and I'd swallow hard like I had a bullfrog
stuck in my throat, and I'd turn as red as a spanked baby's ass.
I remember once with a girl from Scarsdale, which is a very
immoral town, I started to go into a long song-and-dance at
the desk, starting out, "My wife and I live in the country
and we . . ." and it came out in a high squeak like a radio
set that's suddenly gone out of kilter. Then when I tried to
sign the register, my hand shook so bad the writing looked
like it was done by a man a hundred and nine years old.

Now, to go back a ways. I don't ordinarily see much of the
guys I went to college with but there was one, Stan Moresby,
we used to hell around a little together, and one day some-

body told me Stan was manager of the Arcade Plaza Hotel in New York. The Arcade Plaza, as you know, is strictly a class joint with fat ladies leading their dogs around and three or four bellhops old enough to be my father.

Well, I went around to see Stan and after that we had

lunch together a few times and then one day I happened to think about this business with a girl. I figured, we're a civilized people, we ought to have a civilized way of handling this matter, of screwing a woman who is not your wife. So I asked him, "Stan," I said, "what's the best way to work it when you got a girl and no baggage and want to register as man and wife?"

"W'y," says Stan, "the best way is just to pick up the pen and register."

"No," I said. "I mean, you know, if you happen to be nervous about it."

"Well," said Stan, "if you're the type that gets embarrassed about it and don't want to say you just missed the last train to Pleasantville or something like that, then you might use the Niggardly Wife technique."

"Proceed," I said.

"The way it works," Stan says, "is you coach the girl ahead of time what she's supposed to do, and when you walk into the lobby of the hotel, she goes over and takes a chair not too far away from the desk. You go up to the desk and say you want a double room. Twin beds. Like you can't stand to sleep in the same bed with your wife. The desk clerk gives you the register or a card to sign and while you're writing 'Mr. and Mrs.' on it, the girl gets up and walks over to you and says, so the clerk will hear it, 'How much is the room, dear?' That establishes her as your wife, beyond all doubt, and nobody could possibly ask any questions or even hint that there was anything suspicious. So now you say to her, 'Oh, for God sake Myrt,' and then you casually mention that you got no baggage and the chances are the clerk won't even ask you to pay in advance. Be sure to call her Myrt."

You see (Avery continued) how neat it's worked out? It sounded real good to me and one evening a year or so later I was over on East Forty-second Street to see some people in Tudor City and later I stopped in a tavern for a drink. There was a girl sitting alone in a booth and I was at the bar. She was a beautiful thing with coal-black hair and when I say she was stacked, I am understating the facts. I kept looking over at her and she would once in a while look at me and give me just the faintest flicker of a smile. So finally I just picked up my drink and walked over and told her my feet hurt and did she mind, and she said no, crawl in, and we started having some drinks together.

It got late, around two or three in the morning, and she was a little in the bag, and so was I, and finally I sprung the question and she said why not, and we got a taxi and headed for the Arcade Plaza. In the cab I gave this girl her routine, what she was supposed to do, and she bobbed her head and said, "Sure, Mac, I got it."

As we walked into the hotel lobby I noticed that she was a little unsteady on her feet, so I escorted her over to a chair not far from the desk and gave her a quick final briefing. The lobby was empty except for a scrubwoman, and the clerk looked to be half asleep over a copy of the *News*. So I went up to the desk and said I'd like to have a room with twin beds. The guy gave me a card and a pen and I started writing.

This was the point where the babe was supposed to come forward. I glanced back at her, and she was sitting in the chair staring straight ahead as if she was in a trance. I went "Psssst!" She didn't move. I wrote another word on the card, and then I went "Psssst!" again. She still didn't seem to hear me so I gave her a "Psssst!" that almost lifted the carpets off the floor. She wobbled her head around and looked at me and then gave me a silly sort of grin, and got off the chair and came up to the desk. The clerk had heard me doing all that hissing and he was looking from one to the other of us, and now the girl stared him straight in the eye and said, in a sort of snarl, "If this bassard says he's my husbuh, he's bigges' liar eas' th' Mississippi."

The clerk just stood there and stared at her a while, no expression on his face. Then he turned to me. I was furious. I was holding myself in, but I could have strangled that dame where she stood. I had worked out that beautifully organized scheme, and I had watched it unfold exactly the way it was supposed to unfold, as if it had been drafted by a master architect, and now she comes along and with one uncouth crack throws the whole thing out of gear.

The clerk, as I said, looked at me and then he slowly winked his eye and turned around and got a key and handed it to me. I stood there and stared at the key in my hand, still steaming inside; then I handed it back to him and nodded toward the girl and said, "Throw 'er into the street if you feel like it." Then I turned around and walked out and went home.

The moral? You mean you don't see it? It's simply this: a man can fall so much in love with a blueprint that he forgets to put up the building.

∗

∗

∗

16. *Inch and a Half to Go*

I HAD BEEN DRIVING pretty steadily for seven hours and my right foot was beginning to die on the vine. Before long I spotted a big motel up ahead. "Start looking," I said. In five seconds she said, "There's one right ahead that looks like it might be nice." It's always a good idea to let *them* think that *they* did the picking. Saves arguments. So we pulled in and since it wasn't yet four o'clock they gave us a nice room with air conditioning and two-bit television and mattresses guaranteed to throw you through the roof. I hauled in the bags and she went to work at washing out some nylons.

I like to get out of the house on wash day so I walked over to the office and bought a newspaper. In front of the office was a small terrace with summer furniture and a striped awning to keep the sun off. I sat down in a deck chair and began reading about deadlocks at home and abroad. In a little while a thickset man in a white linen cap and brick-red slacks came along and dumped himself into one of the chairs and went to work at the ceremony of getting a cigar going.

"Whew!" he said. "Scorcher, ain't it?"

"Hotter'n a witch's tit," I agreed. Some day I'm going to say something like that and it'll turn out to be an archbishop.

A thin, black-haired man came out of the unit adjoining the office and stood with his hands on his hips, looking around. He had on rope sandals and a yellow pongee shirt and after surveying the premises, he walked over and sat down with us. "Hot," he said. The three of us talked for a while about 301 and speedcops and the number of morons on the road and where we were from and where we were going. The thin man was a history professor from upstate New York and had been touring the battlefields. The big man was from Jacksonville, on his way to New York to attend a convention.

"I'd of been thuther side of Baltimore," said Jacksonville, "but I got messed up on ninety-five early this morning. Came through Rocky Mount and then somewhere north of there, took a wrong turn and next thing you know I'm on something called two-fifty-eight. I must've been half asleep because my wife had the map and told me to take a right, and I took it, and like to never got back on the track."

"As a general thing," said the professor, "it's always a bad idea for a man to ask his wife for directions, especially if a road map is involved."

"Know exactly what you mean," said Jacksonville. "You put a road map in front of a woman and I'll swear she don't know sheep-dip from Shinola. Never been able to understand it. The women must of been standing behind the door when the Lord passed out the geography lessons."

The professor turned and glanced toward the door of his room.

"My wife," he said, "is equipped with an excellent mind, an analytical mind — good in mathematics, plays a fine game of chess. She can make out what Gertrude Stein is saying, she can read a blueprint, but she can't make heads or tails out of a road map. Just a few days ago we were driving in North Carolina and she got me so upset that I told her I'd never even let her *hold* a road map again."

"What did she do?" I put in.

"Well," said the professor, "we were on sixty-four, driving from Chapel Hill to Asheville, and the map was on the seat between us. Usually I keep it in my pocket and when I need to get my bearings I just pull off the highway and waste a few minutes studying it myself. Over the years I've saved myself thousands of miles by keeping the maps away from her. But this time I was in a hurry and there wasn't any way we could possibly go wrong, as long as we stayed on route sixty-four, so I let her take it. We came to a place, Statesville I think, and I followed the sixty-four signs and wound around through the town and stopped for a red light on the main street and she was studying the map and then she suddenly let out a yell. 'Wrong road!' she yelled. 'You're off the track!' I pointed to the sixty-four sign on a pole across the street but she said that was *some other sixty-four!* She said that we had made three or four turns in the town whereas the map showed that the highway ran *straight through Statesville*. Did you ever hear of anything like that in all your life?"

"Certainly," said Jacksonville. "It's a common failing. You've got to expect it of a woman. You have the same kind of trouble with her out in the country too, don't you?"

"Yes," said the professor. "That's where most of the trouble develops. Curves. My wife and I even argue about the terminology of curves — whether it's a hairpin curve or a horseshoe curve."

"Women," put in Jacksonville, "always call it a horseshoe. Men call it a hairpin. It's a hairpin. But I didn't mean that kind of curve-trouble. I meant . . ."

"I know," said the professor. "Time after time I've explained to her that curves don't ordinarily show on a road map. I've explained how the map people don't have room to show every little twist and turn in the road. So she says, 'Well, don't blame *me* then if I can't understand this cockeyed map. It's the map that's wrong, not me.' She says, 'If they made the maps right in the first place, so they showed the road as it really is, I wouldn't have a bit of trouble.' "

Jacksonville gave his leg a hard slap. "Sounds exactly like Priscilla talking," he said. "If I've heard her say it once, I've heard her say it a hundred times. And her two sisters — it's the same with them. They're right, the maps are wrong."

"Well," said the professor, "I'm happy to hear you say it.

I used to think that my wife was a woman among women —
that she was the only one who could look at a map and turn
me north when I wanted to go south. It looks to me as if all
women suffer from some kind of a blind spot, or block,
when it comes to road maps. Take the business of locating a
turn you have to make somewhere up ahead. My wife
will . . ."

"Wait a minute," said Jacksonville. "Listen to this one. I'm
driving on route twenty, out of Tallahassee. I already know
that I want to make a right turn when I get to route two-sixty-
seven. So I say to Priscilla, 'Put your finger on route twenty
and find Tallahassee and then move your finger along west
and . . .' She interrupts me and says, 'Which way is west?'
So I grind my teeth a little and then say, 'Pay attention to
me now, dear. Just find Tallahassee — it's got a little blue airplane alongside it — find the blue airplane and then you've
got Tallahassee. It's on a red one. Put your finger on the red
one and move it along till you come to a blue one marked
two-sixty-seven and tell me how far it is from where we are
right now.' She says she doesn't know where we are right now,
and I say that makes no difference. I tell her, 'Just find Tallahassee. It's on the red one, marked twenty, that's the one
we're on now — TWENTY! A red one. Just find Tallahassee
and then run your finger along the red one till you come to
the blue one marked two-sixty-seven.' Well, by this time we've
maybe shot past the two-sixty-seven turnoff and I've missed
the sign, what with all this discussion about red ones and blue
ones, and trying to keep a checkrein on my temper. But suppose two-sixty-seven is still up ahead of us. If she finally *does*
locate Tallahassee, and gets her finger moving in the right direction, then she . . . gentlemen, you won't believe this . . .
then she has to turn the map around in her lap so the highway on the map is *aimed in the same direction* as the highway in front of us. She has to *aim* the map that way and then
look at her hands a while to find out which is left and which

is right, so she'll be able to find route two-sixty-seven going off to the right. How do you like *that* one?"

"She's not so unusual," said the professor, a bit testily. "You don't need to sit there and brag on her. My wife always holds the map so it's aimed in the same direction as the highway. That's one of the reasons she can't read the names of towns or the route numbers without wrenching her head around sideways. Now, you mentioned asking her about the distance to that turnoff. Step over here a moment."

We got out of our chairs and walked over to his car, which was standing in front of his room. He opened the door next to the driver's seat and pointed to a foot ruler stuck behind the sun visor, above the windshield.

"What do you suppose I carry that for?" the professor asked.

I'm old enough to remember when almost everyone carried a foot ruler in his car. It was used for measuring the gasoline level in the tank, which was customarily under the front seat. The professor's car, however, was a late model with the gas tank in the general neighborhood of the rear axle. A foot ruler wouldn't reach.

"It's not for measuring the gas, is it?" I asked.

"That ruler," said the professor as we walked back to the chairs, "is for measuring miles. There are times when a man wants to know his precise location. Let's say we're driving along route seventeen in New York and we pass through Deposit and then I want to know how far we are from Binghamton. So I ask my wife how far we are from Binghamton. She says, 'Where are we now?' So I say, 'Put your finger on seventeen, a red one, and run it along till you come to Deposit. Go a little distance past Deposit. Then count up how many miles it is to Binghamton.' It usually takes her about three miles to get it figured out. When she finally locates Deposit, and then finds Binghamton, she begins to hum — she always hums when she's feeling good about something —

and she says, 'It's about an inch and a half.' So then I have to calculate it in my mind. I already know that an inch, on the New York State map, is slightly over sixteen miles, because I measured it with the ruler before we started. An inch and a half would be, roughly, twenty-four miles. But *her* inch and a half is a straight line from Deposit to Binghamton, and I've got to make allowance for the twisting and turning of the road. On a highway like seventeen you've got to add about three-tenths of a mile to each straight-line mile to make up the difference. I've learned to work it out in my head. Three times twenty-four is seventy-two. That's seventy-two tenths, or about seven miles. Seven added to twenty-four is thirty-one. So I know it's thirty-one miles from Deposit to Binghamton. Take off two miles that we traveled out of Deposit before I asked her how far it was to Binghamton. That gives us twenty-nine miles. But I've also got to subtract the three miles we traveled while she was trying to find Deposit and then trying to find Binghamton and then make up her mind that it was an inch and a half to Binghamton. Three from twenty-nine is twenty-six, so I know we are twenty-six miles from Binghamton. Is this clear to you?"

"Clear as a bell," I said.

"The important thing," said the professor, "is that by the time I've got it all figured out, I don't give a damn one way or another — I don't care how far it is to Binghamton, I don't care if I ever get there, and I wonder why I ever wanted to know the distance in the first place."

Jacksonville had been sitting through this last recital with a slight smile on his lips.

"I think," he said, addressing the professor, "that you're a little behind the times. You don't need that foot rule. The better road maps you get nowadays give you the information you want. They print the regular scale and then right above that they tell you how many miles in an inch."

"That's a new one on me," said the professor. He stared

off at the sky, thinking about it. "It must be," he finally said, "that all wives do the same thing — measure the mileage in inches. I can't think of any other reason why the map people should print the two different scales. Funny, I hadn't noticed it on any of my maps."

Having contributed next to nothing to the seminar thus far, I now spoke up.

"I know a woman who can read a road map better than a man."

"A married woman?" asked the professor.

"Yes," I said. "She's an actress."

"Oh, well," said Jacksonville, "that wouldn't count. An actress is not hardly the same thing as a woman. What I mean is, we've been talking about wives — housewives."

"Your wife traveling with you?" asked the professor.

"Yes."

"Can *she* read a road map?"

"She doesn't try to, much," I said. "She's about the same as the others. I remember once we drove out of Indianapolis, headed west, and she was studying the map. Suddenly she announced that she had found a marvelous short cut to Chicago. She said it looked to her like it wasn't paved in spots, but it was a direct route and would save us time. She said we could get on it near a place called Dana, Indiana. Well, I pulled up and took the map and she pointed it out to me. She was talking about the state line between Indiana and Illinois."

"Good Lord!" exclaimed Jacksonville. "That's one for the books."

"I didn't finish," I said. "The main point is . . . we weren't even *going* to Chicago!"

Both men were now staring at me admiringly.

"You're not only a member of the club," said the professor, "you can be executive vice-president if you want the job. By the way . . ." He glanced at Jacksonville and then back at me, ". . . there's a little roadhouse I noticed just down the highway. You men be interested in a little refreshment?"

"How far is it?" I asked.

"About an eighth of an inch," he said.

"Let's walk it," said Jacksonville, and we did.

＊

＊

＊

17. A Friend in Brooklyn

NOT LONG AGO I had a letter from Dan Parker, the talented sports columnist for the New York *Mirror,* concerning the recent activities of an old Brooklyn friend we share in common. Mr. Parker's letter took me back to the time of World War II and the day a postal card was dropped into my mailbox. It brought this message:

"Am ready to confess that I alone am responsible for this terrible war we are having. The blame rests on my shoulders and nobody else. Will be happy to give you the details. Best regards."

It was signed: "Foulproof Taylor."

I had all but forgotten him, for it had been nearly ten years since I had last had traffic with him. Now I wanted to see him again, so I telephoned and made a date. It was a blazing hot day when I took the subway to the end of the line in the Flatbush section of Brooklyn. If James Philip Taylor was the cause of World War II, he should be given credit for it, and I would see that he got it.

Few people know him as James Philip Taylor. He discourages the employment of any name but "Foulproof Taylor." He is a telegraph operator employed by a cable company and on the side he is an inventor.

His statement that he was responsible for World War II was not made frivolously. He firmly believes that if he had not existed on earth, if he had not invented the Taylor Foulproof Cup, there would have been no war.

Back in the 1920s an epidemic of fouls brought professional boxing into disgrace in New York. Up stepped Foulproof Taylor with his invention.

"I saved boxing," he explains, "and in saving boxing, I made the reputation of a certain big bum named James Farley. And this big bum James Farley went on to greater things, and put Franklin D. Roosevelt in the White House. And if Franklin D. Roosevelt hadn't been in the White House, there wouldn't have been any World War II. See how simple it is?"

At his modest home in Flatbush that hot afternoon I found out a lot about Foulproof Taylor. He still owns and lives in the three-story frame house that is set close to its neighbors on a street lined with tall trees. On the day of my visit he knew the hour I was coming and he knew I'd be walking from the subway, and I have an idea he watched for me, and when he saw me approaching, he hopped to his piano and began striking crashing chords on it. When I reached the front door he waited until I could see, through the screen, that Foulproof himself was making all that impressive music, then he leaped to his feet and greeted me.

"Ah!" he cried. "I was just after practicing me scales a bit."

In his living room I was startled to see a fire blazing in the fireplace. At least I thought that's what it was, but closer inspection revealed it to be a contrivance for simulating fire — a heap of glass logs and back of them an electric light and a revolving fan to give it a crude flickering effect. It was ninety degrees in the shade and I was already hot and sweating, but now, just looking at that fireplace, I felt as though I would burn up. I started to say something about it, but held my tongue, and found myself somehow liking Foulproof the better for having the thing going. He had here a gismo that he considered both beautiful and artistic. He had company coming — a writer who, he knew, would help publicize his enormous gripe against the injustice in the world — and he wanted to show off his fireplace and to hell with the weather. It was running all the time I was in the house.

We went at once to his basement workroom. "I am the last one-man factory in the United States of America," Foulproof told me. He is accustomed to blurting out strong statements that often have no relation at all to matters under discussion. "Forty years in this country without an arrest!" he'll say. Or, "I am also the blindfolded chess champion of Montreal, Canada."

The basement room was in disorder, with piles of materials, rubber and metal and fabrics, here and there. Foulproof himself is a short, stocky man with a shock of wild, bushy, silver hair somewhat like the frightwig Andrew Jackson had leaping from his scalp. "Bernarr MacFadden once asked me point-blank how I came by such a fine head of hair," he said.

He follows the classic pattern of the inventor who has been duped and robbed at every turn. He inveighs constantly against his enemies and then speaks sadly of the millions of dollars that would be his if justice prevailed in the world. He denounces judges for permitting a thing he calls "daylight perjury." And his pet hate is the aforementioned James A. Farley. He got out his scrapbooks which contain clippings and documents about himself. They contain something beyond that. Whenever he has encountered a printed attack on Farley, no matter how remotely concerned it might be with boxing or Foulproof cups, he has clipped it and pasted it in his books. He always uses strong language when the name of Farley comes up. (Now, in the 1960s, he is angry at a certain prominent doctor who has refused to test out Foulproof's later inventions; he calls this doctor "a holier-than-thou sanctified swine.")

He speaks frequently of his achievement in putting Roosevelt in the White House and causing World War II and he is dead serious about it.

"Here I am," he told me, "an immigrant from England, and look what I have done to the United States and the whole world. I think you'll have to admit I have done quite well for myself."

In his own evaluation, everything that has ever happened to him has been on a colossal scale and usually without precedent. He pulled up his sleeve and showed me four white streaks on his forearm.

"Bit by an octopus," he said proudly. "Not exactly bit, but an octopus grabbed me when I was swimming in the Azores. When you are seized by an octopus like that, a funny thing happens. He sucked the blood out of me so fast, before I could brush him off, that it affected the pigmentation and left these white streaks. Look at the hairs growing out of these scars. I'll bet you never saw scars before in all your life that had hairs growing out of them. It's a medical wonder of the world." You see, even his octopus bites are special, and historic.

I told Foulproof I wanted to get something of his personal history, antedating his becoming an inventor. He said he came to this country in 1894 when he was nine and "nearly dead from the rickets." He was born in Manchester, England, but his father was an Irishman and his mother came from Columbus, Ohio. His great-great-great-grandfather was celebrated in Dublin, he told me, as "Taylor the Quillmaker."

"He made quills to write out of ducks," Foulproof explained. "It gives me satisfaction to think that the old man was known as 'Taylor the Quillmaker' and here I am, his descendant, known to China and back as 'Foulproof Taylor.'"

Soccer has always been a passion with him and he still plays once a week. It was during a game of soccer that he first got the idea for fastening a strong padded cup into an athlete's crotch to keep him from getting hurt. Even as a boy he says he was a chess champion, and in former times he enjoyed billiards as well as tennis.

"Yes," he said, "I have had a full life. I hold a world

championship to this day. Lowered the world's record for the sack race in 1918 at Calgary and it stands today. Sackracing, you know, is an art. Only fools *hop* in a sack race. I put my toes into the corners of the sack, then pull the sack tight with my left hand held at the waist. Then I put the top of the sack over my shoulder, bringing it down so I can hold it in the same hand, pulling it tight against my heels. That way I get a bead on my toes and heels. The right hand I use for balancing. That is the main secret of my success. The others don't have balance and they use both hands to pull up the sack and they always fall down. Incidentally, the day I set the world's record I was timed by a pair of timers from a horse race track. Very authentic."

Foulproof went to a refrigerator which stands in his basement workshop and got out some ale. He was aglow with memories of his achievements.

"When they were building the Panama Canal," he said, "I was working down there and I took sick and they put me in the hospital. It was then that I was hit in the stomach by Dr. Gorgas. He came in and looked at me and thought I was malingering. I'll always remember with fondness that the great Dr. William C. Gorgas hit me in the stomach and knocked the breath out of me with one punch."

Apparently the Gorgas wallop had no inspirational effect on its victim, insofar as inventiveness was concerned. We must come on down to November of 1926 when Taylor's sideline was singing opera.

"I was in the chorus of the opera *Turandot* at the Met," he related, "starring Jeritza and Lauri Volpi. I sang second tenor and I got the job by being picked out of nine thousand voices in eliminations. I was told to go into a room and I went in and found a man sitting at a piano. He struck a chord and said 'Sing Ah.' I did, and I was picked. Somewhere I have a letter from the chorus director complimenting me on my singing at a certain performance. It says, 'Mr. Kahn was highly pleased.' Otto H., you know."

"Now," Foulproof went on, "in this opera there is a Chinese Mandarin with a daughter. In the first scene the stage is crowded with the populace. The Princes are paying court to the daughter. The father is a tough hom-bray. He asks three questions of each Prince and if they can't answer, he chops off their heads. He has cut off fourteen when the fifteenth comes along. The sword is being sharpened on a grindstone. We, the populace, protest against all this senseless bloodshed. The Mandarin orders us dispersed. The guards charge us and force us from the stage. One big bony-legged guard gave me the knee and doubled me up with pain. I said the hell with this. I don't mind singing at the Met but I definitely don't like to get kicked or kneed in the groin."

He thought back to the times he had been crotch-whopped in soccer. "The very next day," he said, "after that bony-legged bastard kneed me in the opera, I decided to do something about it. I went downtown and found a store that sold aluminum and I bought a piece of it. Then I went over to the Bowery and found a trick store and bought two dozen rubber cigars. Trick cigars they were, and sold two for a quarter. I took a triangular piece of aluminum and sewed and glued the rubber cigars around the edge and that night I put it on and when it came time for the populace to be dispersed on the stage, I told that guard to go ahead and knee me good, that he couldn't hurt me. And he didn't. Since then I have been fouled forty thousand times. That figure is up to 1935. After that I lost count. I have even had football players punt me in the crotch. I had Carnera knee me in his dressing room. What a smash! Sent me flying like a shot rabbit. Whenever I walk into a training gymnasium they all holler and line up like a snake dance and take their turns slugging me below the belt. It's accepted practice. They yell, 'Here comes Old Brassnuts, boys, let's get to work!' Then they take their turns, and I love it. I just stand there and smile, even when they lift me off my feet a little."

For four years he saved ten dollars a week "out of a married salary of $32.50" in order to pay the patent lawyers, and then he went on to higher things. He began thinking about the injuries and deaths each year in football, and so he began working on a better type of helmet.

"I took it up to Fordham," he said, "to test it out. That was the time of the Seven Blocks of Granite. They arranged to take newsreels of the test, and I wore a wing collar and charged into the Seven Blocks with my helmet on. It was all arranged that after I charged in, and the Seven Blocks piled on top of me, I'd come out of the mess and run up to the microphone and camera and say, 'I feel fine!' But something happened. I must have held myself wrong. One of the Blocks of Granite hit me in the mouth with his knee. I had bridges in my mouth. In addition to that I thought my leg was broken and my back sprained. But I came up smiling, anyway, and dashed over to the mike and opened my mouth and said, 'I feel fine!' and the words came out all right but also a lot of blood and teeth."

When Joe Louis was training to fight Carnera, Foulproof went to visit the camp at Pompton Lakes. He wore one of his cups, naturally, and walked into a barroom where the sports writers were gathered. The late Hype Igoe was there and Foulproof approached him and asked him to "knee me in the groin as hard as you can." Igoe sent Taylor flying into a wall with such force that Taylor's rear end crashed through the wood. Subsequently the hole was repaired by covering it with a plaque which read:

> *Hypus Igoe*
> *Through this wall,*
> *Knocked Foulproof Taylor,*
> *Cup and all.*

Around sports writers and others connected with the boxing and football trade, Foulproof believes that the best salesmanship consists in having himself beaten and slugged.

When he invented his first beanballproof helmet for baseball players he was forever showing up at newspaper offices, wearing one of the helmets and carrying a baseball bat. Sports writers, working at their typewriters, were accustomed to hearing: "Take this bat and hit me on the head with all your might." Without looking up the sports writers would say, "Hiya, Foulproof." Usually they'd accommodate him, walloping him on the head, often knocking him to the floor, but never discommoding him for long.

Back in the giddy thirties a character named Louis the Barber of Forty-fourth Street put a display of Primo Carnera's ring togs in his front window. Foulproof came along, saw the display, walked in and said, "Why not a cup?" Louis the Barber said for him to bring one in, because Foulproof was then making cups regularly for the Italian giant, and in due course a Carnera cup joined the display.

Foulproof enjoyed standing before that window, mingling with the public and listening to the comment. His name was on the trademark, stamped on the cup, and he'd hear people say: "J. T. Taylor. Wonder who he is?"

"That's what they'd say," Foulproof recalled, "and me standing there beside them in the flesh, unbeknownst you might say."

One day he came along and found the cup had disappeared from the display. He stepped into the barber shop and jumped Louis about it. Louis reached down and picked the cup up from under a chair and said:

"Here. Take the damn thing away and keep it away. Carnera is sore. He says that hundreds of women are pestering him in person, and he's getting from three hundred to four hundred letters a day from women."

"So," said Foulproof, "that was that. I can tell you, though, that man wore the biggest cup ever put on a human being. Come to think of it, I believe I've got one left around here somewhere." He began searching among all the accumulation of junk in the basement. He got down on his knees and began exploring under his worktable. He started talking to a cat that was asleep under the table. Finally he found Carnera's cup — the cat had been curled up asleep in it all the while.

"When Carnera fought Louis," he recalled, "someone stole his cups for souvenirs. The cups were heisted somewhere between his training camp and his New York hotel. I got a hurry call from some gangsters. They said, 'For God's sake Foulproof, you must make a cup for Primo for his fight tonight as he has lost his cups!' So they sent a big bulletproof car for me, and I got together my materials — rubber, aluminum, belting, leg-strapping, rubber cement, needle and thread, and so on — and they rushed me to the hotel overlooking the stadium. Primo was sleeping, so I went ahead and made the cup from memory and in about two hours he got up and tried it on and it was perfect so he grabbed me by my long hair and began swinging me around the room and yelling 'Foul-a-proof! Foul-a-proof!' After that we sat down and played knock rummy until supper. I remember winning sixty cents."

Foulproof recently composed a letter to President Kennedy, asking his aid in getting his new football helmet accepted throughout the nation. He attacked the present type of headgear as "suspension-strap deathtraps that are causing gridsters to die like flies every season." His own patented helmet, he said, "will cut the yearly death toll of young American boys to the bone."

Dan Parker has written many highly humorous pieces about Foulproof over the years, yet he always points out that the Taylor devices have been of great importance in the sports world.

"Not long ago," Parker says, "Foulproof begged me to line up a few TV stations for a demonstration of his baseball helmet. He wanted them to belt him on the bloomin' boko with a bat, a crowbar and a sledge hammer while he made goo-goo eyes into the camera from under the helmet's protective embrace. Several television stations agreed to the deal but then changed their minds, fearing they might fracture the skull that has stopped a thousand mighty bashes without surrendering even a flake of its precious dandruff mulch."

Foulproof was disgusted when he heard he would not be pounded on the head over television.

"A bunch of yellow-bellies!" he said.

＊

＊

＊

18. *This Awful Honesty*

IT IS AN EMBARRASSING THING for me to do, but I herewith make public confession that I am in need of a psychoanalyst. One who does it deep. I am real mixed up and if I don't get myself squared around pretty soon, I'm doomed to a life of degradation and poverty. My trouble dates back to my childhood when I suffered a traumatic experience that is reflected in my everyday behavior today. For years I have existed beneath a dark and depressing incubus, consisting in the main of intense feelings of guilt. When I was a child I was a thief.

At the age of ten or twelve, and over a period of several years, I stole almost everything that wasn't nailed down. I used to sneak into my mother's pocketbook and steal a half dollar, sometimes even a whole dollar. For a time I worked as a soda jerk and I knocked down steadily, taking as much as a dollar and a half a day. There were other thefts of this character. And then one day a sense of shame struck me, and I quit. In a sort of backlash action I became the most honest individual in the United States. I have remained in that unhappy condition down the intervening years. I am today so honest that it is sickening.

And now I have a desperate need to steal, cheat, finagle, crib, pinch, snitch, pilfer — to get some constructive larceny into my life. Only then will I have tranquillity without pills; only then will I be able to sleep soundly. I'm sure that if I could get over my ridiculous honesty fixation I would be a better citizen. I enjoy being a nonconformist but not to the extent that it costs me money.

All around me my fellow citizens are reaping the golden harvest. They are getting the good things of life, and I sit here grubbing away, taking the crumbs, unable to join in their expensive fun and frolic because of that childhood trauma.

Bergen Evans, the celebrated Northwestern professor, has spoken of "the wholly new standards of honesty" which the world has adopted. He actually means standards of dishonesty. And not long ago a famous publisher, appearing on television, uttered the following sentence for the whole nation to hear: "Some of our laws are so ridiculous that I consider it fun to break them."

My distressing mental sickness compels me to obey all laws, so long as they are on the books. I am unable, like many of my fellow citizens, to make a distinction between little laws and big laws. If a sign says "Stop" I take it to mean "Stop" and I suspect that there is a reason for its being placed where it is, even if it is in the middle of the Mojave Desert. Most people apparently do not agree with me; consider the fact that when the authorities want motorists to *really* stop they put up a sign that says, "Full Stop." This leaves the poor, forlorn, bedraggled word "Stop" meaning absolutely nothing.

I remember a few years back when a member of Congress was given a ticket for speeding in Maryland. At first he refused to appear in court, claiming demagogic immunity, but the judge was tough and finally the statesman turned up. He told the court that it is common knowledge all over the United States that a motorist is privileged to drive ten miles an hour above the speed limit without fear of molestation at the hands of the cops. The tough judge said not in *his* jurisdiction and slapped a fine on the Congressman. I thought the defense plea was interesting. In effect the legislator was saying that it's all right to break the law provided you break it by only twenty per cent. If you want to steal a million dollars, don't do it; just steal two hundred thousand. And while we're on the subject of traffic laws, I think of the howls that go up whenever highway police start riding around in unmarked cars, or concealing themselves behind bushes or billboards. The public screams that such conduct is unfair, caddish and agin the Constitution. The public is plainly right — police work should be open and aboveboard, without any nasty cloak-and-dagger atmosphere. When the cops get word that safe-crackers are at work in the First National Bank, they should telephone the bank and notify the crooks that they are coming and give them a sporting chance. The public as usual is right, but my unfortunate sickness compels me to vote a minority opinion. I hold to the fantastic notion that unmarked police cars are an efficient means of controlling the multitudes of idiot drivers who populate our highways.

Our new standards of honesty are reflected in the rephrasing of the old reliable maxims. Nowadays I hear people speak of the *eleventh* commandment, which goes, "Thou shalt not be found out." And the golden rule has become, "Do unto others as you would have them do unto you, only do it first." In many of the published success stories of our time one of the principal ingredients is the subject's cleverness in circumventing the rules. I am not even surprised that this holds true in the case of successful newspapermen, those gallant knights from whose ranks I graduated twenty-odd years ago. The reporter who recognizes no law, no rule of privacy, no locked door, no authority whatever, is quite often the reporter who wins the big prize.

A great many people believe that the popular expression "finder's keepers" means what it says, and that possession is really nine-tenths of the law, or maybe ten-tenths. In 1961 a Los Angeles janitor found a bag containing two hundred and forty thousand dollars in unmarked bills, in denominations of ten and twenty dollars. He didn't even bother to count it. He turned it over to the F.B.I. The bag of money had fallen out of an armored car. Within a month the janitor was almost in a state of nervous prostration because of the abuse he was getting at the hands of friends and neighbors as well as hundreds of strangers who wrote to him and called him a fool and worse for not keeping his mouth shut and holding on to the money. "I wish," said the distraught janitor, "that I'd never seen that money. I wish I'd let it sit in the street and rot. I wish I'd thrown it down a sewer, or burned it."

I need not mention the continuing scandals of the cheating college students, or the revelations in connection with the TV quiz shows. The quiz show ruckus has gone into history and it is probable that those who were guilty of wrongdoing have gone on to bigger and better and more rewarding pursuits. At the time of the scandals, most of the letters to the newspapers took the side of the cheaters, and flash-floods of sympathy and compassion flowed in their direction. We are quick to forgive our sinners. Especially those who steal from us.

One day on a commuter train I heard two men talking about a third. Said one: "Trouble with Fred is, he's always letting himself get slowed down by a lot of loyalties." That's precisely my own trouble. If I could get rid of my nonsensical ethics, I'm sure I would soon be both famous and wealthy. Last year I was visiting in Hollywood and a friend called me and asked me to come to his house to meet "the most interesting man in Los Angeles." My friend didn't tell me who the man was. It turned out that he was famous for one single achievement — he owed more money in back taxes, mostly penalties for cheating, than any other individual in the land. He proved to be very astute, well-informed, gracious of manner and inclined to use the jargon of the lawyering trade. People listened to his opinions with close attention and respect. He was, quite palpably, a man of solid worth.

After Dave Beck, Jr., was convicted of stealing $4,650

from the Teamsters Union, Dave Beck, Sr., told the press: "You boys listen to me. Dave Beck Junior never drank in his life. He never used tobacco in his life. I think on the whole he's an outstanding young man today." O tempora! O mores! O brother! Stealing money is not wrong, just so long as you lead a clean, hardshell moral life. I'm well acquainted with a man who is a top-level corporation executive. He will not say "hell" or "damn" but he permits his underage children to drive cars on the public highways without licenses, and he chuckles when he talks about business successes achieved through piratical methods.

Everybody seems aware of the fact that chiseling on income taxes has supplanted baseball as the national pastime. Recently a well-to-do professional man from New York City called on me at my home in the country. He was eager to buy my house but I told him it was not for sale. He was persuasive, and pressed me hard, and finally talked me into naming the price I would ask in case I did ever decide to sell. Immediately he made his counter-offer, as if I had agreed that he could buy the house.

"We have a little game," he said, "called screwing the government. Everybody plays it, so there's no reason why *we* shouldn't. I'll give you x dollars for the record. Then I'll slip you an additional ten thousand in cash, which you won't have to declare on your tax return." There it was — a chance to swing a real good deal — but once again my ridiculous old honesty got in the way. I wanted to tell that fathead that the game of screwing the government is actually a game of screwing *me*. But I didn't. I knew that such a statement would make me look naïve and foolish, so I held my tongue.

It is the same in the game of screwing the customs men. In my travels abroad I am eternally astounded at the number of men and women who are scheming to cheat the customs and who talk about it, even boast about it. In former times it infuriated me when, arriving back in my native land, my luggage was ripped open and searched as if I were Public Enemy Number One. Then I figured out why the customs inspectors have to behave as they do. Prominent people, wealthy people, world famous people, persist in playing the game of Cheating the Customs. This makes us all suspect, and we must all undergo the indignity of thorough search. Even as I write the newspapers report that American women are buying expensive dresses in Paris and sewing Macy's labels in them before bringing them home. It seems unfortunate that this dodge is not working — the customs men have learned that a French zipper differs from an American zipper. I must admit that I would enjoy participating in the profitable game of smuggling, of outwitting the wily inspectors, but I simply can't bring myself to do it. In addition to my stupid integrity, I am afflicted with the Buff Orpington syndrome. I'm chicken.

My damnfool honesty has led me to turn down thousands of dollars in testimonial money, simply because I never used the products they wanted me to endorse. Many of my friends in show business and the writing trade have no such scruples and fatten their bank accounts with false and fraudulent testimonials. I know one prominent entertainer who glowingly endorsed a moving van company even though he had never owned a stick of furniture in his life. I knew a leading writer who endorsed a brand of liquor, in double-truck ads, though he had not taken a drink of alcohol in thirty years. Another eminent literary figure accepted money for having himself photographed with a cigarette in his hand and with accompanying text in which he said that particular brand was the only kind of cigarette he ever smoked; this shameless character never smokes cigarettes of any kind and is, in fact, a confirmed pipe-smoker and is even said to keep a pipe gripped between his teeth when he is indulging in mattress sports.

The new standards of honesty prevail in all walks of life, and at the national hearthside. Recently I read that the housewives of the nation make off with more than a million dollars worth of supermarket carts each year and that this figure is steadily rising. Another article tells us that employees of stores and warehouses steal upwards of a billion dollars worth of merchandise annually from their employers. Still the moralists shout that people are fundamentally honest. I recall the time a bank in our area put a basket of pennies on a table in the lobby and told the public to make its own parking meter change from the basket. The bank reported triumphantly that at the end of each week there was more money in the basket than had been put there at the beginning of the week. The newspapers wrote glowing editorials about the essential honesty of the American people.

But a leading psychologist remarked that the story might have been different if that basket had been full of ten-dollar gold pieces.

And it seemed significant to me that, at the same time, a concealed movie camera was taking pictures of prosperous commuters, living in our town, stealing dimes and quarters each morning from the "honor system" newsstand in the railroad station.

If I can get the devil of honesty exorcised, if some good psychoanalyst can get me straightened out and make it possible for me to join my fellow citizens in pursuit of the fast and illicit buck, I still want to be a special kind of cheat. I have reference to a thief whose story George Dixon picked up from the F.B.I. The man telephoned the F.B.I. office in New York and said he had stolen a suitcase in Grand Central Terminal. "It's full of blueprints," he said, "and other stuff that looks like secret military information. I've put it in one of the public lockers and I'm mailing you the key. I'm a thief, but I'm a loyal American thief."

That's the kind of thief I yearn to be.

*

*

*

19. Family Reunion

THE BOOKS SAY THAT the vast clan of people named Smith is a heterogeneous brotherhood of mixed beliefs and clashing passions. We are of every creed and color, yet we are capable of unity and we are dangerous when aroused or threatened from without, whether by people named Jones or Johnson or Brown or Hoopingarner. An ancient Scottish branch of the clan gave us our motto: *Touch not the cat without a glove.*

A congregation of Smiths is usually a wondrous thing to behold. I have in my files an account of an old-fashioned Smith Family Reunion held at the picnic grounds on the edge of a Midwestern town some years back. Nearly a thousand Smiths attended, drawn together by feelings of blood brotherhood from all over the United States. Late in the afternoon a male Smith from Tennessee was observed pinching the fatty tissue of a lady who was the wife of his cousin-german. The cousin-german hit the trifler on the skull with a beer bottle. Within seconds Smiths were smiting Smiths with legs ripped off picnic tables and by evening every bed in the town hospital was occupied, and additional wounded lay groaning along the floors of the corridors. Touch not the cat without a glove. Best not touch 'er at all.

My own division of the Smith clan is somewhat less bellicose. It isn't often that we manage to get together in any numbers, but now and then, over the years, there have been raucous little reunions and I have always looked forward to them with eager anticipation. We Smiths who sprang from McLeansboro in Illinois have two important characteristics: we are talkers from who-laid-the-chunk, and we are a laughing family. Get six or eight of us together and we'll sit into the late hours telling stories and laughing — laughing so uproariously that sometimes, even if we're out in the country, we close the windows so as not to keep the neighbors awake.

Just recently I was in Washington on business and I called my sister Jeanne down in Virginia. She said Rita and Arthur were up from Richmond, Marty and Ray were coming over from Clinton, and Lou and John were driving down from Laurel. It didn't take any urging for me to agree to come out as soon as I finished my luncheon date and Jeanne said Don would drive in to Washington and pick me up.

I was in the right mood for such a reunion. I went over in my mind all the new stories I had heard recently, all the gossip I had picked up from kith and kin back in the Midwest, all the arguments I could marshal in support of my peculiar beliefs concerning the human race. I knew that it would be talk, talk, talk and that there would be gales and hurricanes and typhoons of laughter. That's the way it has always been. There would be stories about Mom, an intensely religious woman whose moral strictures were considerably alleviated by a sharp and sometimes earthy sense of humor. I remembered once that she told me she had heard a poem that was sheer loveliness, pure beauty, and I resigned myself to a long session of listening to something possibly about one of the saints, and then she recited:

> *The woodpecker pecked*
> *On the red barn door.*
> *He pecked and he pecked*
> *Till his pecker got sore.*

Someone would surely tell about the time Mom saw the book in the store window, a book titled *Make and Mend*. Being an expert needlewoman she entered the store and approached a girl clerk. "I want to get that book, *Make and Mend*," said Mom. The girl's eyes bugged out like a tromped-on toad frog. She stared at Mom, who was then near seventy, for a long moment. "W'y," she finally said, "I don't think there's any such book as that." Mom said there certainly was and pointed it out in the window. "Oh," said the girl clerk, "my goodness yes. I thought you said *Makin' Men*."

There would be stories about Pop, and it would take relays of garrulous Smiths working around the clock for eighty-five years to ever finish with those. Pop was always one of the saltiest men on earth, a rebel from the word go, a man whose gloriously eloquent profanity I'd match any day against Thomas Wolfe's father, or Huck Finn's pap. In his better cussing days Pop was more like Old Man Finn, "who got to cussing, and cussed everything and everybody he could think of, and then cussed them all over again to make sure he hadn't skipped any, and after that he polished off with a kind of general cuss all around, including a considerable parcel of people which he didn't know the names of, and so called them what's-his-name when he got to them, and went right along with his cussing." Elsewhere I have written of how I inherited two things from my father — that great talent for cussing, plus a double-ended nose.

At the little reunion there would be hilarious stories about Aunt Vieve and about Dicker Smith who, around the time of my birth, was always proclaiming that "Mottomobiles is ruinin' the country." And someone would tell about the time Aunt Nellie Hassett cut a switch and whipped the rooster, because the rooster had pecked one of her cherry pies all to hell. (Aunt Nellie Hassett is known as "The Grandma Moses of Little Egypt" and today, at ninety-three, paints a picture a week. I have just had a long letter from her which concludes with this paragraph: "I know this is a silly letter. You must of inherited your mind from *my* side of the family. Will close as it is time for Huntly Brinkly.")

There would be stories about people we knew in Mc-Leansboro, Decatur, Defiance and Huntington — the towns we lived in successively when we were all growing up. I tell you, I was looking forward to that afternoon in Fairfax County. It had been a long time since so many of us had been together just for reminiscing and laughing. The years had marched by and we were all pretty much middle-aged (which means old as hell); yet this kind of a get-together would make us all feel young and frisky again. I wasn't even thinking about the piling up of the years as Don drove down Gunston Hall Road, once the private driveway of Colonel George Mason, true father of the Bill of Rights.

In a little while we were all settled down on the screened porch, looking off west to a distant green slope where a herd of cattle was grazing. They were just far enough away so that we couldn't detect movement among them and the prospect made me think of a lovely landscape by Petrucelli. (There is no painter named Petrucelli that I know about; it just sounds nice to say that a scene reminds us of a land-scape by somebody important; it makes the landscape so much prettier.)

I got myself all relaxed, with a glass of lager at hand, and prepared to begin the storytelling if nobody else beat me to it.

"We're going to cook steaks and corn out on the terrace," said Jeanne.

"How do you fix your corn?" Rita wanted to know.

"Take the husks off," said Jeanne, "and douse the ears with butter and salt and pepper, wrap them in aluminum foil and put them right on top of the hot coals."

"I'll eat it," said John, "but I won't like it as well as if you'd leave the husks on, drench 'em with salt water and then put 'em on the coals."

"Some people do it your way, John," I said, "but they wrap it in aluminum before they put it on the fire. Me, I've tried all the different ways, and I always go back to the old reliable — drop the ears in boiling water."

"Salted," said Lou.

"God no!" I protested. "That's the worst mistake you can make. I used to always salt the water till I learned better. I found out that salt water makes the corn tougher. What you want to do is put a tablespoon or two of *sugar* in the boiling water."

"Sugar?" said Jeanne. "Sounds *guhhhhhh* to me."

"You just try it once," I said, "and you'll eat sweet corn that's sweet corn."

Ray suddenly spoke up. "I brought over about half a bushel of green beans," he said. Ray is a terrific hand at growing vegetables in spite of the fact that he works for the Department of Agriculture. "You can cook some of them today if you want to," he added.

"I don't think," said Don, "that we've got a bit of fatback in the house."

"Fatback!" said Lou. "Can't you people ever get out of Indiana? Why don't you learn to cook green beans the proper way? You throw in all that greasy pork and then you cook the beans all day and all the good cooks out of them."

"Speaking of beans," I said, before the fatback argument could develop further, "do any of you ever eat *garbanzos*? They're called chick peas in this country but in Spain and Mexico they're *garbanzos*. I've got a recipe for *garbanzo* soup that'll knock your eye out. You cut up a pound or two of link sausages into small bits and fry them till they're almost crisp. Then you boil two or three cups of diced potatoes, and a cup or two of shredded cabbage, and maybe a little chopped onion. Then take a couple of cans of *garbanzos* and drain the juice off and dump them in with the vegetables, and add the bits of sausage. Salt and pepper and let the whole thing cook till the vegetables are done and you've got something — best soup you ever tasted and it's a full meal in itself."

"Yee-yum," said Rita. "It sounds good. Maybe I could drive down to the highway right now and find a store that keeps grabontsoss."

"*Gar-bon-those*," I said.

"Not now, Rita," said Jeanne. "I've got this big meal already planned."

"Hey!" Don suddenly interjected. "I want you all to try my garlic olives." He rushed off to the kitchen and in a few moments came back with a plate of pickled olives and pearl onions.

"Always use stuffed green olives," he said as we began grabbing at them. They were, as the ladies put it, out of this world. "Take a cup or two of olive oil," Don went on, "crush two cloves of garlic in it, put in a teaspoon of celery seed and pour the whole thing over the olives and pearl onions. Put it in the refrigerator for three or four days and then go to work on it. How you like?"

"They're wonderful," I said. "Seems to me you might add a little hot pepper of some kind — not much, just enough to give them a little more zip."

"Not a bad idea," said Don. "I'll try it next time. I've got a jar of whole chile peppers out there. Maybe I'll drop a couple in the next time and see what happens."

"About that garblebones soup of yours," said Marty. "Hey, Jeanne, have you got some paper and a pencil? I want to write it down."

"Bring me some paper, too," said Rita. "I'll give you all a recipe for barbecue sauce I got from a woman, visiting the Orpens a month or so ago, came from Macon, Georgia. It's a barbecue sauce to end all barbecue sauces."

They wrote down my technique for making *garbanzo*

soup. I wrote down the details on the garlic olives as well as the Macon barbecue sauce.

"Incidentally," I finally said, "I've found a food chopper that's the best damn kitchen gadget on earth. It's called a Schneidboy, which is German, I think, for cutting boy. It's got five circular blades, or discs, like little steel wheels, and you simply run this thing back and forth over your vegetables, your onions or peppers or whatever else you want chopped, and it cuts down the chopping time to about one-fourth of what it would take with a chef's knife. I can't for the life of me remember where I bought the thing, and I can't find anybody who handles it. I'd like to buy a dozen and give them as presents."

Arthur now chimed in with his version of the proper method for frying venison steak, smothered in onions and served with brown gravy. Don wrote it down because there's a huntsman in his office who sometimes has venison to pass around. I told about the marvelous venison that's on every menu in Yucatan. John started to tell us how to pickle eggs, the way they used to be prepared in the days of the free lunch counter, but when he got to the part about sealing them up and letting them marinate for at least a month, everybody protested — the waiting period was far too long. I told about my success in growing my own sweet basil and marjoram and outlined my plans for the expansion of my herb husbandry next year.

"Isn't basil what you're supposed to put in spaghetti sauce?" Marty wanted to know. I assured her that it was, that basil is essential to any tomato dish. I agreed to send her a jar of my own hand-grown basil and Lou asked if she could have some too, and so did Rita.

Ray said his potato crop was doing poorly, that it looked as if most of them would be runty. "Listen, boy," said Rita, "don't you remember two years ago when you gave me all those runty peewee potatoes? I love 'em. Wrap 'em up and send me all you can spare."

"You can have them," said Marty scornfully, she being the wife of the potato-grower. "As for me, give me a good old Idaho baked potato. Bruthhhh-errr!"

I got back into the act with the firm declaration that chili (con carne) has no right to be called chili unless a good sizeable pinch of cumin seed is cooked into it. Arthur said that when he makes chili he likes to use half beef and half pork — makes it much tastier. Don says he always stirs in a teaspoon of oregano. I said oregano was fine, and necessary, but not to forget the cumin seed.

Now came a laugh — perhaps the only one of the long session. Rita said she knows a colored lady in Richmond who makes the finest apple pies in the State of Virginia. One day Rita ran into this lady on the street and asked her what it is she uses to give her apple pies such a superb flavor. Said the colored lady: "Jus' cinnena, nutneg, an' sooger."

The recipe-trading went on all the rest of the afternoon. Smiths sitting around with pencils and scratch pads, their brows deeply furrowed as they listed ingredients for this dish and that. It came on twilight and Don cooked the steak and the corn (in aluminum foil with the husks off). At last the hour came when I had to head for Washington Airport.

While I was on the plane flying back to New York the full meaning of what had happened dawned on me. I hadn't even noticed it before, but . . . well, the next morning I telephoned Jeanne.

"Do you realize," I said, "that we spent the whole afternoon and half the evening with scarcely a single laugh among the nine of us? Do you realize that nobody told any funny stories? That nobody mentioned Pop or Mom or Dicker or Aunt Nellie? What on earth has happened to us?"

Jeanne now laughed, long and satisfyingly.

"I guess we've reached that age," she said.

"All we did," I said, "was sit around and recite recipes at one another, and copy them down, and argue about husks versus aluminum foil and Idaho potatoes versus Ray's pee-wees."

"Well," said Jeanne, "I for one thoroughly enjoyed every minute of it. And *you* ought to enjoy it . . . while you can."

"Whadda you mean by that crack?"

"Maybe by the next time we all get together," she said, "we won't be so interested in garlic olives and globlombiss soup. We'll be talking about our stomach trouble, and gout, and heartburn."

"I hope not," I said and then, after a pause, "Listen, how much celery seed did Don say to put in those garlic olives?"

"One teaspoon," she said.

"Thanks. I'm making my first batch right now."

I did make them, and they were super. Out of this world.

*

*

*

20. The Achievement of H. T. Wensel

A FRIEND OF MINE in Washington made the acquaintance, thirty-odd years ago, of a man named H. T. Wensel, who was on the staff of the Bureau of Standards. One day Mr. Wensel called my friend into a shadowy corner of his laboratory and slipped him a document which, he said, might revolutionize all theological thinking. Mr. Wensel has long since disappeared from the scene and today is not even remembered at the Bureau of Standards.

My Washington friend showed me Mr. Wensel's remarkable theory and I copied it down as follows:

Heaven is hotter than hell. The temperature of heaven can be rather accurately computed from available data. Our authority is the best possible, namely the Bible. Isaiah 30: 26 reads, "Moreover the light of the moon shall be as the light of the sun and the light of the sun shall be seven-fold, as the light of seven days." Thus heaven receives from the moon as much radiation as we do from the sun and in addition seven times seven (or forty-nine) times as much as we do from the sun, or fifty times in all as much as we receive from the sun.

Now the light we receive from the moon is a ten-thousandth of the light we receive from the sun, so we can ignore what we receive from the moon. And with this data in hand we can easily compute the temperature of heaven.

The radiation falling on heaven will heat it to the point where the heat lost by radiation is just equal to the heat received by radiation. In other words, heaven loses fifty times as much heat as the earth by radiation. Using the well-known Stefan–Boltzmann fourth power law for radiation $\left(\dfrac{H}{E}\right)^4 = 50$ where H is the absolute temperature of heaven and E is the absolute temperature of the earth — 300° C. (273 plus 27). This gives H as 798° absolute or 525° C.

The exact temperature of hell cannot be computed but it must be less than 444.6° C., the temperature at which brimstone or sulphur changes from a liquid to a gas. Revelations 21: 8: "But the fearful, and unbelieving . . . shall have their part in the lake which burneth with fire and brimstone." A *lake* of molten brimstone means that its temperature must be below the boiling point, which is 444.6° C. If it were above this point it would be a vapor and not a lake.

We have, then, the following: temperature of heaven, 525° C. or 977° F. Temperature of hell, less than 445° C. or less than 833° F. Therefore, heaven is hotter than hell.

Thus the Wensel Formula. I must confess that I do not understand it, just as I was never able to understand heaven or hell in the days when hell was generally thought to be of a somewhat warmer climate than heaven. However, I handed the Wensel paper to Martin Levin, who conducts "The Phoenix Nest" department of the *Saturday Review* and he gave it its first publication. Later it was picked up by the journal of the Phi Lambda Upsilon Honorary Chemical Society and after that, in 1962, it appeared in a book called *The Mathematical Magpie*, edited by my old friend Clifton Fadiman. Mr. Fadiman said he considered it to be transcendental. I don't even know what he meant by *that*. Anyway, old dead-and-gone H. T. Wensel certainly stirred up a bit of excitement. Samuel L. Clemens once said: "Heaven for climate, hell for society." Could it be that people seeking both good weather and pleasant company are now destined to find them in a single place?

＊

＊

＊

21. A Friend in West End Avenue

"I've turned respectable," said Jim Moran. "I may even shave off this beard."

We were walking east on Forty-fourth Street and we had been talking about the time he kidnaped the cat. And the time he shot the crow. And the time he sold the icebox to the Eskimo. And the time he . . .

"I'm finished with all those offbeat shenanigans," Jim insisted. "You are looking at a man who has changed his way of life. I'm now happily married and devoted to my carpet slippers. I have steady employment — more than I can handle. I even have an office on Fifth Avenue. I've quit drinking and gone on a diet and I've got my weight down to a hundred and ninety-five. I'm pushing fifty, and I've turned respectable. No more shenanigans."

We came into Times Square and stopped at the curb and Jim glanced up at the tremendous man-made waterfall which, at that time, surmounted the Bond building. This waterfall, said to have been the largest advertising sign on earth, stretched the whole length of the block and was one of the unnatural wonders of the world. Jim cocked his head a little to one side and stared up at it for a long moment.

"One of these days," he said, "I'm going over that son of a bitch in a barrel. The people in charge of it say they won't let me do it, but I *will* do it, and I'll attract the biggest goddamn crowd Times Square has ever seen. When people first started going over Niagara Falls in barrels and big rubber balls the authorities tried to stop them, but they wouldn't be stopped. And now they tell me I can't go over that thing in a barrel, that I might bounce over the parapet and into the street and kill a pedestrian. Well, just wait and see."

At that moment I began to suspect that Jim Moran really hadn't stopped being Jim Moran at all. The whiskers would stay.

A few days after the waterfall incident Jim turned up at my house in the country with two white sheets. He asked for a drink and said that he and his third wife had gone *puffiffett* and he wanted to know if I had any ant colonies on my premises. I replied that as far as I could make out, my premises consisted of nothing more than one huge ant colony. He took a shovel and went into the woods and after a while was back with two large balls of earth, wrapped in the sheets. Beyond saying that he was removing a thousand or so ants from my property, he refused to discuss his maneuvers.

Several evenings later I saw my ants on television. Jim had them now in a box and he had another colony in one of those glass-enclosed ant houses. He explained to the TV audience that the ants in the box were Mount Kisco ants, while the ants under glass were natives of New Jersey. He said that he was going to introduce some of the Mount Kisco ants into the Jersey ant community.

"Ants," he said, in that solemn, professorial tone of his, "ants are a good deal like people. These New Jersey ants think they are still in New Jersey. The Mount Kisco ants don't know where they are. Now, let's see what will happen when we introduce them to each other."

He took two of the Mount Kisco ants and poked them gently through a little hole in the Jersey ant palace. The camera closed in on the scene until each ant looked to be as big and as unlovely as a moose. The instant the Mount Kisco ants entered the palace, the Jersey ants at all levels began showing alarm, twitching this way and that, wiggling their antennae. The Mount Kisco ants made a few tentative moves, sensing ambush, and then up the ramp came half a dozen Jersey warriors. They pounced upon the invaders and though the Mount Kisco ants fought valiantly, rearing up on their hind legs and snapping like mud turtles, they were woefully outnumbered. Within a matter of twenty seconds they had been vanquished. It was one of the most interesting things I had ever seen on television, even though my paternal feeling for my own ants left me a little saddened, and more than a little angry.

In the last dozen years Jim Moran has widened his audience tremendously through his appearances on television and most of those appearances have been centered around his increasing interest in natural history. He is quite unorthodox in his interpretation of natural law. People who never heard of him in the past, and who knew nothing of his colorful history, now recognize him and salute him on the street, whether he's in New York or Los Angeles or Klamath Falls.

The beard is his trademark — that and his soft, untroubled voice. He is an imposing figure wherever he goes, standing six feet three and seeming to exude a special amiability toward the world. His eyes have been described as "electric blue" and have a magnetic quality.

Several years ago one of those writers who seemed to be obsessed with the gobbledygook of the psychiatrists tried to psychoanalyze Jim in print. He suggested that Jim is loaded with "pent-up hostility" toward the world and its inhabitants, and that he is motivated by "an insatiable craving for publicity." He wrote that Jim's projects "almost invariably involve some elaborate hoax *at the expense of the public.*" The italics are mine, and the unmuffled oaths heard in the background also are mine. Jim is not a show-off. At parties and other gatherings he has never been known to identify himself, when asked to do so, beyond saying, "I do publicity," or, "I do a little work in television." It is a fact that many of the people with whom he has been associated in television are not aware of his earlier career; they don't know that they are dealing with the man who actually sold an icebox to an Eskimo, who truly found a needle in a haystack, who positively turned a bull loose in a china shop, who personally hatched out an ostrich egg, and so on. They don't know these things for the reason that Jim never mentions them.

As for the allegation that Jim operates at the expense of the public, that would seem to be a charge made by a common scold. Those who know him best have always felt that Jim was rendering important and worthwhile service to the public, destroying stupid copybook maxims and knocking down hallowed proverbs. He is the master of the Soft Spoof. He is not a practical joker and he resents being called one. "The thing I deal in," he says, "is the mental hot-foot." He has never set out deliberately to hurt anyone, although he has violated a few minds that needed violating.

I first encountered Jim Moran in 1939. A friend telephoned me at the newspaper where I worked and asked me if I'd like to meet a man who once sold advertising space on the ceilings of Texas barber shops and who, in addition, had sold an icebox to a genuine Eskimo. I hurried uptown and rang a doorbell and a tall, handsome guy opened the door. He had in his hand a thing that looked like a smooth piece of grayish driftwood. The first words he spoke to me were: "Did you ever see a walrus's whammadoodle? Here, have a look at one. Note the graceful curve in it." And he switched at once to the subject of whales.

The New York World's Fair was about to open under the guiding hand of Grover Whalen. Moran said he had come to New York to seek an audience with Mr. Whalen. He wanted to sell Mr. Whalen on the idea of exhibiting a live whale in a "whale-a-torium" at the Fair.

"This is not a gag," he assured me. "I've known about whales and their habits for years. I once led a whale-hunting expedition in San Francisco Bay. I know that a live whale has never been exhibited in this country. I know that people would come in mobs to see a live whale, close up. In six weeks' time I can deliver a live whale at the Fair. The whale and the whale-a-torium will cost fifty thousand dollars. I figure a profit for the Fair of at least a million dollars off an original investment of fifty thousand."

"And you," I said, "what do you get out of it?"

"I wouldn't ask for much. All I want is the concession to sell advertising space on the whale's back. It'll be a cinch. I figure that I. J. Fox alone will take one entire flank." (Historical note: in those days the flashiest advertiser in New York City was I. J. Fox, a furrier.)

The Fair managed to struggle through its two years without a whale-a-torium. Mr. Whalen and his associates were said to have balked when confronted with the proposal that the whale would be covered with advertising. A whale decorated with multicolored ads for furs and soft drinks and cigarettes and panty girdles would, to be realistic about it, look a trifle gaudy. New York City kids, if they know about cows at all, believe that the animal has to squat down on the milk bottles. These same impressionable children, viewing their first whale under these circumstances, could grow up believing that all whales, including Moby Dick himself, resembled the outfield fences in a ball park. Perhaps Mr. Whalen was right. But Mr. Moran was right too. A man can't go to all the bother of capturing a forty-ton whale and delivering it in good health just for the honor and glory of the thing. He ought to get a little something out of it.

And that brings us to an important question in the career of Jim Moran. How many of his exploits have been motivated by crass commercialism? Before attempting an answer, let us examine his past history . . . for the benefit of those who may have come in late.

He was born in the Shenandoah Valley in 1907, son of an attorney and economist. Perhaps the most significant event of his childhood occurred in a kitchen. He was standing by the stove, waiting for a pan of water to come to a boil. Some member of the family came along and said, "You'd better get away from that stove. Don't you know that a watched pot never boils?" Jim had heard the saying before, but now he planted himself firmly in front of the pot, and stared at it, never once removing his gaze from it; and, of course, after a while the watched pot boiled. Jim Moran was on his way.

He had no fondness for school, perhaps because he was eternally being yanked out of one and enrolled in another — his family moved about the country a lot — and he just barely made it through high school. By this time the Morans were settled in Washington, D. C. Jim's first job was selling magazine subscriptions from door to door. Right away he violated the most precious precept of the time. When a housewife opened her door, Jim bowed slightly and said, "Madam, I am *not* working my way through college. I just enjoy making money." This irregular approach paid off for him and after a while he became a door-to-door salesman of fancy radiator covers. He reasoned that the best market for his product lay in the homes of the well-to-do. The problem was to gain entrance to these households. He had a calling card engraved saying simply, *James Sterling Moran, 730 Park Avenue, New York.*

"A housewife in a little bungalow," Jim explains, "knows how to cope with door-to-door canvassers. But a woman in a mansion has had no experience with them. Once you get into her presence you can sell her anything. I'd present this simple, dignified calling card to the butler, and he'd take it to his mistress, and she'd assume that I was someone out of New York society whom she *ought* to know, and in I'd go. Then I'd sell her radiator covers for radiators she didn't even have. If she happened to be youngish, and built, she might even get more than her radiators covered."

From that ancient day when he watched a watched pot

boiling, Jim had always been amused by the willingness of the average person to believe a thing is true simply because it is said over and over again. On a trolley car in Washington he overheard one man say to another, "You might as well try to sell an icebox to an Eskimo." Out of that chance remark came Jim's famous expedition to Alaska. He talked a broadcasting company, an airline and the National Association of Ice Advertisers into underwriting the trip, and in Juneau, after a long search, he found an Eskimo named Charlie Pots-to-Lick who was willing to buy an icebox.

Jim returned to California with two fleas, which he later claimed he got off the hind leg of a husky dog, and two hundred pounds of ice which he had chopped from the Mendenhall Glacier. In Hollywood he talked so convincingly about the special talents of the two fleas that Paramount Pictures paid him seven hundred and fifty dollars for them, and used them as featured players in a Claudette Colbert film. After that Jim sold a small piece of his glacier ice to Dorothy Lamour's press agent, and Miss Lamour was photographed undergoing a facial treatment with this special ice. The remainder was sold to a prominent manufacturer of domestic ice who placed it in a show window with a sign proclaiming: *This Ice Was Made by Nature 100,000 years Ago in Alaska. Laboratory Analysis Shows Our Ice is Even Purer.*

The success of his Alaskan expedition sent Jim off on a long series of fabulous adventures. He had a haystack set up on a prominent street corner in Washington. The executive secretary of the Board of Trade threw a needle into it. Then Jim went to work. It took him eighty-two hours and thirty minutes to find the needle and when he wasn't actually searching he was selling individual straws to onlookers who wanted souvenirs of the historic event.

Soon after the haystack stunt we find Jim in Boston, staging a cockeyed re-enactment of the Battle of Bunker Hill. First he advertised for a dozen men. Two were to have normal vision, two were to be nearsighted, two farsighted, and others were to be bleary-eyed or even cross-eyed. Jim dressed six of these men in American colonial costumes, while the remaining six wore British redcoat uniforms. Jim himself undertook the role of Colonel Prescott, commanding the Americans. He stationed his troops on Bunker Hill and signaled the British to charge. Then, as Colonel Prescott, he uttered the famous cry: "Don't shoot until you see the whites of their eyes!" It was his intention to prove that this was "the stupidist command ever heard on a battlefield." He did prove it, at least to his own satisfaction.

Subsequently Jim dreamed up and executed the following highly successful stunts:

In Nevada, wearing an Uncle Sam uniform, he proved that it's fairly easy to change horses in the middle of a stream.

He sat on an ostrich egg for nineteen days and finally hatched out a baby ostrich, which he named Ossip and which he proclaimed to be his rightful son and heir.

He turned a bull loose in New York's most expensive china shop, proving that a bull in a china shop causes less tumult and destruction than people in a china shop.

He attracted large crowds in Los Angeles by placing in a show window a fragment of Persian rug, somewhat gnawed at the edges, with a sign stating it to be part of a rug taken from the German chancellery and bearing the teeth-marks of Adolf Hitler.

He created pandemonium in a swank Los Angeles night club by impersonating the Crown Prince of Saudi Arabia, complete with robed retinue, and spilling a bagful of phony jewels on the floor, sending some of the movie colony's leading personalities scrambling about on their hands and knees.

He ran for the United States Senate in California on the platform, "What this country needs is a good five cents," and actually managed to corral twenty thousand votes.

There are more — many more, enough to fill a book —

and there have been some that failed. He once questioned the validity of the saying, "Drunk as a hoot owl." He tried hard to get a hoot owl drunk, but the creature refused to swallow the stuff. Wise? Maybe.

I think my own favorite of all Moran performances was one that had its origins in a hangover. Jim awoke one morning in December of 1940, decided he felt too horrible to get out of bed, and reached for a book with the intention of trying to soothe his screeching nerves. By chance the book was an anthology of verse and Jim's eye fell upon the celebrated rhyme:

> *I never saw a purple cow,*
> *I never hope to see one;*
> *But I can tell you, anyhow,*
> *I'd rather see than be one!*

The first line of this verse insinuated itself into Jim's consciousness and stayed there. All day long it kept singing through his head . . . "I never saw a purple cow . . . blah *blah* blah *blah* blah *blah blah*." And gradually Jim worked up a fine hate for Gelett Burgess, the man who had written the verse.

A few days later, at five o'clock in the afternoon, Burgess was in his room at a hotel on lower Broadway. The telephone rang. He was asked to descend to the lobby. He did, and Jim Moran was there waiting for him.

"Mr. Burgess?" Jim asked.

"Yes."

"Just one moment, please," said Jim. He stepped quickly into the street and a few seconds later returned to the lobby leading a purple cow. He jockeyed the animal up to Mr. Burgess, squared her around, and said:

"There!"

Jim had borrowed the cow from the Jersey Breeders Association. By nature she was a fawn color, but Jim rendered her purple by mixing a cosmetic dye with flour and talc and dusting her hide with it. Three of her teats were gold-tipped and one looked to be solid silver. All in all, she was quite spectacular and Mr. Burgess confessed that he would never forget the sight of her as long as he lived.

(At the time it happened I wrote about the purple cow with the gold and silver teats. Subsequently Jim and I were at a party also attended by Gypsy Rose Lee. I introduced them. Miss Lee looked Jim over admiringly. "I heard about the purple cow," she said. "You are a very interesting man. I'd like to have you stop in some time for cocktails." Said Jim: "I'd be happy to come." Said Gypsy: "Be sure to bring your paint pots.")

It is true that commercial promotion has been involved in most of Jim's iconoclasticisms but many of them, including the adventure of the purple cow, have cost him money. His techniques are radically different from those of other publicity men. He dreams up his project and then looks around for someone to pay the bill. Let us take the case of the ostrich parturition as an illustration. Back in the early years of World War II, Jim got on his ostrich kick. He was fascinated by ostriches as he had been fascinated by whales a few years earlier, and by walrus parts before that. He read everything he could find on ostriches and he told me, around 1943, that some day he was going to hatch out and become the father of a baby ostrich. Nothing happened for several years and then Betty MacDonald wrote *The Egg and I,* and in 1947 the book was filmed in Hollywood. Jim went to the producers with his egg-hatching idea and they put him, so to speak, to set. He wore a feathered costume in the hatching pen and at night roosted in a special bed which made it possible for him to transmit rump-warmth to the egg without breaking it. Reporters and photographers came in a steady stream. The pay-off for the movie studio was simple — a sign above the coop saying, *The Egg and I.*

It has been said that Jim's restaging of the Battle of

Bunker Hill was a promotion stunt for a manufacturer of optical glass. Jim denies it. "That one was on the house," he says. "I paid for it out of my own pocket. The same thing goes for quite a few of my projects, especially the earlier ones. I never tried to make a fat profit out of them. All I've ever wanted is a roof over my head, enough to eat, two suits of clothes and money to replace broken guitar strings." He made that statement about ten years ago. We shall see, shortly, that his philosophy in this matter of Spartan living has changed a bit.

He has said that he would be quite happy to eliminate all commercial considerations from his debunking activities. He believes that he is contributing a little toward the sanity of the human race, and he resents the opposite belief — that he is a screwball, adding to the world's insanity. He feels that one of the big foundations should establish a moderate fund to finance his special operations so that he wouldn't have to go around looking for commercial sponsors. By "moderate fund" he has in mind something on the order of ten or twenty million dollars.

"I'd accept less," he says. "Right now, for the price of plane fare and one shotgun shell, I could bring an end to the American Civil War. I would furnish the shotgun. As you know, they're still fighting that war like fury. The reason for this is that the last shot of the Civil War was never fired. At least I can find no record of it. I'd like to go down to the Mason-Dixon line and stand astraddle of it and aim a shotgun into the air and fire the last shot of the Civil War. Then it would be over and done with, and we wouldn't need to hear another word about it, and Bruce Catton could go somewhere and pick himself some goober peas."

Let us go back a couple of paragraphs to that avowal by Jim that he prefers the simple life, and then look at the way he lives today. Each of his three wives tried to understand him but they couldn't cope with the magnificent brainstorms that seized him, sometimes in the middle of the night. When a big idea hits him he has to tell it to somebody. If his wife prefers her sleep and refuses to listen, he gets on the phone and calls a friend and talks perhaps an hour. It might be said, too, that he has polygamous instincts and this may have had something to do with the breakup of his marriages.

In any event, this hairy philosopher, this Golden Gaekwar of West End Avenue, lives today in the dod-glangdest apartment ever seen outside ancient Hindustan and even there you'd not likely find its equal. I have had a tour of the premises with the satrap himself, clad in an ankle-length brocaded silken robe once worn by a Japanese shogun of the Ashikaga family, and on his head a saffron-colored skullcap which he got from the noodle chef at Sou Chan's Chinese Restaurant. The apartment has ten rooms and five baths and Jim describes the overall décor as rococo baroque with trim. It occupies the entire floor and has its own elevator landing and a closed-circuit television hookup which shows who is coming up on the elevator.

I can provide a mere sampling of the furnishings and fixtures of this fabulous pad. The living room is almost seventy feet long and features a great variety of musical instruments, including a custom-made concert grand piano; two classical guitars of expensive make; two medieval lutes; the four basic instruments of India's orchestras, acquired by Jim in Calcutta, namely, the sarod, the sitar, the tampura and the tabla; various ukuleles, banjos, mandolins; assorted drums from all over the world; flutes and recorders from Nepal and Tibet and Japan and other faraway lands; a great assortment of percussion instruments from around the world, things to rattle, whack, thump, scratch, shake, pick, hammer, tap, thud, snap, rap, crunch, pluck, squeak, blow, bang, crackle and wallop. Also a Tibetan Buddhist horn and a five-foot music box from Vienna.

There are statues and busts here and there, and about

three thousand books touching on a great variety of subjects, with very little fiction. One entire room contains masks which Jim collected from thirty-five countries, and there is an enormous closet filled with more than three hundred hats, helmets, caps, tarbooshes, berets, and other kinds of headgear. Jim also has a collection of several hundred costumes, including resplendent military and naval getup and many oriental robes.

And the antique lace. "I am," says Jim, "the only non-faggot lace collector I know about. Handmade antique lace is great art, and is fast disappearing from the world. Nobody is learning how to do it and the techniques are so difficult that we've probably seen the last of it."

Miscellaneous items in the apartment are an Inca chief's huge mace, that whammadoodle off a walrus, one Norden bombsight, one latest model lie detector, thirty pairs of medieval-style boots, a Sharp's rifle that was used in the Civil War, two jeweled Ghurka knives, a Zulu war club, a ship in a bottle given to Jim by his good friend Burl Ives, hundreds of fine recordings, fifty varieties of spices and herbs, thirty kites including one of the whirling rotor types, a Fat-O-Lator, bound volumes of the National Geographic covering 1915 to 1950, a hypnosis machine, a fine microscope, much photographic equipment, a porcelain elephant from Saigon, and so on and on and on.

Jim has long been a master cook and when he lived in Hollywood he was always in demand among the movie stars and producers as a "guest chef." He specializes in esoteric dishes, leaning toward curries and shashlicks and such, and he is full of little culinary gimmicks that delight the women-folks. Roy Rogers and Dale Evans still talk about the time Jim cooked dinner at their home and introduced them to a subtle innovation — ground coffee sprinkled lightly over a green salad. "At first," says Dale Evans, "it doesn't sound too good, but wait'll you try it. I wouldn't eat a salad nowadays unless it had coffee sprinkled on it."

Jim plays most of the musical instruments in his apartment but he is known best as a classical guitarist of great talent. He once played regularly with a group known as the Beverly Hills No Refund Philharmonic, whose other members included, from time to time, Ben Hecht, Jack Benny, Harpo Marx, Orson Welles, George Anthiel, Charles Lederer and Benny Goodman.

His friends congregate frequently in his big apartment and they include writers, musicians, painters, sculptors, actors and occasional nondescript characters picked up off the streets of Manhattan. These informal soirees are often musical although sometimes the guests just settle down and listen to Jim talk. He may be in a mood to deliver one of his incomparable lectures. He can spend an hour and a half talking about the life and habits of the white ant, or termite. He can talk entertainingly for another hour about the sex life of the date palm, which he investigated during a sojourn at Indio, California. Or he might get out a recording he made years ago to accompany one of his most hilarious lectures. He stands beside the record-player and tells of the period in his life when he was a sound engineer, engaged in recording certain native American noises that some day would be extinct.

"This particular recording," he says, "was made so that we might preserve one of our nation's most distinctive sounds. I have reference to the toilet flush."

Then he sets the record going and it consists of a long series of toilet flushes, with Jim explaining each one in detail, narrating the circumstances under which he got it on wax, pointing out the mellifluous tones to be found in certain flushes, the rasping, chattering notes of others. Throughout the lecture he employs the terminology of the musician in analyzing the flushes, including the one taken in the gents' room just off the floor of the United States Senate, and including also the one captured on a moving Pullman car. This lecture is delivered in Jim's customary dead-pan

manner, with praiseworthy dignity and with never a suggestion of vulgarity — it is as serious and as solemn as any
one of the wonderful laxative commercials we hear so much
today on television. It is, in fact, a fine satirical commentary on almost every illustrated lecture ever given.

Many ridiculous things have been written about Jim
Moran in the past. He lets them go unchallenged. Almost
all the published sketches of his career contain the statement
that he is an expert marksman. He has never challenged that
one.

"It's nice to be known as a sharpshooter," he says. "Something masculine and dashing and romantic about it. It also
keeps outraged husbands from coming at you too hurriedly.
But my reputation as a marksman is based on one single
shot. I was riding in an open car with a Washington columnist
one afternoon. We were somewhere out in the Virginia
countryside. I opened the glove compartment to look for a
map and saw a pistol. I got it out and was examining it
when suddenly I noticed a crow flapping along some distance ahead of us. 'Watch this,' I said, and raised the pistol
and pulled the trigger. Great God, you should have seen the
feathers fly! I just turned and grinned at my friend and
shoved the gun back in the compartment. From that day on
he went around telling everybody that I was the greatest
pistol shot on earth, and the story spread, so now I'm always
described as a marksman. I haven't had a gun in my hand
since that day I shattered the crow. If I *did* have one, I
wouldn't be able to hit Sophie Tucker in the ass with ten
tries."

I mentioned a Fat-O-Lator as one of the items in the
apartment. This is a machine which, Jim explains, has fourteen thousand moving parts, each part moving in a different direction. He would add more parts but he can't find
any new directions. The Fat-O-Lator was inspired by the fat
shortage during World War II. Jim reasoned that there ought

to be a method for storing up fat in good times for use in bad times. Since we are now enjoying prosperous times, there is an oversupply of fat and the machine was designed to reclaim it for storage.

"Millions of Americans, including myself," says Jim, "are on reducing diets. Suppose we had just one million people who are each losing two pounds of fat per week. Where is all that fat going? It has to go somewhere. Well, it's in the atmosphere. It stays in the air, sort of a thin mist, moving around like a low pressure area, or just hanging there in the sky like an occluded front. In its movements, this fat pursues a general pattern. In Seattle, for example, the people are exposed to waves of Eskimo and Siberian fat, which is inferior fat because of its large blubber content. But the fat front moves on down the coast so that San Francisco picks up Seattle fat and then Los Angeles and Hollywood get San Francisco fat. Over Hollywood the front picks up a couple of midriff pounds of Jayne Mansfield and a pound or two of Diana Dors, whose real name incidentally is Diana Fluck. The front travels on toward Texas with this precious burden. I like to think of a good clean American boy, lying in a field in Texas, knowing that somewhere overhead hovers two pounds of Jayne Mansfield. Such a boy will be a better American for that knowledge; he will grow up to be a better man. I don't believe he should think too much about the Diana Fluck fat. It is English."

Jim explains that his Fat-O-Lator is far from being perfected. It is self-lubricating, of course, and while it succeeds in extracting a great deal of fat out of the atmosphere, it has its faults. If one tiny part breaks down the results can be unfortunate — under such conditions the Fat-O-Lator has been known to bring in lean meat, and that's bad for somebody.

Another of Jim's inventions is the Ground-O. A small silver plate, made from a Mexican coin, is set into the sole of a shoe. A hole is cut in the sock so that the bare flesh of the foot makes contact with the silver. At the back of the shoe is another hole, from which a key chain extends, dragging along on the ground.

"Almost all of us," Jim says, "are walking around loaded to the eyebrows with dangerous static. We get it from television. If you are watching television and you are sitting in a line between the television set and the transmitter, it stands to reason that the waves are passing straight through your body. But *all of them don't get through.* Some of the static is retained in the body, and it builds up steadily. The result is that, after a while, you begin to behave in an eccentric manner. You go around talking to yourself in the sonorous accents of Walter Cronkite. You have a vague feeling that singing commercials concerned with soapsuds are coming out of your nose. I'm as much a victim as you are. Just the other day my teeth started to ache and suddenly I began giving myself the seven o'clock news. This happened because I was not wearing my Ground-O."

The grave manner in which Jim expounds such theories on television is natural with him; he is at bottom, as you may suspect, a very serious man. There is, in fact, one surpassingly serious note in his life. A dozen years ago in California Jim met and talked with a philosopher and in the course of their conversation Jim admitted that he, in common with many of his fellow citizens, was thoroughly bewildered about life and religion and science and human endeavor. The California philosopher steered him to the works of Alfred Korzybski, a Polish-American scholar and engineer who founded a system of educational discipline which he called *General Semantics.* His theories are set down in a book called *Science and Sanity*, and they embrace the fields of anthropology, biology, botany, conditioned reflexes, education, entomology, genetics, mathematics, logic, physics, neurology, ophthalmology, physiology, psychiatry, and for all I know how to tell when a steak is medium rare.

The California man gave Jim this eight-hundred-page

book. "Take it home and read it carefully," he instructed. "When you get through, start over again. And after that, read it again, and then again, and keep reading it the rest of your life. Each time you reread it you'll get more out of it and some day you may even come to understand the system in all its details. If you ever do, you'll be one of the few truly civilized human beings in the world."

Jim has lost track of the number of times he's read the book but he's still at it and his enthusiasm for the Korzybski teachings increases with each passing year.

Sometimes when he's visiting at my home he'll sit for hours talking about General Semantics, trying to explain it to me, telling me I should take it up and achieve the passionless peace of imperturbability, which comes with the annihilation of disturbing desires. I tell him it is all very interesting, and he talks about it beautifully, but that if I have any disturbing desires left, I want to keep them. They'll go away quick enough.

*

*

*

22. Another Triumph for Never-Never Land

AMONG MY NEIGHBORS is an excellent lady named Henriette
Granville who came to the United States years ago from her
native Vienna. She is an American citizen now and one day
she said to me: "There are only two things in this country
that I will never be able to understand as long as I live. One
is baseball. The other is peanut butter."

If you stand beside her in the matter of baseball, if The
Romance of Stan the Man, or The Adventures of Mickey
Mantle, bore you, then you'd better skip the next two or
three chapters, for they are about the new and improved
game of rounders. Ignorance about baseball is ignorance; ignorance about peanut butter is purely a matter of personal
taste — I have a daughter who spreads it on her buckwheat
cakes.

Let us begin this seminar with a report on a startling discovery I once made respecting the origin of ballplayers. By
origin I mean place of birth.

A dozen years ago some people in Hollywood acquired the
motion picture rights to a novel of mine concerned with the
doings of a New York baseball team. Two writers were put
to work on the screenplay and when they had finished, the
director brought it east for me to read.

Unlike the classic Writer-versus-Hollywood pattern, I was
not outraged by what they had done to my story. They had
switched the ball club to Brooklyn but that was all right.
The one thing that did give me a slight shock was the man-

ner in which the California screenwriters had the ballplayers talking. Every one of them talked as if he had been born and reared in Brooklyn, saying "dem" and "dese" and "goil" and "erster" and "awright awreddy" and suchlike.

It was necessary for me to recite the facts of life to those screenwriters and I did it by long distance telephone. I was tolerant of their mistake, knowing that they were Californians, and knowing also that Californians were apt to be confused by major league baseball. This was in 1950.

"Big league ballplayers," I told them, "don't come from Brooklyn, with one or two exceptions. The great majority of them come from places like Arkansas and Oklahoma and Texas and Georgia and the Carolinas. The talk you hear around a ball team is usually hillbilly talk, and never Brooklynese. It's like listening to a bunch of farmers. Get it straightened out or you'll be the laughingstock of North America and the Spanish Main."

In time the picture was made and I saw it. The language of the ballplayers still didn't suit me — they all talked as if they came from . . . well, from California. That certainly wasn't right but it was better than having them speak the colorful and mysterious language of the Gowanus.

Time passed, and occasionally I'd catch myself speculating on the geography of baseball, wondering why it is that the players are usually a backwoodsy sort of people. Then one winter's day the subject came up in the barber shop where I do most of my baseball arguing. I said flatly that ninety per cent of all big league ballplayers were country fellers with a strong aroma of cow manure hovering about them. I nearly fell out of the chair when both barbers, Vince and Ernie, agreed with me.

All baseball arguments in smalltown barber shops end up with intemperate yelling, and this was no exception. We agreed on the general principle, but quarreled over the details. I gave it as my opinion that South Carolina produced more ballplayers than any other state.

"Sheez!" exclaimed Vince. "How crazy can you get? Most of them are from Texas — anybody knows that."

Ernie spoke up and said that the both of us were in need of mental hygiene. He said Oklahoma. So I decided the time had come to resolve the question. I went down to New York and the offices of *Sports Illustrated* where they had certain employees who were modern-day marvels, able to do the same work as UNIVAC and the other mechanical brains that sit around clanking out analytical thoughts. I got together a list containing the names and birthplaces of all the big league players of that particular year (this was just before the leagues expanded). I sprinkled a little sassatate on the list and fed it into our human UNIVAC and after a while it kicked a sheet of paper into a box and we had the answer. It was a cruel sort of blow to me because it showed conclusively that the state which produces the greatest number of major leaguers is . . . California. And in second place, Pennsylvania. And after that, New York, Illinois and Michigan be-

fore we got to North Carolina. Oklahoma and Arkansas were far down the list, though Texas occupied seventh place in the ranking. And where was my choice, my own dear South Carolina? In twenty-first place with six ballplayers.

Conclusion No. 1: the gallus-snapping rube is a minor factor in major league baseball.

Conclusion No. 2: a barber shop is an excellent place to get a haircut.

✳

✳

✳

23. The Romance of Baseball Records

ONCE UPON A TIME in the faraway land of Lower Manhadoes, I was sitting at sup with a group of sports writers and someone suggested that we all get on a subway train and journey uptown to see the new Crosby picture. What he actually suggested was that we all "go up to Leone's and get really barreled" but I choose to put it the other way, since sports writers are among the heroes adored by American youth.

All present agreed that it would be bully to go see the new Crosby picture — all save one. This fellow said: "Hell's pecker, I can't do it. Got to go back to the office and do the filberts."

"Judas Priest!" exclaimed a confrere, employing a vile expletive he had picked up from years of contact with Branch Rickey, "haven't you done *them* yet?"

There was a considerable discussion in which I took no part for the reason that I was baffled. What did Williams mean when he said he was going back to do the filberts? How does one *do* a filbert? Cook it? No, not likely in a newspaper office, though daffier things take place there. I happen to know that there is a creature called the filbert mouse; maybe he meant he was going back to the office and do *in* some filbert mice.

At length it was decided that the rest of us would have a couple more and wait for Williams while he was doing the filberts, provided he did them with celerity. He hurried off and in a few minutes I timidly asked what he was going to do when he did them. It seems that the sports pages of his newspaper carried a column beneath a stock head: FIGGER FILBERT. This was the name of a nonexistent person who was daft about the mathematical aspects of sports events, particularly baseball. Each item written into the "Figger Filbert" column had something to do with figures, most of them being copied out of the record books which are devoted to the various divisions and subdivisions of the sporting world.

The filberts had to be done, I was assured, or there would be a large beef from the readers. They told me that every sports fan wants his daily ration of figures and wants it straight; in other words, this character Figger Filbert was no myth — he was every American sports fan. As of that evening, the great night of doing the filberts and seeing the new Crosby picture, I became keenly interested in the whole science of baseball statistics, with special reference to the making of new records.

Up to that moment I had believed implicitly that we were a nation of arithmetic haters. I knew that one of the most common expressions to be heard in our country has always been, "I can't add up a simple column of figures." I believed that when the President of the United States sat down to compose his budget message he first flexed his fingers (and thumbs), knowing that he would be counting on them for the next few hours.

But I was wrong. We are all Figger Filberts, even those of us who are not rabid sports fans. And our appetite for figures is never satisfied. We love to see a record shattered and if not that equaled and if not that, *almost* equaled. The instant a record is broken, the moment a NEW MARK IS SET, we begin yearning for the new mark to be bettered. The Weather Bureau has known of this universal weakness for years and scarcely a day passes without a meteorological record being broken. And better even than the Weather Bureau, the newspapers and the radio and television people know about

it. Says the weather story: "A new all-time record was established yesterday, the coldest January 16th since 1924. The low for yesterday was four degrees above zero. On January 16th in 1924 the low was three above zero, hence yesterday was the coldest January 16th since the January 16th we had in 1924. Brrrr!" (That last word in the weather story is put in for humorous effect. You'd be surprised how many readers will snicker and giggle over it.)

A report of this nature thrills the populace and excites comment even though there have been, since January 16th, 1924, maybe eight hundred winter days in which the thermometer dropped below three.

Suppose our little January the 16th cold spell had the aspect of a blizzard. What does the public want to know, most of all, about the blizzard? Storm's toll, of course. The banner lines in the newspapers give the answer: STORM'S TOLL MOUNTS TO NINE IN CITY. And who are these nine who fell before the blizzard's icy blasts? Just damn near everybody in town who got killed or dropped dead on the day of the storm. Among them you might find a sixty-year-old man whose heart stopped while he was looking at another man shoveling snow; had the weather been balmy this man might likely have died the same day while watching a neighbor whip a baby. Another storm victim is a boy hit in the head by a chunk of ice thrown by another boy; had the day been sunny and warm, the kid who threw the ice probably would have brought down his victim with a rock. Included in storm's toll is a housewife whose husband shot her between the eyes because she was using too much coal on the fire. Several of the victims were killed in auto accidents; two days earlier when the streets were dry and the sky cloudless, twice that many had been killed in auto accidents. It all seems a little stupid until you consider that newspaper readers gobble it up and rush around informing one another that the storm took a toll of nine.

Theater owners have always been great people for records. I well remember the days when the Paramount Theater in Times Square was enjoying the sound of crashing attendance records. Sometimes it would be a motion picture that shattered all records at the Paramount; other times it was Benny Goodman or Frank Sinatra or the same Crosby that was in the new movie we all went uptown to see. Every few months, year in and year out, existing records were broken at the Paramount. How did it come about? Did they keep adding seats in the balcony? Was the auditorium constantly expanding, like stretch pants? Did they institute new rules permitting girls to sit in the laps of their boy friends? I used to get nervous about it, awaiting the day when the Paramount would reach the saturation point, and then go beyond it, exploding at the seams and killing everybody trying to get a taxi at the Hotel Astor.

Even in the years before baseball became a prime entertainment on television I spent many delightful hours listening to the crash of batting and fielding and pitching records by way of my radio. One afternoon I was listening to a broadcast of a game in which a batter slammed one straight at the pitcher. The ball struck the pitcher on the head and bounced to the shortstop, who threw to first base in time for the out. My old friend Red Barber quickly credited the pitcher with an assist on the play and then continued:

"If you're thinkin' this is a world's record, then have another think. The record for this kind of a play was established long ago down in Texas. I don't have the precise data at hand but I can give you the main outlines. The batter hit the ball, a sizzler. It struck the pitcher on the forehead and bounced straight back toward home plate. The catcher came forward, grabbed the ball, fired it to first and the runner was out. That was the last out of the game. The pitcher was lyin' unconscious on the mound — knocked cold by that drive. He got an assist on the play and he was the winnin' pitcher, but he didn't know anything about it till two days later." Mr. Barber paused, then concluded, "So, you couldn't rightly call the play today a world's record, or even *equaling* a world's record, because the pitcher wasn't knocked unconscious."

Among the choice world's records entered in my own private files is one concerning a certain Chet Laabs, who was playing ball twenty-some years back. One season Mr. Laabs took to hitting home runs indiscriminately. On a summer afternoon I was listening to a game in which he was working. He had stricken homers in the three games preceding this one, and now he had just stricken another.

"I believe," said the announcer, "that it's a new record. He's hit five homers in four consecutive games. Fans, I do believe that is the world's record for number of home runs in four consecutive games."

There was a mumbling in the background. The statistical backstop at the sportscaster's elbow was challenging this statement.

"No," said the announcer, "no, I'm sorry, it's not a world's record for Laabs. Tony Lazzeri holds the record for number of home runs hit in four consecutive games. Lazzeri hit seven and Laabs only has five. *But* . . . Chet Laabs has six innings to go in today's game and he might . . . I say he *might* equal or even, well, maybe I'm getting out on a limb here, but . . ." His voice dribbled off into little nothings, and then came a long pause.

"Look at it this way," he finally resumed. "Chet Laabs hasn't equaled the record, but one thing is pretty certain. He most certainly now holds the record for home runs hit in four consecutive games *considering elapsed time*. He holds the record there, all right. You see, Laabs started his home run streak in a night game — night before last, when he hit two. Then yesterday he hit homers in both games of a double-header and now, this afternoon, he's already hit another one. Boy! That's easily the most home runs ever hit in four consecutive games *played in forty-eight hours*. Let me explain it a little more carefully. You see, when Lazzeri set the record they didn't have night games, so *his* home runs were hit over a longer period of time than Laabs's home runs, so even though Lazzeri hit *more* home runs in four consecutives games, Laabs has hit more home runs in four consecutive games played closer together, in point of time, I mean, than Lazzeri, and what's more, Laabs can . . . just a minute . . . Walker takes a ball, low and inside . . ."

That's what the man said. He said that. Maybe this world's record set by Laabs is a little confusing in print but I assure you it was crystal clear, and altogether convincing, as it came over the air.

Fans, in my next chapter I'm going to discuss the one single reason I am disappointed in the baseball record books. Right after this commercial message.

*

*

*

24. Rectifying the Record Books

In 1962 there was published in the United States a remarkable volume, the *Guinness Book of World Records*, put together in England by a couple of men named McWhirter. Its publishers claim that it covers all world records, from the high jumps of Watussi tribesmen in Africa to the record thirty-one piglets thrown by a sow named Liz in 1955.

These McWhirters, I must say, come up with some splendid world records, such as the following:

Heaviest human of all time: Robert Earl Hughes of Fish Hook, Illinois, who reached 1,069 pounds early in 1958.

Most service as Best Man at Weddings: 48 times, by Mr. Walter Gant, a bachelor of Yorkshire.

Highest recorded jump by a porpoise: 16 feet, by the female Nellie, at Marineland, Florida.

World record for shortest will ever admitted to probate, name of testator uncertain (case of *Thorn* vs. *Dickens*). The will read: "All for Mother."

That's enough. You can see that these boys tried to cover the field. But they are European and quite skimpy on the subject of baseball (and peanut butter). They are, in fact, wholly inadequate on baseball, but then it is my contention that the fat books of baseball statistics issued in the United States are likewise inadequate.

The statistics are not complete, and do not give an accurate picture of the baseball season. Many times during each succeeding summer I have personally observed new records established, or I have heard about them, and I know they will not be included among the official statistics. Off-hand I think of the precedent-shattering performance of Ed Ofer, the knuckle-ball pitcher, during a July game in Chicago. With nobody out in the top of the first inning, Ofer walked the first two men to face him. His catcher, Ears Eakin, called time and trotted to the mound. Eakin began to talk soothingly to the pitcher, intent upon steadying him down. But Ed Ofer interrupted him, saying: "Listen. You git on back behime the plate and mine yer own dam business. You do the ketchin' and I'll do the pitchin'."

Is such a sterling and confident declaration to go unrecognized and unrecorded in the history of the game? Not while I'm able to raise my voice. I propose that in the future the annual record book carry a fat appendix, setting forth all those special achievements which are today beyond the province of the cool-blooded statisticians.

Certain spectators as well as certain players have recently turned in performances worthy of historical recognition, and to me they are fully as important as the switch-hitter who got the most singles off left-handed pitchers in the three middle innings of an American League game while having a sore wrist heavily taped.

Following are a handful of the world records I have compiled:

MOST RECKLESS MANAGER AWARD

To Wolfie Brenner. Every time he went to the mound to talk to his pitcher during the 1963 season, he deliberately stepped on the whitened base line.

FOUL BALL LEGION OF HONOR

To Benjamin Barstow, Washington fan. He was seated in the lower stands off first base when a high foul ball came arching downward. All around him men and boys shrieked and leaped in the air and tore each other's clothing. Mr. Barstow sat with arms

folded, staring straight ahead. Amid all the banging and scrambling and screeching he was heard to say: "Who wants a dern old baseball?"

DON DRYSDALE TROPHY

To Jack Cochise, New York Mets outfielder. In the clubhouse before a game with Los Angeles he quietly removed the insignia METS from the front of his uniform shirt and played two and a half innings before anyone noticed it. When Manager Stengel demanded an explanation, Cochise said: "I'd ruther not be identified with this club."

BUSINESS ENTERPRISE AWARD

To J. Leeford Shanklin, of Peetang, North Carolina. He executed the business coup of the year in baseball, obtaining by artifice the eating tobacco concession for the National, the Three-Eye and the Piedmont leagues.

CONSERVATION OF NATURAL RESOURCES CUP

To Fog Burbitt, Minnesota relief pitcher. He refused, throughout the season, to ever warm-up in the bull pen, contending that "it wears out muh strenth."

OVERSEAS PRESS CLUB MEDAL

To Cecil Dugdale of England. Visiting in New York he was escorted to a ball game by a sports writer who envisioned a hilarious account of the Englishman's dumbhead reaction. In the first inning Mr. Dugdale said nothing until Colavito hit a ground ball to short. Then the Englishman spoke: "That would have been a sure double-play ball if Tony had been playing two and a half feet to his right."

OPTIMIST CLUB TROPHY

To Pasquale O'Toole, Boston fan. He attended a game between the Red Sox and Detroit in which Monbouquette was the Boston pitcher. In the top of the first inning Monbouquette's first pitch was hit to third base and the runner was thrown out. Exclaimed Mr. O'Toole: "Holy jayz! Monbouquette's got a no-hitter goin'!"

AMERICAN ARBITRATION ASSOCIATION CUP

To Virgil Brinks, umpire. He was back of the plate in a Cleveland game when Gig Chaney came to bat. The count went to three and two. On the next pitch Chaney didn't move and Umpire Briggs called "Strike three!" Chaney immediately began kicking dirt, beating the ground with his bat and uttering swear words. Whereupon Umpire Brinks said: "Okay, Gig, okay. Keep your shirt on. If you thought it was a ball, it was a ball. Go on and take your base."

LEAGUE OF FREETHINKERS RIBBON

To Bud Hayden, first baseman. Walking through the lobby of a hotel in Kansas City, he spied a hairpin lying in full view on the floor. Instead of giving forth a wild cry and leaping for it, he simply glanced at it and said to his companion, "Ain't women slovenly?"

SPECIAL PULITZER PRIZE

To Donald Weatherwax, Houston fan. He was hit in the head by a home-run ball belted by Willie Mays. When he regained consciousness the club management offered to give him the ball that struck him, autographed by Mays. He said: "No, thanks. But I'd love to have it autographed by J. Frank Dobie."

ADVERTISING CLUB PLAQUE

To Bill Frennet, who hit .323 for the season. Offered one thousand dollars to endorse a certain make of baseball bat, he turned it down, saying: "I hate bats. Damn old wooden things!"

HUMANE SOCIETY SCROLL

To Vincent Popperly, Baltimore fan. When one of the Baltimore players was knocked unconscious by a beanball and carried off the field on a stretcher, he was the only person among the 3,862 spectators who refused to commiserate with the fallen warrior, saying: "He ast to play baseball, didnee?"

BRONZE STAR FOR DECENCY

To Porky Susskind, shortstop. He consistently encouraged his teammates by slapping them on the shoulder instead of on the posterior. Asked by reporters why he didn't pat lower, as the other players do, he said: "They won't leave me do it to ladies on the train so by God I won't do it on the field."

HORTICULTURAL SOCIETY RIBBON

To Fig McKnight, center fielder. He called time and ran all the way into the dugout. The TV announcer said he was after his sunglasses. It developed later, however, that he had come in to complain to his manager as follows: "They's too much peat moss in that turf out yonder."

BREWERS BLUE RIBBON

To Siegfried Schwartz, Milwaukee fan. He took top honors in the County Stadium at Milwaukee, drinking twenty-six bottles of imported beer between the first pitch and the seventh-inning stretch without once leaving his seat.

ARCHIMIDES SOCIETY TROPHY

To Posey Fabricant, outfielder. This enviable prize was given Mr. Fabricant for two examples of first-rate scientific thinking during a single season. The Mets outfielder refused to ever go to bat without wearing his wrist watch, claiming: "If I tooken it off it'd thow me off balance." And in a game at San Francisco, after he had struck out three times in a row (wearing his wrist watch) he explained to his teammates: "It's jist that I'm allergic to home plate. Ever time I git within six foot of anything made outa rubber, my eyes begins to wotter."

These are but a few examples of what I have in mind, and I trust the reader will note how so many of these fine ball-players speak in the accents of California. I do hope that from now on these and other similar records will be passed along to posterity, so that posterity will not grow up believing that our national pastime was nothing more than a great big wonderful game of arithmetic.

✳

✳

✳

25. Crying Need for an Unobtrusive Midget

BEING A PERSON whose aptitude tests and butt end both in-
dicate a strong affinity for soft chairs, I have been taking my
baseball almost exclusively on television during the last few
years. On those rare occasions when I do get to a game, the
picture never seems quite correct. Even when I'm sitting in a
field box the perspective is cockeyed and the players are distorted and out of focus. I sometimes have the feeling that I
should get out of my seat and make my way to the rear of
the stadium and fiddle with the knobs which the repair man
says I should never fiddle with — knobs, in this case, that are
as big as washtubs. And in the ball parks I have trouble
guessing what's going on because most of all I miss the
learned chatter, the erudite chitchat, of the sportscaster.

It is time that somebody put in a good word for this small
breed of dedicated and garrulous men. I'm genuinely
shocked by some of my friends, including of course my
neighbor Avery, who, while watching a ball game on television, keep up an acidulous attack on the commentator, crying out such things as, "How does that prig hold his job?" or
"Why doesn't somebody strangle th' creep?" That's no way
to talk about people with whom I have to live, week after
week, all through the summer.

There's ample room for criticism, but let's leave intemperate name-calling to the science of government. The men
who telecast the ball games are in a tough spot. It is necessary for them to talk without first thinking about what

they're going to say and (though an amazing number of us do the same thing in ordinary life) that is not necessarily a sensible practice. Almost all of us who sit in our living rooms and gripe at the sportscaster would, if we were suddenly shoved into his chair at the microphone, proceed to make ineluctable idiots of ourselves. (,My don't he use big words though! An ineluctable idiot is merely an idiot who is short-weight in the eluctable department.)

Some of the newspaper writers, being a modest lot, amuse themselves from time to time by letting off broadsides at the TV boys, charging them with being flannel-mouthed and wren-headed. The newspaper writers complain because the sportscasters talk a great deal about the personal whims of the ballplayers, discussing their preferences in food, their superstitions, their childhood orneriness, their Pullman-car idiosyncrasies and a multitude of other matters which have little to do with the proceedings on the field.

Well, I'm firmly on the side of the TV boys. When a batting star like Musial is in a slump and comes to the plate, I like to be told that he has started eating his breakfast backward each morning in a desperate effort to improve his hitting. I enjoy looking at a close-up shot of a ballplayer at bat while someone tells me that he can dance the Russian *kazatski* and has a birthmark shaped like a beer bottle.

In this present mood of tolerance (which may not last long), let us consider the fact that the TV sportscaster is often blamed for faults that lie with the program director or one of the technical crew.

Says the sportscaster: "Here we go again — a little dog has just run onto the playing field."

Sometimes we see the little dog, but sometimes we don't. The sportscaster continues talking about it, describing the frantic efforts of players and coaches and umpires and cops to capture the invader . . . and the camera fastens itself on the scene at the plate, or on the pitcher, and stays there.

Directors and cameramen should be ever alert for little

dogs on the playing field. Those little dogs are important. They are fun to watch and they represent the confusions of modern living, the eternal foul-up that accompanies the forward march of technological civilization. For centuries it has been the nature of little dogs to run on the field whenever they see people in short pants playing with a ball. But in this instance they are complicating more than a game — they are interfering with . . . well, with a big business operation. The public is always on the side of the little dog and against those who would drive him off and frustrate his atavistic impulses. The public wants to watch this drama, and the public is entitled to watch it.

The technical people also are responsible for the occasions when we are given inadequate picture coverage of rhubarbs. It would be possible today for IBM to rig some sort of an electronic device which would call balls and strikes unerringly and do away with the plate umpire. If such a machine came into use, baseball would die. You can't argue with a machine. The antics of an enraged manager tangling orsoles with an equally enraged umpire is worth, in my book, fully as much as one home run or a run-down between first and second.

We who sit at home may hear, occasionally, a distinctive kind of murmurous buzzing from the crowd, and after a while the announcer tells us what we already know: "A couple of fans seem to be having a mild disagreement." We may catch a glimpse of a part of the crowd — everyone standing, faces turned away from the game, trying to see the mild disagreement. But *we* never see it. We know that these mild disagreements between fans frequently take the form of crashing blows to the snoot, shirts ripped off, flying legs and arms, and this sort of boyishly innocent tiffing is a thing we would enjoy watching at close range. The TV people have those zoomar things. They could haul us right into the middle of mild disagreements, but for some reason they don't do it. Perhaps it's a shortage of cameras. If it is, well then, by god, let them put an extra camera into each ball park. Call it the little-dog-and-mild-disagreement camera, and give us what we're . . . well, what we're not paying for.

One of the most common examples of technical goofing comes with the Flipped Lid on Ball Four. The umpire calls ball four and the batter trots off toward first base. The camera follows him — at a time when nothing interesting can happen to him, short of his being struck by lightning, and the camera stays on him while he adjusts his crotch components and picks up some dirt and confers with his coach. Meanwhile the sportscaster is describing it: "Whitey Ford didn't like that last call. He's storming down off the mound, yelling his head off. Man, he's on fire!"

He's on fire, but we at home can't see the flames.

One of the main advantages of looking at baseball on television is, or should be, the acquisition of behind-the-scenes information, lowdown and poop. If I am sitting in the stands and Casey Stengel bowlegs it out of his dugout and begins a violent recitation with gestures, the chances are I won't know what the ructions are all about. But if I'm at home, I expect the sportscaster to tell me the reason for Stengel's irascible conduct. Many times he is unable to do it. He'll say, "I don't know what it is Casey's sore about but, man, he's on fire!" I want to know who struck the match and I want to know it right now.

This sort of thing could be corrected. It seems to me that the TV and radio people could hire an unobtrusive midget with an inquiring mind and get permission for him to range back and forth between the dugouts during a game, and to phone up to the broadcast booths somewhat as follows:

"Hey Russ, guess who this is. Shorty. Ole Orph he claims Aunt Nellie tooken his foot off the rubba and bocked but Barlick he says he dint, so Orph he calls Barlick a nonprintable name and Barlick he slung him outa the game. No, I won't tell you what name he called him. Wudges think I am, vulgar?"

This unobtrusive midget, in addition to scouting the dug-outs and circling around the livelier rhubarbs, could pick up authenticated gossip in the bull pens, follow injured players into the clubhouse and determine immediately the nature of their wounds, and he could spend part of his time spotting celebrities in the field boxes. There are usually a few notables present at the ball games and the customers at home like to get a glimpse of them, whether they be crooners, prizefighters, politicians, movie stars, astronauts or ballplayers out of the Queen Anne period. In New York the camera seldom shows anybody but Toots Shor, and Toots Shor is no longer a celebrity at a ball park; he is a permanent fixture, like the fungo circle.

If the sportscasters ever draw up a code of conduct to govern their profession, I would recommend that they abolish Pitch Description. Let them say that a pitch is a strike or a ball after the umpire has made his ruling, and let them refrain from describing the category of the pitch itself, unless it's in the dirt or ten feet over the batter's head. I know that this practice should be discontinued from having conducted a little experiment. I had the television set turned on and I tuned in the same game on the radio. The two sportscasters were members of the same TV-radio team, and I listened to them describe each pitch. The man on TV would say, "Strike one, a fast ball hit the inside corner." At the same moment the radio man would be saying, "Strike. He cut the middle of the dish with his slider." It went on like that all afternoon, one man calling a sweeping curve, the other describing it as a blazing fast ball; one saying it was outside, the other saying it nearly hit the batter.

The sportscasters' code should certainly take a stand on the question of baseball witchcraft. I have particular reference to the superstition under which nothing is to be said about the fact that a pitcher has a no-hitter going. Time after time I have sat through the middle innings of a ball game listening to an announcer trying to say something about something without saying anything about it. In former times this superstition was much simpler than it is today. If a pitcher had a no-hitter going and one of his teammates said to him, "Hey, stupid, you know what? You got a no-hitter goin'!" then sure as shootin' the next man up would belt one. In fact, among ballplayers themselves it is traditional that *nothing whatever* is said to the pitcher while he has a no-hitter going. Ballplayers fear the whammy much more than they fear nuclear attack. Somehow the voodoo sickness has passed over into sportscasting. And the avoidance techniques that have been developed are so intricate that I sometimes have difficulty following them.

Let us suppose that Bo Belinsky has a no-hitter going against the Yankees. Up to a certain point, somewhere around the fourth or fifth inning, it is permissible for the sportscaster to say, "For the Yankees — no hits, no runs, no errors." But beyond that point in the game, he is forbidden to give the line score in such an abrupt and forthright way. He can say, "It's zero straight across," or something on that order. The cameraman can still focus on the scoreboard, showing the zeros, just so long as nobody says anything about it. Thereafter the announcer walks a verbal tightwire. He speaks of the growing tenseness of the crowd. He says that old Bo Belinsky is out there pitching his heart out, maybe making baseball history. He says, "Up to this point only one Yankee has been on base, and *he walked.*"

Where is the line of demarcation? I know that the fans at the park can say to one another that Belinsky has a no-hitter going. *They* don't have to keep the faith. I know that in homes and in taverns and in barber shops it is perfectly moral and proper for listeners to speak in a forthright manner about what is going on. So why does the sportscaster have to play along with the boys in the Los Angeles dugout? Personally I don't put much stock in the science of the whammy, but sometimes when a pitcher has a no-hitter going against *my* team, I feel like rushing down to the ball park and choking a few positive words out of the sportscaster who's protecting the bum.

Finally, I have one serious indictment to make. There is something in the id of the average sportscaster that will not permit him to ever admit he is capable of making a mistake. He will sometimes go to fantastic lengths to alibi his own blunders and lay the blame for them elsewhere, sometimes right in the lap of God Almighty. I have collected a few examples to illustrate this point.

The sportscaster says: "There goes a screaming liner over field. Felipe Alou's under it . . . wait a minute. It's in there, in the upper deck! That ball was dropping straight down toward Alou's glove and then all of a sudden *it took off!*"

What does he mean, took off? I'm not too well educated in the behavior of airborne baseballs, but it frightens me a little to think about the eccentric parabola of that one. Usually we are told that the wind was responsible. I'm fairly well informed on wind, but not the kind of wind they have around ball parks, where it blows in all directions at once, including straight up and straight down.

The sportscaster says: "There goes a screaming liner over the third baseman's head. It's curving foul. It's a foul ball." While he's speaking we at home have seen the umpire proclaim it a fair ball. The sportscaster now continues: "Folks, I swear to you that left field base line *seemed to move.* It looked to us up here like that ball curved foul, but we were screened out by two or three players over there, and we were watching the base line. It had every appearance of a foul ball."

It did not. It had every appearance of a fair ball.

The sportscaster will say: "That's Don Mossi warming up in the bull pen. No," he corrects himself, "it's Aguirre. Aguirre's out there throwing *exactly* like Mossi."

Or the sportscaster will say: "There it *goes!* A clothesline drive into right. He oughta get two. Hold it. It's a foul ball.

But let me tell you something — that ball certainly looked like trouble as it left the bat."

The hell it did. It didn't look like anything as it left the bat.

If you watch baseball on television and listen to the announcer carefully, you'll often find him creating alibis for himself throughout the game. He doesn't seem to realize that his listeners would much prefer that he confess to being a human creature and say, as Dizzy Dean sometimes says, "Scuse me, folks. I'm ignernt." Let the sportscaster study the career of Ed Sullivan, a man who has achieved vast fame and considerable fortune through unremitting fumbling and blundering — and learn that the people love Sullivan and identify with him, largely because of his mastery of half talk (double talk divided by four).

Please understand that I bring all these matters up in a spirit of friendliness and good will. I'm even willing to concede that there are sportscasters who come close to perfection. But the more I think of those alibis they are forever throwing at us, the more I wonder how some of the jerks hold their jobs. Somebody ought to strangle th' creeps.

*

*

*

26. A Friend at Townsend Gut

THE LAST TIME I was up (down) to Boothbay Harbor on
the Maine Coast I stood on the wide veranda of a trim white
house with light blue shutters and looked at the waters of
Townsend Gut.

Scattered over these waters are hundreds of prancing
buoys, each marking the location of a lobster pot. A lobster
pot is a miniature two-roomed Quonset hut constructed of
wooden slats; a fifty-foot length of rope leads from the pot
to the surface, and is supported at the surface by two buoys.
One of these markers is a wooden block and five or six feet
distant, at the end of the rope, is an empty quart beer bottle
plugged against leakage. Since each pot must be pulled up
daily, emptied, rebaited, and then hauled to a new location,
and since a dozen or more lobstermen fish these particular
waters, it is necessary that the buoys be given distinguishing
characteristics, the way golf balls and range cattle are sometimes labeled with their owner's mark. In Townsend Gut
there were seventeen pots whose wooden markers were
painted white and blue, with the beer bottles painted the
same shade of blue — the blue of the shutters on the house
that overlooks them.

The white-and-blue house, which is called Slipshod
Manor, and the white-and-blue pot buoys belonged to
George Rockwell — the same Doc Rockwell whose name is a
legend to the people who remember the golden days of
American vaudeville. Historians of the period have called

him "the greatest monologist of all time." His most famous act had him in white coat, big black-rimmed glasses and stethoscope. He appeared on stage with a withered banana stalk which he represented to be the human spine, and he delivered a lecture in mock-chiropractic that was one of the great comedy performances of show biz history.

Doc lives the year 'round in the house with the blue shutters but Doc no longer pulls the pots with the blue beer bottles. Yet in the time of my visits to Slipshod Manor, lobstering was a passion with him. From the front of his house wooden steps led steeply down to the rickety dock where he kept his boat. And each day, seven days a week through the lobstering season, Doc would descend those steps, prepare his keg of fragrant bait, and set out across the water to pull his pots — an operation that absorbed about three hours a day. Usually he rode alone but sometimes visitors were up from New York and then the boat might carry as many as five or six passengers. The Great Monologist, here on the coast of Maine, standing in the prow of his boat, wearing boots and a rubber apron as he pulls his pots, would deliver a brilliant, crackling, running commentary on the art of lobstering, on life beneath the surface of the sea (he *seemed* to know more about it than Rachel Carson), on the whims and prejudices of the Maine lobstermen, on the delights and cruelties of human existence along that ragged coastline.

Through the winter months he worked at the endless preparations that a lobsterman must make against the arrival of the fishing season. He built his own lobster pots, and knit the funnel-shaped nets that went into each pot, and repainted his markers and his beer bottles. All winter long he'd vow that he'd quit come springtime, but he didn't give up until he sprung a disc in his own banana stalk. Lobstering, he always said, was a thing that got into a man's blood. During the season he often crawled out of bed before dawn and paced the floor, impatient to be off, eager to get into his boat and make the rounds to find out how many big lobsters and how many little lobsters and how many *legal* lobsters had fumbled through those hand-knit nets and trapped themselves. On a day when he got, say, twenty-five lobsters of a size which may legally be retained — the legal limitation being gauged by the length of the shell back — he'd come whooping in to the dock as if he had pulled up a Saratoga trunk filled with pirate gold.

Doc is a small, dark-featured, wiry man now in his seventies, though he looks nearer fifty. He comes close to being the most consistently interesting man I've ever met. He has, of course, the practiced capabilities of the veteran actor — the talent for mimicry, the expressive hands that contribute so much to the art of story-telling, the memory for attitudes as well as anecdotes. But there are many in the world who have those qualities; they are not altogether the things that make Doc Rockwell, to me, a man of infinite variety and charm.

He possesses the most boundless curiosity that, I do believe, has existed in any man since Benjamin Franklin lived. His energy, both physical and mental, verges on the nuclear; though he no longer lobsters, though he is living in virtual seclusion from the frenetic world he once knew, each day of his life is a daffy caper. No problem of the human race is too big for him to tackle, or too small. Want the Einstein formula explained? Doc will explain it and in the act keep a roomful of people rocking with laughter, and in the end they'll each feel that they *almost do* understand it.

If anyone has ever wondered what becomes of the multitude of "How to —" books that are published each year, part of the answer may be found in the white house with the blue shutters. Doc has them all. If the whim came upon him (and it might) to build and operate a gristmill, he has a book that tells him how to go about it. What's more important, he has read it, even though the passion to become a gristmill proprietor has never so much as brushed him. If you encountered him on the road and told him that you wanted to build a gristmill and operate it and that you knew nothing of how to go about it, Doc would take you by the hand and lead you to a spot in the shade and set you down and say, "Now. To begin with . . ." and he'd lead you through the entire project specification by specification; and in the telling he'd make the building and operation of that gristmill sound like the ultimate flowering of man's genius. He cannot play the violin, because he's never tried, *but he knows how.*

There are people who still try to drag Doc back to New York and show business. Once Billy Rose enticed him out of Maine and put him in a musical show called *Seven Lively Arts.* Doc enjoyed that season on Broadway because it gave him an opportunity to indulge one of his long-neglected hobbies — attending small conventions. Now I must admit that I consider the American business convention to be a searing pain in the ass, and most of the people I know feel the same way, but not Doc. He took a room in one of New York's big commercial hotels and each morning when most theatrical people were sleeping, he'd be down in the lobby studying the bulletin board which chronicles the day's events. It was the kind of hotel where there are always meetings and small conventions in progress in the lesser public rooms, and Doc would choose the one that appealed to him most and attend it. It might be dentists, or sandhogs, or theosophists, or scout-masters, or herpetologists, or manufacturers of small arms. Doc would pick his meeting and enter it briskly, smiling and nodding as he'd take his seat. Usually he would have a notebook and pencil and, if challenged, he'd pass himself off as a writer doing research. Once settled he'd bend his attention to the proceedings; in many cases the speakers, acutely aware of this fellow who was concentrating so intently on their words, would find themselves directing their remarks straight at him. His motive was never clownish, never suggestive of the practical joke. He attended such meetings because he wanted to find out about things. All things. He's curious about snakes and small arms and scoutmastering and theosophy and dentistry and sandhoggery.

During the 1940s Doc was lured away from Maine once each winter long enough to make a guest appearance on the Fred Allen radio show in New York. Allen referred to this annual event as "Man Hog Day" — the day on which Rockwell emerged from his hibernation, cast his shadow over the land by way of the radio, then hurried back to his roots and his nuts. A date would be set for Doc's appearance on the show, perhaps a month or six weeks in advance. Thereafter, up to the time of the broadcast, Allen's mail was loaded with scripts coming down (up) from Maine. Doc began writing a new script every day, would get it half finished, send it off to Allen, and then the next day start to work on an altogether new one.

He should, in fact, have been a writer. Many of his friends are writers and they have pestered him to abandon all other pursuits and devote his time to affairs of Thalia, the muse of comedy and bucolic poetry. He has a little shack set on stilts down at the water's edge, once devoted to operations relating to the capture and cooking of lobsters. Sometimes he takes a portable typewriter down there and begins writing at a furious pace. He'll finish a story or an essay and carry it back to the house and settle down to read it. Invariably his critical sense tells him that the thing is too long. Got to be cut down. So he returns to his typewriter to rewrite it, to compress it, and always the second draft turns out to be twice as long as the first; so he rewrites that one for size and it comes out still longer, and he goes at it once again and comes up with a manuscript near book length, and then he throws the whole thing into Townsend Gut and takes a nap.

Therein lies his recurrent complaint against life; in his own view he is a little man bucking a world that is too big for him — leading a life of clamorous desperation. He considers his existence to be a parade of horrible frustrations and he has tried to evolve a personal philosophy to combat his sense of ineptitude. It is a philosophy which, in large part, is made up of comic bitterness. The last letter I had from him, written in the dead of winter, told of a new and hopeless war against Fate. The town had been hit by a bad snowstorm, the town plow broke down, and this was most tragic because that was the day the A & P was running a special on center-cut pork chops. Then they got the plow fixed, just as Doc finished shoveling all the snow off the sidewalk in front of Slipshod Manor. Along came the plow and threw it all back on the sidewalk. Doc resumed his shoveling, throwing it back into the street. The plow returned and once again snowbanks covered the sidewalk.

"I will never give in," Doc wrote, "and *they* will never give in, so we will keep it up until we wear out the snow."

There was the time Doc bought a summer hotel in Southport, which is his town. He no more than got it running when it caught fire and burned. Doc stood and contemplated the smoking ruins and said: "Oh, well, I don't care. The salt cellars were always getting plugged up." He went home and painted a sign which said, "Gone Out of Business," and returned and nailed it onto a charred stud. All through that day the smoking ruins were attracting little crowds of tourists.

Maine people are quite peculiar, as are all people, and that afternoon a man telephoned Doc. "I saw that sign you painted where the hotel burned down," said the man. "It's sure a good job of sign-paintin' because it's drawin' a lot of trade. I'd like for you to paint me a sign that says Fried Clams." Doc did it, and that really got him started in the sign-painting business, which now takes up a good part of his time.

His two-car garage was always so crowded with miscellaneous junk that he could never get even one car into it. Alton Cook, the movie critic who is a warm friend of Doc's, tells about the time Doc inspected his crowded garage and arrived at a decision to clean out some of the old furniture that was stored in it. He drove over to Boothbay Harbor to consult with a dealer in secondhand furniture. When he returned home he had not sold a thing, but had his station wagon loaded with *more* secondhand furniture — he hadn't been able to resist the bargain prices. And all this additional stuff, of course, went straight into his garage.

But one day he did clean it out and it is now his studio. There is a sign outside saying:

SOUTHPORT INSTITUTE OF ART

FINE — MEDIUM — COARSE

He doesn't need to solicit business but once he offered to contribute hand-painted directional signs showing people the way to the hospital. Each one was a pointing finger with a band-aid around it.

When he isn't painting signs he is turning out cartoons for John Gould's weekly, the Maine *Enterprise*, or a monthly humor column for *Down East* magazine, or trying to outlast that snow plow. Each spring he puts in a vegetable garden and by midsummer he is swearing that he'll never do it again.

"The soil on my place," he says, "is a heavy clay, and after a rain the sun comes out and bakes it into a sort of flattened-out crockery, so that I have to cultivate it with a cold chisel. Nothing prospers except the bugs, even when I drench them with Bordeaux Mixture — which is another name for synthetic tobacco spit."

Year after year he has tried to grow potatoes and year after year the Colorado beetles destroy the plants.

"The Colorado beetle," says Doc, "is a magnificent animal, and I hate him and would like to see him burn in hell. Sometimes, though, I think of him as an innocent bystander, full of faults, yes, but those faults belong to mankind and not the bug. Originally he had no appetite for potato plants — didn't know what a potato plant tasted like. He lived quietly in the Rocky Mountains and ate sandburrs and never tried to get out of jury duty. Along came our revered pioneers in their covered wagons, carrying potatoes. Those beetles got one taste of potato plant and went crazy. What did they do? They *walked* all the way from Colorado to Maine. That's a long walk for a potato beetle. In fact it's a long walk for anybody. Any bug that walks that far is bound to arrive hungry. It wouldn't be so bad if they'd just strip my potato patch and go away. No, that's not enough. They pupate in my ground. Right on my property, they *pupate!* It's almost more than flesh can bear!"

One year in the middle of the growing season a neighbor came to Slipshod Manor and asked to borrow Doc's hoe. The neighbor had started home with the implement when Doc called him back. "Look, my friend," said Doc, "do me a big favor. Don't bring it back." And on another occasion he stood and looked at his sickly garden and observed: "It would be cheaper just to eat the fertilizer."

Several years ago I wanted some biographical material from him and sent an airmail letter asking that he get it off to me as quickly as possible. At length his reply came, saying:

"I'm rushing this answer off to you, two weeks late. I've been trying to jot down the stuff for you, but there's a debilitating factor. In recalling all the things that I've tried to do, I have to live them all over again, and I'm worn out from all that lost motion."

In subsequent talks with him I've learned that he was reared in Providence, Rhode Island, and that his full name is George Lovejoy Rockwell. He believes his unflagging curiosity is both inherited and acquired from a grandfather who lived in Nova Scotia. Doc spent several of his boyhood years with his grandfather.

"He reached a hundred and four before he died," says Doc. "He was a man who remembered everything he ever saw or ever heard or ever read. When I knew him he had lost his eyesight and I spent many hours reading to him. He never just sat and listened. I'd read a paragraph and he'd stop me and begin arguing with the author. I learned from him the proper way to read. Most people read as if they were a piece of machinery gobbling down words. You've got to stop and think and argue with the writer or you really don't get much out of reading. My grandfather taught me that, and he taught me another thing — he believed that no provocation is great enough to warrant a man's ever getting mad."

Doc tries to practice that precept, even though his attitude toward the world is compounded of pessimism and a deep sense of futility. He once sat down at his typewriter to do an essay, and started it in this manner:

Once upon a time there were a lot of bees who broke their backs all summer gathering honey. When cold weather arrived, the farmer took all the honey and sold it and with the proceeds spent the winter in Florida.

That's as far as he got with it; he thought there ought to be a lot more to it, but I for one don't agree. I think it's quite complete.

"Human beings," he once told me, "are engaged in nothing more than a game of polite meat-snatching. You've seen two dogs fighting over a piece of meat. The only difference between the dogs and the humans is that the humans can talk and the dogs can't. If dogs suddenly acquired speech they'd still go after that chunk of meat, but not with their fangs. They'd talk. Like statesmen. They'd try to *reason* each other out of it. They'd refine their methods but aim for the same result — getting that piece of meat."

Once I asked him what field of human endeavor he would choose if he had it all to do over. Since he knew so much about so many trades and professions, I thought he would surely have an interesting answer. He did.

"I'd be a fairy," he said. "And by this I don't mean an elf. I once had a partner in a vaudeville act and he was a fairy. He was one of the nicest guys I've ever known. But the important thing was, he had friends in every town and village in the United States. We were on the road all the time and every town we hit, we'd get off the train and I'd be standing there in the cold, all by myself, and there would be a whole committee of joyous fairies there to greet my partner, and find handsome accommodations for him, and feed him and give him drink. My God, those people are better organized than the Elks."

At one time or another Doc has investigated every religion known to man, working up a tremendous enthusiasm for one, only to forget it completely when he has discovered another. During one period of his life he was a food faddist, inventing his own remarkable diets. He lived for months on a diet of raw vegetables and a beverage which he called

Vitafizz — a mixture of milk, lemon juice and bicarbonate of soda. Another time he decided that the proper diet should consist solely of beer and green salads. And there was a brief spell when he was accustomed to going into a New York restaurant and saying to the waiter, "Bring me my chemicals." His chemicals were hot milk, hot water and after-dinner mints. He'd combine the milk and water, then stir in the mints, and drink it down.

The manner in which his curiosity drives him into strange alleys is illustrated by an experience he had in New York a dozen years ago. He had decided to publish his own magazine, written entirely by himself and called *The Mustard Plaster*. Seeking a quiet place to write, he hit upon the reading room of the New York Public Library. One afternoon he picked up a book from the table where he had been working and casually started reading it. By chance it was a law book. He came back the next day and finished it, and then ordered more law books and read them, and in the end he knew about the law.

His lobstering operations were always economically unsound. He intended for the business to pay for itself but he usually gave most of his catch away and when he did take his lobsters to market the proceeds were seldom enough to pay for the gasoline consumed by his boat. His ambition all along was to gain unquestioned acceptance from the other lobstermen. He wanted to belong to their fraternity, their hot-stove league, and yarn with them through the winter months, for he considered them to be the greatest set of characters he ever met outside of vaudeville. For a while he thought that he had gained acceptance. Then one day while I was visiting him the two of us went to a little grocery store in Southport to get some beer. A woman waited on Doc and when he put the money on the counter he remarked, "There goes my hard-earned lobster money."

The woman gave him a sly, cynical look, and said:

"Posstime!"

We were back in the car before Doc realized the full importance of what she had said. Lobstering a pastime! A hobby! So that's what the natives thought of him! It upset him so much that he decided he would either quit lobstering altogether, or enlarge his operations to a point where no one would dare laugh at him.

The following morning we were out pulling the pots, and Doc was a bit on the glum side. He dragged in a pot, perched it on the prow of the launch and began removing and measuring lobsters. "This," he said, "is Number Twelve."

"Not by my count," spoke up Harold Matson, the literary agent. "I figure that one is Number Eleven."

They argued over the count from then until the boat reached Number Seventeen, by Doc's count, or Number Sixteen, by Matson's reckoning. Meanwhile Doc delivered a lecture on the lobsterman's problem of keeping an accurate count of the pots that have been pulled and the pots that remain to be pulled. Here was a good example of the importance of an accurate tally. If Doc's count were right, then all the pots had been pulled and the day's work finished. If Matson were right, there was another Rockwell pot somewhere, probably loaded with fine lobsters. We spent the next hour cruising around looking for a white-and-blue buoy that we might have missed, and found none.

During the ride back to the house Harold Matson had an idea. He is a man with a fabulous mind; ask me someday about his Cashew Nut Theory. He pointed out that Doc maintained seventeen lobster pots in Townsend Gut. Doc should buy seventeen croquet balls, and put them in a box in the boat. Each time a pot was pulled and baited, he should drop a croquet ball into it. Then when the box had been emptied of croquet balls, the day's work would be finished. No bother about keeping count in his head. And the next day, reverse the procedure: take a croquet ball out of each pot and return it to the box and when the box contained seventeen croquet balls, then day is done.

Doc let the idea stew around in his head for a while and then gave it his cyclonic endorsement, announcing that by means of the croquet ball technique, he was going to confuse and revolutionize the lobstering business.

"These old-time lobstermen," he said, "who think I'm doing this for a 'posstime,' spend hours and days and weeks arguing and quarreling over the most trivial details of their business. For example, they've been arguing for years over why a lobster goes through the second net in the pot. He goes through the first net to get at the bait but before he eats the bait he pokes around and finds that second net with a hole in it and, like a pure idiot, he goes through that one — into the second compartment, away from the bait, and there he stays, trapped. Why does he do it? There have been fist fights over the issue. Any little detail of that kind will set the lobstermen to fussing for months. Now. Here's what I'll do next season. I'm going to get those seventeen croquet balls and start using them — *but I won't ever take them out of the pots.* I won't use them to keep count — just leave one in each pot. I'll not say a word about it to anyone but within a few days the story will get around that Rockwell is using croquet balls in his pots. A few days more and they'll start coming to me, snooping around, trying to find out what I'm doing. *Then's* when I'll fix their wagon! So they think my lobstering is a posstime! I'll just manage to drop a hint that since I started using croquet balls I've increased my catch by, say, thirty per cent. You know what'll happen then? The factories that make croquet sets will start getting orders from Maine . . . *for croquet balls alone.* No mallets. No wickets. No stakes. No instruction books. Just balls. Before long they'll be getting orders for croquet balls by the tens of thousands, and they'll be thrown into confusion. They'll call an emergency meeting of the board and they'll send a vice-president up here to investigate. They'll tell him, 'Eph, you go on up to Maine and find out what the hell has got into those people that they want so many croquet balls without no mallets. Maybe they've got up a new game. We ought to keep abreast.' And the vice-president will come up here and find out the truth, and send back word that they've got to re-tool, unless they can figure out a new market for mallets *without balls.*"

When I got back home after that trip I kept thinking of the plan to put a croquet ball in every pot. I did a lot of talking about it. Then I met a man from Salinas, California, named Emmons, and told him about it and he came up with the solution to the problem of the surplus mallets. They could be sold to the abalone fishermen of California, who employ a wooden mallet to pound out abalone steaks. Thus a sort of balance could be achieved: croquet balls to Maine for the lobstermen, mallets to California for the abalone fishermen.

Alas, it never worked out at all! A few days later someone told Doc about the Jehovah's Witnesses and their beliefs about Armageddon and Heaven. He immediately abandoned croquet balls and began investigating these strange ideas. He wanted to find out if there might be something in it for him. There wasn't.

*

*

*

27. One Coat of White

(A Short Story)

EVERYBODY KNOWS by this time that we first met Lautisse on shipboard but few people know that, in the beginning, Betsy and I had no idea who he was.

We were on the *Queen Elizabeth*, coming back from our first trip to Europe. The second day out I was wandering around the boat deck and somehow blundered into his hideout — a little nook into which he had dragged his deck chair.

We had caught glimpses of him before and, in fact, Betsy and I had used him in a little game we played aboard ship — trying to guess what business different people are in. I looked at the bushy hair blowing in the wind, the ragged gray beard, the pullover sweater and the sandals, and violated my own rule by saying I thought he was an artist, a French artist.

Betsy snorted at me because we had long since agreed that people don't often *look* their business. She said she thought he was either a Greek archbishop or a member of the British parliament.

When I poked my nose into his hideaway he raised his head and gave me as nasty a scowl as you ever saw in your life. I started to back away, mumbling an apology, and then his expression changed.

"Wait!" he called out. "You are an American?"

His English was good, and he asked me if I had a moment to help him with a small problem. He wanted to know if there was a United States Senator named Boat or Ferry. I couldn't think of any, and he showed me the ship's daily puzzle which he was trying to work. In this particular puzzle someone had taken the passenger list and rigged up a series of trick definitions. One definition, for example, was "Stone-like female tennis player." Listed among the passengers were a Mr. and Mrs. Pendergast Marble, so the answer was Alice Marble.

I squatted down alongside of him and puzzled over the one that had him stumped. The definition was, "Senator who crosses a river." I thought of Senator Ford, the old-time raconteur, but there were no Fords on the passenger list, and then I got it — Senator Bridges. There was a Miss Ethelyn Bridges on board.

My bearded friend began chattering excitedly in French, swiftly lettered in the name "Bridges" on his puzzle sheet, and then leaped from his chair and went flying off down the deck.

I didn't see him again until the next day, just before lunch, when he came into the main lounge, grabbed me by the arm and drew me off into a corner. For a moment I had the sensation of being in the grip of an international spy.

"Look!" he said in a hoarse whisper. In the palm of his big hand he was holding a man's wallet, made of pigskin. "The prize!" he said. "The first prize, I won it! You, my friend, are responsible. Come and have a cucktell with me."

I went with him to his stateroom and he got out a bottle of some kind of brandy and poured a couple of slugs and we sat down. He introduced himself as Monsieur Roland and kept thanking me for my help with the puzzle. Then he began asking me some questions about myself and my business, and I told him I sold oil burners. I had to explain what an oil burner is and he damn near floored me by saying he had never seen one in his life. A real rube.

We sat there talking for at least an hour, and had another brandy, and finally he asked me if I could keep a secret. I crossed my heart and hoped to shrivel and then he said, "I am Lautisse." He might as well have said, "I am Alice Marble." It didn't register with me, but I played it straight and pretty soon we broke it up and went down to lunch.

I told Betsy all about it and when I mentioned the name Lautisse she said she hated to admit that I was right in the beginning, but she was pretty sure he was an artist. So after lunch we went up and talked to the ship's librarian, asking him a few innocent questions and then dropping the name of Lautisse. In short order we found out that my new friend was probably the world's foremost living painter.

I told the librarian we had seen some of Lautisse's pictures somewhere in Europe and that we were interested in the man, so he dug around and found a book with a biographical sketch and a photograph. The man in the picture didn't have a beard, but he was Monsieur Roland all right. The thumbnail sketch told about some of his famous paintings, and how at the age of fifty-three he had suddenly quit and retired to a villa near Juan-les-Pins on the Riviera. He hadn't painted a lick in a dozen years and was on record as saying he would never touch another brush as long as he lived. I judged from the sketch that he was disgusted with the human race. It wasn't too clear.

Betsy decided I was obligated to him socially and talked me into sending a note to his stateroom, inviting him around for a drink.

Well, we got to be real friendly with him, and he told us how he was a bitter man and hated people because they were stupid and couldn't get along with one another; he said he lived alone on the Riviera, except for his servants, and never saw anyone; and how he had decided on a trip to America where he understood people were at least as stupid as elsewhere.

He said he disliked for people to recognize him, so he had grown the beard to hide his identity, and every now and then he'd pull out that pigskin wallet and turn it over and over, admiring it, and winking at me.

He planned on spending a month in New York and it was Betsy who suggested that he come up to our place for a weekend.

Our house in Westchester isn't pretentious, although I sometimes say it's pretty elegant in the basement. We have the best damned oil burner on earth down there. We have ten acres and we're a little off the beaten path, and I like it.

Lautisse arrived on the noon train Saturday and I met him at the station. He had on a business suit now, and a felt hat to hold down that mop of hair. We had promised him that we wouldn't have any people in and that we would respect his desire to remain incognito and that we wouldn't try to talk to him about art.

Driving out from the station I asked him if he wanted to do anything in particular like play cards or go for a swim or walk in the woods, and he said he just wanted to sit and relax. Betsy had laid in some French wine and she was going to order some frogs' legs but I talked her out of it; I figured a Frenchman might take it as an insult if Americans tried to serve him frogs' legs. The same as if you had a Swiss for a guest and insisted on shooting an apple off his head with a bow and arrow.

So we sat around all afternoon and Lautisse looked at a ball game on television for about five minutes, and couldn't make anything out of it, and I took him down in the basement and showed him the oil burner, and he couldn't understand that either. Mostly we just sat and talked. He was pretty socialistic in his views, but then you come to expect that sort of thing from artists and authors and people like that. I needled him a little about it, but not much. He was pretty sour about Americans, how money-mad we are, slamming ourselves around in search of dollars, but I reminded him that in recent times the people of Europe have been getting a little money-mad on their own hook. Or, rather, on *our* hook. He got a bit snappish at times but he didn't actually lose his temper. I barbecued some chicken on the outdoor grill for dinner and we had a couple of bottles of wine and about eleven o'clock we were all in bed.

I was up at seven-thirty the next morning and looked through the papers while I had breakfast and then I remembered a job I had to do. Our vegetable garden is alongside the garage, enclosed by a white picket fence which I built with my own hands five years ago. A neat white picket fence, about four feet high, with a two-foot apron of wire fencing around the bottom to keep the rabbits and woodchucks out.

There are a million chores around a place like ours, and most of them I leave to Andy, who works one day a week for us; but that garden fence is my pride and joy and now that it needed a coat of paint, I wouldn't dream of letting Andy do the job. I had no idea when our guest might emerge from the sack, so I got out a gallon bucket half full of outside white, and a three-inch brush and an old kitchen chair. I was sitting on the chair, stirring the guck loose from the bottom of the bucket, when I heard footsteps, and there stood Lautisse. He was wearing the same costume he had on the day I met him on the ship.

"Had breakfast?" I asked, and he said Madame was fixing it for him. I said I had been getting ready to paint the garden fence but now that he was up, I'd postpone it. He threw up his hands and protested — I should march with the painting. He came up close and looked into the bucket and then without saying anything, took the stick out of my hand and began dabbling around in the paint. Then he gave me an intense, questioning look, and said, "*Terebenthine?*" He had me for a minute, and then I knew he meant turps, and told him we call it turps, and he said I needed to add a *soupçon* of turps.

I don't like to have people tell me how to paint a fence, but then I realized that this guy knew his business as far as mixing paint is concerned, so I went and got the jug of turps and he took it and carefully dribbled in about half a pint,

stirring briskly, and lifting the stick now and then and letting the paint trickle off of it, all the while making little ooo-
la-la expressions like a French chef testing his cake batter.

"Now!" he finally said, and I moved in with the brush,
but he seized it from my hand and said, "First, I show you!"
And he started on the nearest four-by-four corner post.

I'm no Tom Sawyer — I wasn't looking for anybody to
paint that fence. In fact I wanted to paint it myself. I let him
finish two sides of the post and then I interrupted.

"I'll take it from there," I said, reaching for the brush.

"No, no, no, no!" he yelled, just like a little child, and he
increased his pace, which was rapid to begin with. He had
finished the outside of half a dozen pickets when Betsy
yelled from the kitchen door that his breakfast was ready.
He didn't hear her, so I told him.

"No, no!" he said with an impatient wave of the brush.
"No breakfast. I will paint the fence."

I argued with him but he wouldn't even look up from his
work, so I went in the house and told Betsy. "You know
very well," I said, "how sometimes I like to get a paintbrush
in my hand, and you know how I feel about that fence,
and . . . goddamn it that bum came out there and prac-
tically *wrestled* the brush away from me, and if I don't do
something to stop him, he's going to finish the *whole*
fence!" Betsy laughed at me. "Let him paint it," she said.
"Let him do whatever he wants to do. He's having a good
time."

I went back to the Sunday papers but every now and then
I'd get up and go out and watch him for a couple of minutes.
He was painting furiously and while I must admit that he
was doing a pretty good job as far as the fence was concerned, he was about the sloppiest painter I ever met up
with. He was beginning to get spots and splotches on his
shoes and his pants and his sweater and there were little dots
of white on his face and in his whiskers. I tried to talk to
him but all I got was a series of grunts and it was obvious

that he wasn't listening to me, so I finally told him to holler when he got tired and I'd come out and take over.

He never did holler. He spent three hours at it and finished the fence, all four sections of it, inside and out, and himself to boot. You should have seen him when he walked around the house to the terrace where I was sitting — he had white paint *all over him*. He still had the brush in his hand, but you couldn't tell where the brush ended and his hand began. And he was beaming.

"I finish her!" he exclaimed. He was as happy as a kid with a new astronaut suit, and all my resentment faded; that is, until he held that soggy brush out toward me and said, "Now you better clean." He escorted me back to the garden to examine his handiwork. He had me stand off at a distance and look, and then move up closer and inspect the pickets, recommending that I note "her smoothness" and the absence of streaking and so on. Then he looked at his hands and called for "many more turps" and it took him another hour to clean himself off and change back into his business suit.

Some time during the afternoon he asked me if we were anywhere near Chappaqua and I said it was very close by and he wanted to know if we had ever heard of Gerston, the sculptor. We had heard of him, of course, and Lautisse said that he had once known Gerston in Paris and thought well of him, and would it be possible to get him on the telephone? I got Gerston for him, but he talked in French and I have no idea what the conversation was about.

He went back to town on the 10:31 that night and at the station pumped my hand and clapped me on the back and said I was a fine fellow and that he hadn't enjoyed himself so much in years and that he wanted Betsy and me to come in to New York and have dinner with him some night.

We didn't hear anything from him or about him for ten days and then the story broke in the New York papers. Some AP correspondent on the Riviera got wind of Lautisse's se-

cret trip to New York and cabled the New York office, and
somehow they found him. He denied his identity at first but
they had him cold and so he confessed all and gave them
an interview. Along toward the end of the story was a paragraph saying:

Since his arrival M. Lautisse has spent all of his time in New
York City, except for a weekend at the home of Mr. and Mrs.
Hervey Gregg in North Westchester. He met the Greggs on the
ship coming over.

The newspapers made an enormous fuss over him, like
they do with all big celebrities, and of course *we* were in
trouble immediately. All of our friends came down on us
like a ton of bricks for not letting them know about that
weekend. Some of them accepted our explanation, but two
or three of them got mad and stayed mad . . . till later.

The day after the story broke a reporter and photographer
from the *Daily News* arrived at our place while I was off
selling oil burners, and Betsy did the honors. They wanted to
know every single detail — every move the great man made,
every word he uttered, and Betsy told them of course about
the garden fence. They took pictures of it, and more pictures
of the paint bucket and the brush and the jug of turps and
the next morning the *News* had quite a spread. It was a
long story, done in a humorous vein, and the headline said:

LAUTISSE PAINTS AGAIN!

It gave us a sort of funny feeling, all this publicity, but we
didn't have much time to worry about it. Early on the same
day that the *News* story appeared, an excitable little man
arrived in a chauffeur-driven limousine. He leaped out of the
car, rushed up to me, grabbed me by the shoulders and began shouting: "Where is it? Where is the fence?" I knocked
his hands down and demanded to know who he was, but he

kept yelling things like, "Has anybody else been here?" and "Show me the fence!" I had to get tough with him to simmer him down and finally he said he was Mr. Vegaro from the Millard Galleries, and he wanted to see the fence that Monsieur Lautisse had painted, and so I took him out and showed it to him.

He stood before that picket fence like a man in rapture, clasping and unclasping his hands and making little squeaking noises, and crying out, "Magnificent!" and "Superb!" and things like that. Then all of a sudden he quieted down, wrenched his eyes away from the fence, stared at the ground for a moment, and said:

"Mr. Gregg, I would like to buy your fence. I will give you five hundred dollars cash for it."

He no more than got the words out when another car came roaring up the driveway and out popped two men. They came at us with a rush, waving their arms wildly, screeching, "Stop! Stop!"

When Mr. Vegaro saw them he turned into a wild beast, and charged at them, screaming that he had got here first, calling them thieves and bandits, and I thought for a moment there would be a real wingding but it was all noise and no blows struck.

All three men now swarmed around me, shouting and gesticulating and clawing at me, and so I now loosened my larynx and let go, and did a little yelling on my own. They calmed down and I said that if they wanted to behave like gentlemen, I would be glad to take them into the house and find out what it was all about.

It turned out that the second two men were from the Widdicome Galleries and they, too, wanted my garden fence, because it had been painted by the great Lautisse.

"You people," I said, "are either drunk or crazy. Don't you realize that a garden fence is a garden fence, and a bucket of white paint is a bucket of white paint, and that Lautisse put the paint on the same way I would have put it on, or even my wife, or anybody else that went to work painting a white fence?"

All three of them looked at me as if I were the one who was drunk or crazy. Didn't I realize that Lautisse had not held a paintbrush in his hand for twelve long years? That Lautisse had sworn he would never paint again? That a single painting by Lautisse was worth as much as a quarter of a million dollars?

"Look, gentlemen," I said, "I'm a businessman, an oil burner man. I don't know anything about painting. I mean painting pictures. But I do know a thing or two about painting a fence. A mule could have held a paintbrush in his teeth and done almost as good a job on that fence as Lautisse did."

"A thousand dollars for the fence," said one of the Widdicome men.

"Twelve hundred!" said little Mr. Vegaro.

"Fifteen hundred!" cried the Widdicome man.

"Hold it!" I yelled. "I'm beginning to think you guys are serious. How on earth are you going to get fifteen hundred out of that fence?"

"Good Lord, man!" exclaimed the second fellow from Widdicome, "don't you realize that your garden fence is a *genuine Lautisse*? Don't you realize that some of the wealthiest people in this country are dedicated Lautisse collectors?"

Little Mr. Vegaro had been twitching with excitement. Being outnumbered didn't affect his vocal powers. Now he exploded.

"You Widdicome bums!" he cried, facing his competitors. "I know exactly what you're up to. Mr. Gregg, let me speak! These men will take your garden fence to Texas. They have clients in Texas, oil people, *nouveau riche*, incredible jerks, people who'll pay any price that's asked. That's not where this magnificent fence belongs. Me . . . Mr. Gregg, I have a client, one of the most distinguished leaders of industry in this country, a man with his own private gallery attached to his residence in Connecticut. That gallery is big enough for my client to set up your fence as the centerpiece of his whole collection, and there it will stand, surrounded by some of the greatest works of art that exist in this country — including four original paintings by Lautisse. Mr. Gregg, I appeal to you. Two thousand for the fence."

One of the Widdicome men called Mr. Vegaro a lying whippersnapper but I held up my hands and demanded order. By this time my business sense was coming awake. I'm a little ashamed that it took me so long to catch on.

"Gentlemen," I said, "the fence is not for sale. Not at this moment. I need a little time to . . ."

"Three thousand!" broke in the Widdicome bidder.

"Save your breath," I said. "I need some time to think it over. I have a sentimental attachment for that fence. I built it with my own hands. Set the posts myself. Drove every nail and every staple in it. It would be a difficult thing for me to part with it. I'm proud of it."

"Great God Almighty!" exclaimed Mr. Vegaro. "You can build another one! You can build *fifty* fences! Four thousand dollars I offer!"

Four thousand dollars . . . another trip to Europe, this time in style . . . yet I really did want time to think. I told them finally that I'd make my decision in the next few days.

Those next few days were bedlam. We had to have the telephone disconnected — there were calls from Detroit, Indianapolis, Atlanta, Honolulu, Miami Beach, St. Louis, Mexico City. At least another dozen art galleries and museums sent people. By the end of the second day I was being offered twenty-five thousand. The next day fifty. And one weird character arrived in a hired limousine after flying in from California. He had on purple slacks and when he got out of the car he darted his eyes around the premises and then made straight for the tool shed. It turned out that he had been tipped off by a movie mogul that Lautisse had also painted the tool shed. He was making offers for the shed before he ever got to it, and then he discovered that the tip had been phony — the shed hadn't been painted in three years. He was crestfallen, of course, but he began making offers for the garden fence. He wasn't within forty miles of the top bid and I told him so and he finally went away muttering to himself.

By the fourth day I had to ask the local police to put a roadblock at the foot of my driveway because all kinds of wild people were running over the premises — Lautisse fans were beginning to arrive now, and more reporters and cameramen. Then on the fourth day Gerston came sauntering in — Gerston, the sculptor from Chappaqua. He got past the cops because they knew him and he had a big grin on his face as he introduced himself. He went out and sat down on the terrace.

"I've been having so much fun reading about your fence," he said, "that I simply had to come over and visit the scene of the crime. Decided what you're going to do about it?"

I was certainly happy to have somebody from close to home, somebody who knew about art, to talk with. And he convinced me that I should not sell the fence yet — that I should permit the Palmer Museum in New York to exhibit it for a couple of weeks.

"I'm curious to know," he said, "how the public reacts to this thing. I'm wondering if the public is as interested as the gallery people."

Gerston gave me an interesting sidelight to the whole affair. He said one reason the gallery people and their experts were so hopped up was that Lautisse had never, in his active years, used a bit of white paint.

They came up with a big van and a crew of seven men and pulled the fence out by its roots — but oh, so carefully, so tenderly, with much crying out of, "Easy now!" and "Watch that corner!" and "Don't get a scratch on it!" They took it apart at the four corners and hauled it down to New York and set it up in a big room at the Palmer Museum. Two days later they threw the room open to the public and I went down myself to have a look. Hundreds of people swarmed into that museum, and I couldn't help laughing when I saw my fence — *it had a fence around it.*

Gerston phoned me occasionally from New York. He was keeping in close touch with things, and reported that each day the crowds were growing in size. The exhibition was to end on a Saturday and Gerston called that day and asked if I would come in and meet him at the museum on Sunday. He was grinning slyly when I picked him up in the lobby.

"Brace yourself, Gregg," he said, "because you may get a shock in the next few minutes."

He led me to the room where my fence had been exhibited and I *did* get a shock when we walked in. The fence had been wrecked — sawed up into sections — and the sections were standing around the walls of the big room.

"What in the name of . . ." I began.

"Don't get excited," said Gerston. "Please notice that each section is approximately square. Altogether there are thirty sections. Now, come along and let me show you something."

He marched up to one of the fence sections and bent down, pointing at the bottom of the end picket. "Lean down here," he said, "and have a look." I leaned down, and there was a word scrawled in black paint at the lower corner. It took me a few seconds to recognize it. It was the signature of Lautisse.

Gerston stood up and waved his hand over the room. "Every one of the thirty sections," he said, "bears the authentic signature of Lautisse."

"But . . . I don't get it!" I exclaimed. "Why . . . what . . . where is he?"

"Lautisse sailed for home early this morning, laughing," said Gerston. "But late last night he came over here, got down on his hands and knees, and signed each of these thirty panels. Now you've *really* got something to sell."

And indeed I did have. With Gerston's professional guidance, twenty-nine of the thirty sections were sold within a month's time and the average price was ten thousand dollars per section. There were buyers clamoring for the thirtieth section but I didn't want to sell it. It's hanging now over the mantel in our living room, and please believe me when I say I'm sentimentally attached to it.

I was so confused by everything, and so busy during the period in which the fence sections were being sold, that I gave little thought to Lautisse himself, and especially to his motive for signing the sections. But after it was all over, I stopped one day at Gerston's house and we sat down with a couple of drinks and I began talking about Lautisse.

"He was genuinely fond of you and Mrs. Gregg," said Gerston. "He hadn't the faintest notion when he painted your fence that it would bring on all this hullaballoo. But when it did, he was vastly amused. I've never seen him laugh so uproariously. And it was *his* idea to have the fence cut into sections. I went with him that Saturday night and we supervised the job of cutting the sections, and then he got down and signed each one. He simply gurgled with pleasure all the way through the job.

"But," I put in, "it still doesn't make sense. I got the money, he didn't."

"He didn't want any of it," said Gerston. "He wanted you and your wife to have it."

"I don't get it," I said. "We weren't that close to him. After all, we never *did* see him after that one weekend."

"Well," said Gerston, "I'll be truthful with you. I think the old boy's mind is beginning to wander."

Somehow I didn't much like the implication. "What makes you think that?" I asked.

"Oh, just general observation, I guess. For example, I remember that when he was down on all fours signing those fence sections, he stopped at one point and took out his wallet and stared at it without opening it, and I heard him mumbling something to himself . . . and I'll swear to you he was talking about some Senator."

"What Senator?" I asked, straightening in my chair.

"It sounded like 'Breedges,' " said Gerston.

28. *You Know Me Alwyn*

(A Love Story)

I HAD DINNER WITH some friends and then went back to my
hotel with the intention of hitting the sack early. There was
a big newsstand at one side of the lobby and back of the
counter a classy redhead. A real sex wagon. Her skin was as
smooth as a satin muff and she had big eyes that suggested a
childlike innocence until you looked closer and caught that
warm, purplish glow. I tell you I'd have crawled eighteen
miles over broken beer bottles just to . . . but I'm a little
long in the tooth for that sort of thing. I made a total of one
flippant remark and she looked at me as if I belonged in
the pig department out at the stockyards. So I began shop-
ping around for something to read and my eye fell on a
book. It was a reprint of Ring Lardner's *You Know Me Al.*
I had read it back when Coolidge was jigging around in
war bonnets, but now I had an urge to go through it again
— possibly because I was in Chicago, the locale for most of
Jack Keefe's adventures.

I took it over to a corner of the lobby where there was a
battery of comfortable leather chairs and sat down and studied the picture on the cover — a representation of a real slob
ballplayer. I'm the type of baseball fan who is attracted to
the game by the refreshing individuality of the characters
who play it; my rounders heroes have been guys on the order
of Dizzy Dean, Baron Poffenberger, Casey Stengel in his playing days, Art (The Great) Shires, Smead Jolly, Pepper Mar-

tin, and the peerless Babe Herman. Some of these I never saw play, but I know all about their personalities.

Sitting there in the hotel lobby I started reading the letters of Jack Keefe. I had negotiated about six pages when I heard a man's voice nearby.

"Say, Virgil," he called out, "do you think Coker's a schizo?"

I glanced up from my book. Four young men were occupying chairs off to my right. There was something familiar about them and I stared from one to the other and then a valve opened in my head and I got the answer. They were ballplayers. Not only ballplayers, but members of my favorite team, the New York Loons. I knew the Loons were in town playing the Cubs but it hadn't occurred to me that I might bump into any of them.

I had never seen these four in street clothes but I recognized their faces and their haircuts. They were seated in a semicircle and three of them had been reading. Alwyn De-Kalb, the Loon second baseman and the one who had asked the question about Coker, was holding a book in his lap. I could read the title from where I sat and it was something like *You Can Always Tell a Harvard Man Without Trying*. Virgil Wilson, the fence-busting left fielder, had been reading one of those sixty-cent eggheady magazines. Dayton L. Clay, Jr., the first-string catcher, was halfway through a book about the Nigra Question. And RFD Poteet, the rookie pitching sensation from the clay hills of Georgia, was half dozing in his chair, his long chimpanzee arms hanging down and his knuckles resting on the polished floor.

DeKalb, Wilson and Clay were dressed conservatively in business suits but RFD Poteet looked like something that had escaped from the back tent at a carnival. He had on brick-red slacks, a chartreuse sports shirt and a sports jacket that might have been woven by the Navajo Indians when they weren't feeling too well.

I don't believe in eavesdropping on people so I fastened

my eyes on my Lardner book and pretended to read. I didn't miss a word of the conversation that followed.

"Alwyn," said Virgil Wilson, "I make a practice of never trying to apply abnormal psychology to people in baseball. To be perfectly honest with you, I failed that course at USC."

Dayton L. Clay, Jr., now entered the conversation. "We had a professor of psychology at Tulane," he said, "name of Weathersill, one of the most understanding men I've ever known, but I didn't take his course. Sometimes I wish I had."

RFD Poteet had come suddenly awake and was sitting staring from one to the other of his teammates. There was an eager alertness about him, as if he were looking for an opening to get into the conversation. Now he spoke. "Too-lane," he said slowly. "I know whirr that is. N'yawlins. I played ball in N'yawlins two years ago when I was with Nashvul. Th'owed me a two-hitter there oncet."

The three others smiled in his direction and it was easy to detect an air of condescension in their manner. RFD didn't appear to notice it and went right on. "I'd a had a three-hitter out there today if it hadna bin fer that ole bug that flew in my eye in the sixth. Banks he couldna touched me if it hadna bin fer that ole bug. Seems like ever time a bug comes around I be John Dog if he don't fly right straight in my eye when he coulda flode in Banks's eye easy as not. Seems like . . ."

Poteet looked up and saw that his three companions had returned to their reading. I felt a little sorry for him. His fast ball, they say, is as good as Walter Johnson's ever was. He sat there and looked at his teammates and swallowed hard a few times, his big Adam's apple rising and falling. He started to say something further, then thought better of it, and let his knuckles down onto the floor again.

After a while he yawned as big as a rain barrel and then got out of his chair and went strolling off across the lobby.

As soon as he was out of earshot the others put down their reading matter.

"What a character!" said Alwyn DeKalb.

"An absolute natural," agreed Virgil Wilson.

"*Pithecanthropus erectus* in person," said Dayton Clay.

"It's hard to believe," added DeKalb, "that Mother Nature still turns them out like that."

"I feel a little guilty," said Wilson, "sitting here and reading and ignoring him, but I get enough of his talk around the clubhouse. Mind you, I realize he's a rare specimen, a primitive, you might say, but I'm way behind on my reading. Sal McKenzie told me about this article on George Szell and I must say it's a first-rate evaluation of the old boy's genius. I'm beginning to think that Szell comes close to being one of the truly great men of the twentieth century. I mean in the arts, of course."

"Pfaugh!" exclaimed Alwyn DeKalb. "I'll argue that point with you from now till breakfast."

"Okay, okay," said Wilson pleasantly. "I already know how you feel about Bertrand Russell the Nonpareil."

"Please, fellows," spoke up Dayton Clay. "Please don't get started on Bertrand Russell again. But as long as we're on the subject of magazine articles, let me tell you about a brainstorm I've had. I'm thinking about trying my hand at one."

"The Science of the Passed Ball?" suggested DeKalb kiddingly. "Or, Two Years Behind the Plate?"

"Let's not get comical," said Clay. "Jim Brosnan can write about baseball. No, I have something more serious in mind. There's a wonderful quarterly I used to read at Tulane called *American Speech*. I'm going to start taking notes on our provincial friend Poteet. His speech pattern is, in a sense, almost classical. You may have noted certain influences in his enunciation which, I believe, can be traced to the perimeter regions of the Dismal Swamp. And there's a strong overlay of phonetic irregularity that's reminiscent of the Outer Banks.

I think that, with enough research, I could do an essay about him for *American Speech*."

"Sounds like a fun thing," said Virgil Wilson.

"You fellows can give me a hand with it," said Clay. "Anything good you hear from him when I'm not around, jot it down. Anomalous preterites, and past participle forms, and that sort of thing."

DeKalb and Wilson agreed to assist in the collection of material for the catcher's essay. Out of the corner of my eye I saw RFD Poteet, who had been wandering aimlessly around the lobby, now edging his way over toward the newsstand. I got out of my chair and strolled over in the same direction. The alluring redhead — she'd make a man gnaw the knobs right off a dresser drawer — was still back of the counter and I came up behind the rookie pitcher just in time to hear her say: "Maybe you'll learn better than to come out here and fool around with our boy Banks. You must be his cousin or something." She gave him a provocative smile.

"No, honeybunch," said RFD, "I ain't related to him. It jist so happens that one of your dern Chicago bugs flew in my eye and made it wotter and the plate was in a kinda haze. I kin beat them Cubs inny day in the week long as I oney got to play nine min, but what they done out yonder today was to th'ow nine min and a bug at me."

He flung back his head and laughed uproariously, and the redhead laughed right along with him. "RFD," she said, "you are sure a whizzer. I believe you *could* beat the Cubs some day if Banks broke both his legs or something."

"Sweetthing," said RFD, "I would like to refer you to the record book. I have beat the Cubs three times and they have beat me oncet, with a sist from a bug."

The redhead laughed until her eyes were wet. "RFD," she said, "you simply *kill* me."

"I go fer you too, dear," said RFD. "Listen, what time you git offa work?"

"Wooden you like to know?" she answered teasingly.

"Tell you what I'll do," he said. "Next time I face that bum Banks I'll think about how beaudiful you are and then I'll say to myself, 'This here one is fer the redhead,' and then I'll haul off and rare back and strike th' big bum out on three pitched balls. I garrantee it. Jist fer you, Sweetthing."

"You mean you really would?" she said, her big eyes growing even bigger. "You'd remember to do it? You'd think about *me* before you pitched to Ernie?"

"Cross my heart," said RFD, crossing it, "and hope to die. Now, what time you git off?"

"Ten-thirty," she said, "but you got to be in early, don't you?"

"I ain't a relief pitcher," RFD told her. "Le's not fergit I pitched today, except *I* would like to fergit it. There ain't a chance I'll be used tuhmarr, less maybe Coker wants to send me in as a pinch hitter."

"That's a laugh if I ever heard one," said the redhead.

"What's the matter, don't you read the newspapers?" he demanded. "Dint you people out here in the sticks hear about me hittin' that triple offa O'Dell in Frisco? Well, how about it? How about me and you?"

"To tell you the truth, Mister Poteet," she said, affecting formal tones, "I am somewhat flattered. You go over and set down and when you see me closing up this trap, give me a chance to powder my nose and then meet me five minutes later out on the corner."

"Yes sirree bob sir," said RFD, glancing at the lobby clock which showed twenty minutes to ten. "You got any new comic books?"

"Only a few," she said. "Oh, say, wait a sec! One of them's a double-jointed doozie. It's about baseball. Here, let me get it." She went to the far end of the magazine rack and came back with a comic book of the horrifying type. "It's about this guy," she said, "this ballplayer, that's got a grudge against the second baseman, I mean on the other team, and so he puts this deadly poison on his spikes and spikes the second baseman when he slides in, and he drops dead, and then the other fellas on the second baseman's team, they find out about it, and so that night they . . ."

"Whoa!" cried RFD. "Don't tell me how it comes out fer crimenently sake. Lemmy have it."

All this time I had been fooling around the magazine rack, not eavesdropping at all, but now I bought a pack of cigarettes. RFD gave the redhead a big wink and took his horror comic back to his chair, and I returned to mine.

"RFD," I heard Alwyn DeKalb say, "you know very well what the boss said about those comic books. He doesn't want you reading them in public places like this. Why don't you stick it in your pocket and take it up to your room?"

"I'm gonna read it rat here," said RFD, a note of defiance in his voice. "I seen Coker readin' one in public last Thursday night on the train. And anyways, this here one happens to be about baseball. Maybe I'll learn me somethin' out of it."

"In what way is it about baseball?" asked Dayton Clay, glancing up from the Nigra Question book.

"I ain't read it yet," said RFD.

"Well," cautioned DeKalb, "go ahead and read it but you better get rid of it before Coker catches you with it."

So now we all settled down to our reading. It took RFD about twenty minutes to get through the comic book, twenty minutes of alarmed snortings and grunts of astonishment, with an occasional "Whew!" Then he put it down in his lap.

"Great Lord-a-mercy!" he said. "They cut off his head and cut him all up in pieces, arms and legs and all, and they used his cut-off head fer home plate, and his legs and arms fer the bases, and his . . ."

"Please!" cried Virgil Wilson.

"Well, you guys *ast* me what it was about," said RFD.

"I'd rather not hear any more about it," said Wilson.

"Have it yer own way," said RFD, "but this one I'm gonna

keep and read over again." He folded the comic book and put it in his inside pocket. Then he dropped his knuckles to the floor, slouched himself down in his chair, and half closed his eyes. They weren't fully closed, though. I could tell that he was watching the redhead across the lobby. And the clock.

After a while Virgil Wilson yawned and stretched. "Where's McKenzie this evening?" he asked.

"Sal and Everett went over to the Field Museum," said DeKalb. "That Melanesian collection."

"Sometimes," said Wilson, stretching again, "anthropology bores me. Well, I need a good night's rest. Anybody for bed?"

DeKalb and Clay got up and the three men started walking away. After a few steps, DeKalb turned back.

"How about you, Phenom?" he said to RFD.

"Not me," said RFD. "I'm gonna stay up a wholl longer. I go to bed now and I'd have nightmares about that fella they cut all up in pieces."

So they left, and after a few minutes I recalled my own resolve to get some sleep. I got out of my chair and left the field to RFD Poteet. Up in my room I got into bed and finished *You Know Me Al.* I'd like to report that it's just as good as it ever was, although there were moments when I felt that I was reading medieval history rather than American humor.

*

*

*

29. The Woofinwhiffle Excitement

CAME A DAY WHEN I was at work in my study, minding my own business (meddling in the affairs of other men). I was writing a reminiscence of my childhood in the Midwest, and I had reached a point in my narrative where I was discussing the glories of transportation in the horse-and-buggy days, and suddenly, as so often happens, I found myself stuck. There was a word I wanted and I couldn't get it. It wasn't even on the tip of my tongue.

Back yonder, as we senior citizens say, there was a gismo, or hootnanny, that was part of the equipage of almost all horse-drawn vehicles. In a buggy it reposed on the floor, close beside the driver. It was of metal, probably cast iron, and was usually circular in form, about the size of a dinner plate. It was maybe two and a half inches thick and weighed, I should judge, twelve or fifteen pounds. It was employed as a tethering or hitching device to keep a horse from wandering off. The heavy disk had a depression in its center and set into this well was a metal loop or ring. One end of a strap was attached to this ring. Whenever a driver wanted to leave his buggy or wagon for any length of time, he'd drop the metal anchor overboard. Then he'd climb down and snap the other end of the strap onto the horse's bit.

I felt almost positive that this iron instrument had a common name for it was among the commonest of objects in my childhood. I felt equally certain that I had heard that name, many times. I have what is called a good ear for such things, but I couldn't drag this one out of the store-bin of memory. So I went to the books.

My reference library is a good one and I figured it would take three or four minutes for me to find the colloquialism I was after. I tried Roget's *Thesaurus* and *The American Thesaurus of Slang* and some old Sears Roebuck catalogues. No luck. I tried the more recent *American Dictionary of Slang* (in which I am cited as an authority on several vulgar matters not related to the horse or the buggy). I searched the word books and the phrase books and the *Oxford English Dictionary* which comes in thirteen whopping volumes, and H. L. Mencken's bulging works on the American language. I consulted Phil Stong's *Horses and Americans* and prowled through several *fin de siècle* novels. Still nothing. I found hitching post and hitching block and hitching rail and hitching rack — but no word describing my iron platter.

Now, as is customary in cases of this kind, I began lying in bed at night and talking to myself. Not deliriously, but almost. I somehow got the idea that if I groped around, experimenting with letter combinations, I might stumble on the word I sought. Could that doo-dad have been a crufty? No. A flonk? A midger? A grawb? A yopyop? An orpdog?

At last, grown thoroughly angry, I turned to my wife who was raised in a little town in Missouri and sometimes can remember things as they were in medieval days.

"Oh, sure," she said blithely. "That whatchamucallit. It kept the horse from running away. Now, let me see. What *did* we call it?"

She stood around and tapped her foot and pressed a finger to her cheek and came up with nothing, so I told her to get back to her arnin'. Soon after that Margaret Lorini from Mahopac and Marie Michau from Pleasantville came for lunch. My wife asked Margaret if she remembered the name of The Thing, describing its functions briefly.

"Of course," said Mrs. Lorini. "I know exactly what you mean. In New York City the milk wagons always had them. Let me think just a moment. I'm certain they had a name that was short and colorful. It'll come to me in a moment . . ."

It didn't come to her. Marie Michau, a native of South Africa, said that she too knew precisely what we were talking about, that they had these horse-restrainers in her homeland, and that she would be happy to write to Cape Town and get me the name that was used there, but I said never mind, that it would probably turn out to be fusselhasset or goomafroom or dugchumby and I wanted the American name for it. I had a feeling that things were getting a little far afield.

That evening I found that my wife was still bugged by the problem and had telephoned some people named Williams who live a few miles from us and who have a reputation for being horsey. I scolded my wife for this act because I knew the Williamses are racehorse people rather than surrey drivers and the item I had in mind is not in use around racetracks. But she insisted that horsey people probably would know about all things horsey, and Mrs. Williams had promised to call her back. She did, late that night. She said she and her husband and some of their horsey friends had been sitting around wrestling with my problem. They knew the doo-dad, or woofinwhiffle, that I was concerned about, and they had been putting the ends of their fingers together and staring at the ceiling and thinking hard, seeking the word. They had not yet found it.

My wife now phoned another neighbor and old friend, Blanche Barns, who promptly grew vexed with herself because she couldn't get the word off the tip of her tongue, where she said it was. "I've seen a million of the darn things," she said, "and I'll get the answer for you in just a moment." She didn't, so I took over and talked to her husband, Frank, who is about eighty and who grew up on a farm in middle New York State. He, too, had seen a million of them. "It so happens," he told me, "that my own family never used one." I neglected to ask him why and later on *that* became a secondary worry — for what earthly reason did that upstate Barns family carry a grudge against the use of a . . . a . . . a you-know.

Frank Barns got to telling me about how he used to court a certain freckle-faced girl when he was a young fellow, and he went into ecstasies in his description of his buggy and all its glistening accessories, and he said that medical science has proved that freckle-faced girls are much more reliable than girls without freckles, and he quoted Sir William Osler on the subject. I got him back to his buggy and he said it had a patent-leather dashboard, and brass lamps, and the lamps had big red glass rubies set into them, and the shafts were made of ash and varnished, and the harness was a handsome tan color, and his horse was a sorrel named Sal and usually wore a rosette at her ear. Frank could even recall that the top to his rig was of stylish pantasote, but he couldn't remember the name of the do-hickey I was after.

About this time Ira Greer, who brings milk to our house, arrived on the scene (in a truck) and I remembered that he came out of Nebraska and so I asked if he could think of the word for The Thing. "I'll be darned," he said. "Hadn't thought of that . . . that . . . that thing in years. Everybody had 'em. Let me see, now." He pondered a long time. He looks like Raymond Massey and does an impressive job of pondering but this time the results were skimpy. He couldn't think of the name of the diddledywhackus. He went out to his truck and sat behind the wheel a while and then finally drove off, brow furrowed.

A couple of days later Blanche Barns called and said she hadn't been getting any sleep, trying to think of it, and so she was writing to a woman friend in Utica, Ethel Sautter. I can't remember why this lady in Utica was rated as an authority in the field, but she was, and by this time both my wife and I were acting dyspeptic, tossing at night, muttering crazy words. So I remembered our old friend Mister Dick in

Dallas, an antiquarian of sorts, and decided to splurge by telephoning him, and did, and he hemmed and hawed on the phone for a while and then got to talking about whip-sockets and when I finally got him back on the proper track he said that in the Tennessee hills where he grew up he seemed to remember that they called it a stay-put. I had a feeling that Mister Dick had made that one up on the spur of the moment, and asked him to give some more thought to the problem, and he said he would, and just before I hung up he said, "Could it have been a hoss-bobbin?"

Soon after that Mr. Greer arrived again. He said that he had gone to see our town's last surviving blacksmith, who said: "Sure, I know what you mean. I can make you one in no time at all. No, I don't know the name of it. You want one?" Mr. Greer didn't want one, and next went to call on an old guy who used to have a horse-drawn taxi around town. This man took Mr. Greer into his barn and showed him one of the dinguses, authentic and standard, and said that he used it nowadays as a sort of anvil on which he repaired broken tire chains. This old man was a Scot and a classicist; he said that *he* would be inclined to call the thing a hard-hobble, but that in Scotland, as he remembered it, they called it a tether-weight.

Stay-put, hoss-bobbin, hard-hobble, tether-weight . . . none of these words would do. It had to be something catchy in a short, slangy way — a grawb, a crufty, a midger, a yopyop. My wife's mother wrote from Missouri that she had communicated with an old horse trainer who said the term was hitching-iron. Too straightforward and simple for my purposes.

Now Mr. Greer telephoned. "I've made up my mind," he said. "I'm going back to Nebraska on my vacation. I *know* I can find out the name of it and I won't leave Nebraska till I do." I told him I thought that was carrying things a little too distant, and then the thought crossed my mind that maybe

Marie Michau had packed and sailed for South Africa to get the word for me.

A letter came from Ethel Sautter in Utica. She had scouted the antique shops in her area and the best she could do was the simple word "tether." But she recommended that I write to a man named Townsend in Williamsburg, Virginia. This Mr. Townsend, she said, would know the answer if anybody knew it. I called Blanche Barns to let her know I had heard from Mrs. Sautter and she said: "I'd just as soon you had never brought the thing up in the first place. Frank hasn't talked about anything else but that fancy rig he had and that horse Sal, and that frump of a freckle-faced girl he was courting. I'm about to go mad."

Mister Dick telephoned two or three times from Dallas, at his own expense, saying it was a halter-iron, and then changing to ground-frog, and finally suggesting nag-anchor. It was his money. Then a telegram came from Dodge City, Kansas, sent by vacationing Ira Greer, who seemed to be circling Nebraska. The message: "Boot Hill authorities call it Dead Man."

I heard that the horsey Williamses were still sitting around with the ends of their fingers together. Frank Barns was talking about a trip back to the York State county where he used to sit behind his patent-leather dashboard, freckle-faced frump at his side. Mister Dick continued to phone from Dallas, and was having a high old time secretly inventing names for me. Mr. Greer came home empty-handed except for stories of adventures on the Great Plains. I found myself reading in the early novels of Sinclair Lewis and loving them, and digging into other books about the Midwest. Everybody was all wrought up. I ran into an old friend from North Carolina and asked him about it, and he said that down there they simply called it th' arn. But he'd hurry home and dig around for me. I said don't get Harry Golden started and off he went.

I was almost willing to settle for th' arn, but not quite. I decided that the thing to do was to let matters stand. Everybody was having a good time. I didn't really *want* a definitive answer. Things were better just as they were. So, throw out the midger! Cast off the yopyop! And let's all leave well enough alone!

*

*

*

30. Never a Yopyop, Nor Ever a Dugchumby

SUBSTANTIALLY as it stands in the preceding chapter, I wrote out an account of my search for the word, and it appeared in the *Reader's Digest*. The last line of the *Digest* article was an appeal: Don't nobody tell me! And that was the title of the article itself. It has always been true that if you want the public to do a certain thing, advise them not to do it, *order* them not to do it.

It was wintertime back home but I was in the fabulous little town of Papeete, Tahiti, and on a February morning I walked into the office of Dave Cave, a transplanted American who rents automobiles to tourists. Mr. Cave looked up from his desk and said, "Hobble." His copy of the latest *Digest* had just arrived from the States and he had been reading about my search for the name of the hootnanny.

Dave Cave got out his dictionary and showed me that a hobble is "a fetter for an animal" and he grinned in a superior sort of way and said that was it. I knew it wasn't but I refrained from disputing him — I had no awareness of the fantastic things that were happening back home. Hundreds of letters were pouring into my home and into the *Digest* offices a mile down the road. The discussion had fanned out across the United States and into Canada and Mexico and thousands of men and women, most of them past fifty, were making inquiries and prowling through libraries and cross-examining antiquarians and writing letters, all in search of the right word for that old-time horse-holder. In the light of all the excitement it seems a wonder that mass meetings were not called. The Smithsonian Institution, that great storehouse of American memorabilia, became actively involved. And a Mrs. D. M. Shaw of British Columbia wrote: "One half of the continent of North America is asking the other half of the continent, 'You know those things that . . .'"

When I got home from the South Pacific the mail was stacked high in my office. The letters were, in many cases, epic narratives of adventure — stories of screwy experiences of people in search of the word, and stories out of the horse-and-buggy age. Many of the letters were loaded with nostalgic sentiment. The mention of that iron platter had taken people back to a pleasanter era — a time when jets were not crashing to earth, intercontinental ballistic missiles were not poised around the country, women sewed on buttons, people were not being slaughtered wholesale on the highways, good bread was baked in the home and switchblade knives were used for skinning fish. That little article had projected folks back to their youth, and they poured out their tales of the better days.

Some people suggested that a kind of mental telepathy, or extrasensory perception, had been at work — for *they* had been wondering about the word for The Thing at the same time that it was nagging at *my* mind. Some letters told of how the hitching device had shown up on the television show *Gunsmoke* at about the same time my article was published. A character named Doc had thrown one of the iron platters out of his buggy, and immediately the program's producers began getting mail, asking for the name of it. The corresponding vice-president of the program *Gunsmoke* answered these inquiries, saying it was a hitching weight.

Then, too, a great many correspondents advised us that the woofinwhiffle had been mentioned in a story by Barbara

Luther in a recent *Ladies Home Journal*. Miss Luther's fictional people were shown buying a supply of The Things to use in weighting down some helium-filled balloons. She called them horse weights. Other people mentioned the novel *Andersonville* in which the author, MacKinlay Kantor, wrote: "He dropped Molly's block on the ground and snapped the catch against her bridle." A bum sentence, poorly wrote. And a man in Atlanta said the right name was killick — he had read it thus in an old issue of the *Saturday Evening Post*.

From Michigan came halter-hitch and frog. One Kansas correspondent said that in the olden days the thing was called a frog because it was customarily painted green. Yet a woman in Texas insisted that the correct name was hootenanny whoa. She was kind enough to specify that the "whoa" was pronounced "woe."

Mrs. Ethel Hofer of Chicago Heights went to work with great energy, making inquiries all over the land. A harness dealer in Arkansas told her it was a hitching ball and an old man in Sidney, Illinois, said it was a dolly. A lot of people, like Mrs. Hofer, dropped whatever they were doing and set themselves to find the word or die trying. Mrs. Dorothy Scheer of Philadelphia badgered horsey people along the Main Line and including those of the Devon Horse Show. She searched the dictionaries and encyclopedias in a big university library. She had local broadcasters appeal to their listeners for help in the same urgent tones they normally used in asking people during snowstorms to put out something for the birds.

"I consulted harness makers and the cowboy outfitting shops," she wrote me. "I wrote to Midwestern friends, and a professor of rural sociology. A Japanese girl said her father knew the word in Japanese but that she had forgotten it. I asked university professors for help. It seemed odd that we knew the distance to the stars, the gases on the planets, the character of calories and vitamins and the mysteries of outer space, but a simple object existed in the world and we didn't know its name." In the end Mrs. Scheer came up with the correct answer, which we shall get to eventually.

Take also the case of Mrs. May L. Dieckhoff, of Fort Atkinson, Wisconsin, who described herself as a fanatic on antiques and said she had forty-two scrapbooks treating of that subject. "I kept the telephone wires hot," she said, "have written dozens of letters, called our museums, written the Farm and Craft Museum at Cassville, and to the State Historical Society. I've been having a good time."

At random I have picked some of the names that came in the mail: weigh, wait, drop hitch, toe hitch, The Weight, tether stone, hitching pod, clog, tether block, donnegan, hoochie, single weight, hitching iron, hitch dog, bob, quoit (pronounced quote), plug, ground halter, dumbjack, drag, hobbler, oxen-tie, hamper, The Plumb, stump, hitch, knot, plunker, stomper, hitching toggle, lackey, hangstring, swock, jerk.

Several correspondents called attention to the fact that the Amish people of the Pennsylvania Dutch country still travel by buggy and use the thingamajigs and that *they* surely ought to know the name. One correspondent said that the Amish called it a buggy-stopper, another said they call it a tie weight, whereas the truth seems to be they call it *Das Gewicht*. Someone else informed me that he had asked a professional jockey about The Thing, and the jockey had said it was a tie weight. I'm inclined to be somewhat suspicious of a jockey who sets himself up as an authority on horse-restrainers.

The feverish search for the word was given great impetus by several newspaper columnists around the country. An example is Earl E. Buie, top columnist for the San Bernardino *Daily Sun* in California. A man named Louis W. Wright of Big Bear City wrote to Mr. Buie that he had read the *Digest* article and had not been able to sleep nights or hold still daytimes, and would Mr. Buie's readers perhaps know the answer. Mr. Buie asked them, in print. Now *he* began to have sleepless nights — people from all over Southern California, a happy and carefree and well-adjusted lot, began telephoning him night and day, telling him tether rope, buggy hitch, throw weight, clog, tie pad, stand weight, fetter, bridle brake, hold-back, clak, trammel, curb drag, pound, pad, anchor iron, whipple hoppet, hitching hob, snub block. Mr. Buie, himself the son of a blacksmith, said that he could remember the name he called The Thing one morning when he stubbed his toe against it. "But, alas," he wrote, "I know it was the wrong name as my mother, overhearing me, washed it right out of my mouth with lye soap."

Many correspondents went to old mail-order catalogues to get the answer. Others consulted the catalogues of long-gone harness manufacturers. An expert on patents dug into the records and came up with fourteen inventions classified under the general heading of "horse-weights." Senior citizens of St. Petersburg, Florida, wrote that their numerous circles were abuzz for weeks after the article appeared, arguing heatedly over different versions of the name. A horseman in Ohio looked at the animal used to illustrate the *Digest* article and said it was an outrage — "a dray horse with hame harness and no head-check." He said that other horsemen would be so disgusted with this artistic error that they would likely cancel their subscriptions. A man in Massachusetts ignored the basic question and said the things were of no earthly use — "the horse could shake his head up and down as he walked, dragging the weight with him." A man in Oakland was even more original, contending that The Thing *never had a name*. "It was always the driver who dropped it overboard," he said. "He never had to tell a passenger, 'Put out the —.' He did it himself and never told himself to do it out loud. So it didn't need to have a name."

An Iowa correspondent reported having known an old mail carrier who grew too feeble to tote the weight, and took to hooking the strap alone to the horse's bit, and this proved effective. Someone else reported that a horse will stand still out of habit if a mere length of thread is snapped onto his bridle.

A Mr. Hyatt wrote from California that it was a bridle hobble, adding, "Any nut should know that — I should know as I was born in Idaho 30 years too soon." Mr. Hyatt confuses me a little. Another reader in California wrote that I should "take the three words Santa Claus uses most and you will find what's bothering you your own self." I'm still working on that one. Best I can do is "ho-ho-ho." Still another kindly correspondent suggested that if I searched long enough I would find the answer somewhere in Boccaccio's *Decameron.* People are essentially good.

A doctor in McAlester, Oklahoma, said the thing was called a stob and in his region the word was part of a colloquial saying: "Throw out the stob" — meaning cease, halt, desist. A Massachusetts man said he tossed and writhed in bed at night, trying to locate the word, and then one night the fire alarm sounded, and he sat bolt upright in bed and cried out, "The Plug!" Too bad. A San Francisco man said it was called The Pound "because it was shaped like the pound of butter that came from the old-fashioned butter mold." Another man in Honolulu said it was a horse-wait and that "in the winter it was heated, wrapped in a woolen blanket, put under Grandma's feet and referred to as a Carriage Stove." Charles O. Williamson of Montana, author of *Breaking and Training the Stock Horse*, notified us that it was a hitchin' arm.

A registered nurse in San Bernardino suggested that, in producing such a trivial magazine article, I was indulging in "a form of mental exhibitionism" and that, as the British put it, my head wants seeing to. I wrote her that I was worse off than she thought, and that any day I might turn up at her hospital and conduct myself provocatively in her presence.

So at last we came to the answer, and it was disappointing. Don H. Berkebile of the Smithsonian Institution reported that when the article appeared the telephones started ringing in his office. The inquiries precipitated an argument among members of the staff, each of whom had a name to champion. Mr. Berkebile went to work in the spirit of a true antiquarian. He consulted forty-five old catalogues. "The idea never occurred to us," he said, "that since it was a weight for hitching horses, it might just be called a hitching weight."

And so it was called, in his catalogues and in old Sears Roebuck and Montgomery Ward catalogues dating back into the nineteenth century. So it was called in Everett B. Wilson's book, *Vanishing Americana*, as well as in the *Ashley Book of Knots*. So it was called by a majority of the people who wrote to us. Unquestionably it was known by other names in specific geographic localities, but the most widely accepted term was hitching weight, or, more properly, hitchin' weight. Consarned if the *Gunsmoke* people warn't right.

Thus we close the book on hitchin' weights. Some people tried to lure me off onto Bridle Rosettes and Whiffletrees and Hame Guards and Cruppers and Gleason Bits. One woman wrote: "Oh, when are we going to have another game in the *Reader's*? They are such fun!" And the most alarming of all was a note from Carrie Ida Pierce of New Orleans. She said that she knew the true name of the thing but she would not tell it to me unless I helped her out in another direction. *She* wanted to know the name of a gadget, a metal prong on the end of a pole, which was used to turn off the gas-burning chandeliers that hung from the tall ceilings in the long ago.

I don't want to know it. If anybody so much as sends me

a postal card about it, I will call down the Ancient Curse of the Lesser Antilles on him. He will wind up with an assortment of social diseases, stacked one on top of the other, just like planes over Idlewild on a foggy, foggy day.

✳

✳

✳

31. *A Friend in the Slightly Wild West*

EARLY ONE SUMMER MORNING I was wandering around the
lobby of the Blackstone in Chicago, trying to figure some
way of cornering the wheat market without hurting anybody's feelings, when I came face to face with an old friend.
He was dressed for the trail and was wearing a pair of six-
shooters as big as chain saws.

"Come on up to the room," he said. "Dale's up there
autographin' a stack of books and we can have a visit."

The "room" turned out to be an elegant suite. We ordered
up some coffee and sat around and talked and laughed, and
what we talked and laughed about most was the story I'm
about to tell.

A score of years have gurgled down the drain of history
since that July day in 1943 when *Life*, an unbiased magazine
of vigorous opinion, hit the stands with a biographical article on Roy Rogers. The sketch of the "King of the Cowboys"
was written by me and the front cover of the magazine
was devoted to an impressive photograph of Roy astride his
celebrated horse, Trigger. Before we get to the *real* story, let
us have a look at that original magazine article, considerably
abridged:

The manufacture of personalities through a process known as
The Old Build-up has long been one of Hollywood's most noted
contributions to world civilization. No better example of the
hand-tailored human exists today than Roy Rogers, who has

been trumpeted into the splendid title, "King of the Cowboys."

Rogers is a bashful and naïve man in a community of rabid exhibitionists. He is not much given to introspection, yet sometimes the cackle of his chickens awakens him at dawn and he lies in bed and lets a small thought rattle around in his mind. He thinks: "It ain't me."

It ain't him. He is playing a part not only during the hours he spends before the camera. He is under compulsion to play it almost twenty-four hours a day. He has done a good job of it, for he reigns today as Hollywood's top cowboy star — a position which entitles him to something more than a footnote in the encyclopedia of American mythology.

A cowboy, it has been said, is nothing more than a field hand on a horse. Yet since the first blossoming of Buffalo Bill, the cowboy has been an authentic American hero. As pictured today on the screen, he is as far removed from truth as Broadway Rose is from Mrs. Cornelius Vanderbilt. He is the protagonist in the American morality play. He is purity rampant — he never drinks, never smokes, never shoots pool, never spits, and the roughest oath at his command is "shucks!" He never needs a shave, and when it comes to fist-fighting he seldom takes on a single opponent; he beats their brains out in groups. He always wins the girl, though he doesn't kiss her. He kisses his horse. His immense public would have him no other way. [Listen reader — remember that this was written twenty years ago.]

An ordinary Hollywood actor might play the role of a kindly clergyman by day and in the evening get cockeyed and wallop his wife with an extremely rare Sèvres cider jug. Roy Rogers and other cowboy stars must comport themselves in private life with all the propriety attributed to Eagle Scouts. Roy actually doesn't smoke and he never takes a drink in public. On rare occasions, such as when he faces a frightening newspaper interviewer, he'll take a Scotch and soda for the purpose of oiling his larynx.

Rogers landed in motion pictures because he could finger a guitar and sing cowboy songs that cowboys never sing. He can look back on a long string of semi-eminent predecessors, for the history of western pictures is almost the history of the movies. The first of all movie stars was a former vaudeville actor named Max Aronson who changed his name to "Bronco Billy Anderson" and as writer, director, producer and performer turned out one horse opera a week for 376 consecutive weeks. It is worth noting that Mr. Aronson was afraid of horses and woefully inept when mounted on one.

Between Bronco Billy and Roy Rogers a succession of cowboy stars ruled the celluloid range and became American idols. Many of them disliked horses and some were more than a little gun-shy. William S. Hart was a Broadway matinee idol who went West for a vacation and stayed to become mildly immortal. Tom Mix was close to being a real cowboy, having served as a United States deputy marshal in Oklahoma before Hollywood gave him a job worth, in the end, about eight million dollars. He didn't even have to be taught how to shoot a pistol.

Considering his personal background, Roy Rogers has about as much right to play cowboy as has Louis B. Mayer. He grew up on an Ohio pig farm, nursing an ambition to become a dentist. His real name is Leonard Slye and when he first started in pictures he was called Dick Weston. [Leonard Slye sounds more like a true cowboy name than either Dick Weston or Roy Rogers. At the time this *Life* article was published the champion rodeo cowboy was a hearty fellow named Homer Pettigrew.] The Slye farm was at Duck Run, twelve miles north of Portsmouth, Ohio. The future Roy Rogers had a thoroughly rural upbringing. Today he still speaks his native grass-roots language and it has never been necessary for directors to coach him in the lingo associated with movie cowboys. He was saying "git" long before he learned the song about the little dogies. And he was Leonard Slye for his first twenty-five years. Members of his family have difficulty remembering he is now Roy Rogers. Around his house when strangers are visiting they often refer to him as "Leonard I Mean Roy."

At thirty Roy is still essentially a farmer boy, though a trim and handsome one. At his six-acre "ranch" in Encino he spends much of his spare time fussing with his chickens and his pigeons. His literary tastes run to pulp fiction and the funny papers. His first wife bought a bookcase and subscribed to the Book-of-the-Month Club and the shelves are almost filled now. Roy, who is honest in all things, says, "I ain't read a one of 'em."

He much prefers his game of darts. He is adroit in all games involving physical skill. His greatest single talent is the coordination that athletes must have, and in physique he is pretty close to perfection. He's an expert rifle shot but confesses he's less skillful with a pistol. When he goes hunting in the hills he usually employs a bow and arrow and has brought in several bobcats from these expeditions. This hobby once led the Republic Studio publicity men to put out a story describing Roy as part Indian. He says it ain't so. (Originally the publicity department called Roy a native of Cody, Wyoming, whereupon the citizens of proud Cody sent word that they'd better cut it out or there would be bad trouble, mebby even bloodshed. They cut it out.)

Back on the farm Roy was always one of the most expert slingshot artists of his neighborhood. Today he has a dozen homemade slingshots lying around the house. He is deadlier with a slingshot than with a Colt. Last year he was on tour in Oregon when he noticed a certain tree called a vining maple. It attracted his eye because it was full of first-rate slingshot prongs. Throughout the Oregon tour Roy spent his spare hours searching for vining maples and cutting prongs from them. He filled up the rear end of a station wagon with them and now he says he has enough slingshot prongs to last him a lifetime.

He rides a motorcycle to and from work. He hasn't worn "city" clothes in several years. His studio — still vigorously at work creating a fictive personality out of this amiable hay-shaker — demands that he dress as gaudily as possible in order to attract attention to himself in public. At first Roy, the shy country boy, didn't like it. In the beginning he acquired cowboy clothes of conservative color and design. Now he is becoming more accustomed to his job and appears in dazzling regalia.

He gets a thousand fan letters a day and 999 of them are complimentary. The greatest compliment ever paid him, however, may not have reached his ears. Wearing his tight-fitting white cowboy suit one evening at a hotel in Hollywood, he was introduced to one of the screen's most glamorous actresses. As he walked away from her she stared after him, sighed, and remarked:

"There goes the handsomest behind I ever saw in my life."

Thus the significant portions of the *Life* article, with its rather unusual ending. Within a very few years after the appearance of the article, the bashful young man became the top moneymaker among all Hollywood performers. So the question now presents itself: was *Life*'s big splash in any way responsible for Roy's enormous success?

Writers of the Broadway-Hollywood school love to think they are personally responsible for the fame of people about

whom they've written. Frankly, I'd enjoy thinking that I contributed to the success of Roy Rogers. The truth is, however, that my article almost ruined the young man.

Because of that biographical sketch Roy developed a sort of psychosis about his butt. There were times when Art Rush, his personal manager, thought seriously of hog-tying him and hauling him to the psychoanalysts. For two long years after that article appeared, all the people around the famous young man were engaged in a subtle campaign aimed at making him forget about his behind.

Six or seven years afterward I was in the Beverly Hills Hotel and one afternoon Art Rush walked into my room and said:

"That part about the handsome behind — you probably made it up — but if you didn't make it up, would you mind telling me which actress said it?"

"I didn't make it up," I said, and I told him the name of the lady who actually uttered the remark, in my presence.

"I can laugh about it now," said Art, "but let me tell you, there were times when I'd have enjoyed strangling you." And he told me what had happened.

The day in 1943 when that issue of *Life* went on sale, Roy Rogers opened a personal appearance tour at a large theater in Chicago. The management of the theater had a huge blow-up made of the complete article and placed it in the lobby where it all but covered an entire wall. The concluding bit, containing the viewpoint of the anonymous actress, appeared by chance at the eye-level of the customers at the ticket door and most of them read it as they stood in line.

Roy came onstage for his first show, splendidly caparisoned in his finest cowboy costume. He played the guitar and sang a couple of songs. Then he began talking about his horse. He arrived at a long pause in his discourse; before he could resume, a cry came from somewhere back in the auditorium:

"Turn around, Roy!"

A roar of laughter billowed up to the stage, and with it came another cry:

"Turn around, Roy, and leave us see it!"

Keep in mind that Roy Rogers was, at least in those days, perhaps the shyest of all Hollywood stars; the boyish bashfulness that he brought to Hollywood was never a studied pose — it was genuine.

He stood there in the glare of the spotlight and blushed a deep crimson. He was so embarrassed that he couldn't talk. And the cry of "Turn around, Roy!" was taken up by the entire audience. At last he made a halfhearted attempt to sing one more song, struggled through to the end of it, and then made his exit — walking sideways from stage center to the blessed sanctuary of the wings.

The next show was worse. The audience howled incessantly for him to turn around, and the whole routine of his act was disrupted. He couldn't talk and he couldn't sing and, what was worse, he was unable to laugh it off, or even to grin. He simply stood there and suffered while the audience bellowed in chorus: "TURN AROUND, ROY!"

Before that day was over Roy was having tantrums. He wanted to quit, to cancel his tour. They managed to convince him, however, that this was no more than a one-day phenomenon, that by tomorrow the audiences would not be concerned over his hinder parts. But tomorrow came and again it was "Turn around, Roy!" the moment he stepped onstage, and it was "Turn around, Roy!" until he disappeared from view — still walking sideways.

The horror pursued him and taunted him for two solid years. Almost every time he stepped in front of an audience, even in remote, parochial sections of the country (such as New York), someone would sound the cry, and it would be taken up and amplified into a roar.

Roy developed a strong obsession. He made every effort to conceal or disguise the object of all this public adulation. He grew bitter about it.

"They don't wanna see me — Roy Rogers," he'd say. "All they wanna see is my behind. Why the hell don't you just cut it offa me and put it out there on a table and let them look at it?"

He began altering his clothing. The tailor who fashioned all his costumes reported one day to Manager Rush:

"What's got into Roy? He wants me to make his coats longer, so's they almost hang down to his knees. And now he's started telling me to make his pants baggy in the seat. We can't have that — it's against the laws of nature. They got to be tight across the seat. Roy says he wants them to droop. He says he wants his pants made so's they would fit Trigger. I won't do it. It would ruin my reputation."

There were long and bitter conferences on this one matter alone, with everyone trying to convince Roy that he was treating an asset as if it were a liability. He had grown morose about the hateful haunch that Nature had given him. It may even be that he was jealous of it. Sometimes he would speak of it as if it were a ham, bent upon stealing scenes from him, and sometimes he called it names.

It took a lot of doing and some expert help but they finally brought him around and the tailor resumed the production of tight-fitting pants, and Roy wore them. The cries of "Turn around, Roy!" continued and while they embarrassed and infuriated him still, he got so he could force a grin and then quiet the customers down and sing them another song. In time he found that he no longer had to make his exits in the clumsy sidewise manner and then, after two years, conditions returned to normal.

Art Rush told me, in fact, that the overall effect of the experience was probably beneficial.

"Today," he said, "if an audience started yelling 'Turn around, Roy!' I think Roy would probably turn around and let them see it."

That day in the Blackstone we didn't talk much about it.

Instead Roy told me a story about another thing that had happened to him in Chicago along in the early 1950s. He had been out walking on the boulevard, wearing a sky-blue cowboy suit, and people crowded him to the wall, asking for his autograph, wanting to talk to him. Back in his hotel suite he thought about how nice it would be for a change to walk the city streets without being recognized. It had been a dozen years since he'd worn a business suit, but now he called in a haberdasher and ordered one, a plain blue serge, and a pair of black oxfords, and a white shirt and plain necktie, and an ordinary hat. He put all these things on and went for another walk. Nobody gave him a second look. He enjoyed the sensation so much that the next day, when he boarded The Chief for Los Angeles, he was still wearing his civvies. He lounged in the club car and no one recognized him and then, walking through the moving train toward his bedroom, he arrived in a vestibule between cars and came face to face with a man walking in the opposite direction. The two stared at each other and Roy recognized a former resident of Duck Run, Ohio. But before he could say a word, the other man cried out:

"Great God Amighty! Of all people! Leonard Slye! Whirr the hell you been all these years?"

*

*

*

32. Confessions of a Woolgatherer

FOR A WHILE I thought I was getting calcium deposits in the joints of my skull, the way it happens to a ballplayer's elbow. The symptoms were quite disturbing, even a little weird, and I began to have daymares in which the top of my head was being trepanned off. It was a happy moment, therefore, when I found out that I have merely been gathering wool, and that woolgathering is a pursuit that is almost universal among people who lurk about in my age bracket. It is a form of disorientation, sometimes called absent-mindedness, and if practiced within reasonable limits it can be a good thing for humanity.

Woolgathering is by origin an English institution. In bygone days there were people who wandered aimlessly about England's countryside plucking fragments of wool left by sheep as they brushed against fences and bushes. These people were not interested in textile production; nobody knows what they did with the little tufts and wisps of wool, unless perhaps they went around and put them on *other* fences and *other* bushes. Nor were they trying to neaten up the fences and bushes in the interests of a more attractive community. They simply had, in a physical manifestation, what I have in my head. In short, they were nuts.

The English not only originated woolgathering; they have always been most expert in its figurative practice. There are many stories about Englishmen who were accomplished woolgatherers. Not long ago I heard of an aging, aristocratic

Londoner named Mr. Dewhirst who was a guest at a dinner party in the home of a certain Lady Baggley and who found himself seated next to the hostess. During the dinner Mr. Dewhirst's mind began to pluck wool, and he fell under the illusion that the party was being given in *his* home, and that *he* was the host. He turned to Lady Baggley and in a loud voice said, "I'm quite upset about it but, really my dear, this is a wretched dinner." His hostess drew back as if someone had slapped her across the face with a Dover sole. She fixed him with a stare of astonishment but before she could utter a word, Mr. Dewhirst continued, "I must explain that this is the cook's night out and this sickening mess was churned up by the kitchen maid, who deserves to be stoned in public. I'd recommend that you not eat any of it if you value your good health." *

That's as far as the story went. I don't know what happened afterward. I don't want to know and I was not amused, for it brought to mind a series of things that had recently been happening to me.

On two different occasions, within a single week, I locked myself out of my office, leaving both keys inside. Each time I had to shatter a glass panel on the door to get back in. And each time I had to call a carpenter to replace the broken glass. The second time he came I didn't like the way he looked at me.

Along in that same period I picked up the phone and dialed a number. There were half a dozen rings at the other end and then a man answered. During that brief passage of time I forgot who I was calling. I should have been forthright about it and, employing the customary hollow laugh, explained my insane lapse of memory but instead, when he said "Hello," I said, "Who is this I'm calling?" The man

---

* The English language is a marvelously supple, fluid and flexible instrumentality. For the benefit of my younger readers, may I say that "to be stoned in public" does not mean, in this context, what they think it means.

(whoever he was) hesitated in obvious confusion and then finally said, with more than a suggestion of sarcasm, "You're asking me?" I felt trapped and panicky and said, "I must have dialed the wrong number," and then I hung up. The real bad part of it was that I wasted the rest of the day sitting around trying to think who it was I had called, and I never did get the answer. I just *know* it was something very important.

Soon after that a letter came from a local woman asking me to perform a minor service for the committee which she headed. Her letter somehow got shoved under a pile of old Brazilian sheet music on my desk and a month passed and then I found it. I was embarrassed — caught between a rock and a hard place. I decided to make a clean breast of my dereliction. I telephoned the lady and began apologizing to her. I said that I was normally quite punctilious about correspondence but that the painters had been in and upset the place and somebody had strewn Mesopotamian shards all over my office and that I really wasn't the kind of person who . . .

"But," she broke in, "you *did* answer my letter. You wrote a very *gracious* answer."

"Good God!" I exclaimed. "What did I say in it?"

She told me and we got it all straightened out except that by now I was pretty well convinced that my brain was shriveling up like an aged potato. The worry continued to haunt me until that Saturday when my wife and I were invited to spend the afternoon at the home of Dr. Ferdinand Wake. We were going to sit around on the terrace for a few hours and then broil some steaks.

This Dr. Wake is widely considered to be a man of superior intelligence. He's a general practitioner and a fine surgeon and buys books and paints in oils and grows glads and can adjust carburetors and knows a great deal in the way of applied psychology. While he and I were alone on the terrace I decided to tell him about my disintegrating mind

— about locking myself out of my office, about the phone call to nobody, about the unwritten letter that was written. And so I did.

"Ah!" he said with a deprecating wave of the hand, "you shouldn't disturb yourself about that sort of thing. You're just getting a little smooth on the tooth. It's perfectly normal for you to . . . by the way, do you know Judge Glenn?"

I said I knew him only by reputation. He is one of our leading citizens, formerly a county judge, a director in the bank and a public speaker of some eminence.

"The Judge," said Dr. Wake, "is possibly the most absent-minded man I've ever known, and I've known some dandies. He's a woolgatherer in a classic sort of way. I wouldn't be surprised to learn that he was the original of the man who put out the clock and wound the cat."

Dr. Wake now told some stories about this Judge Glenn. One of them concerned the time that Mrs. Glenn went to a luncheon party up on Grove Street. She asked the Judge to pick her up at four o'clock. When the other ladies at the party heard about this arrangement they all laughed fit to kill, and Mrs. Glenn laughed right along with them. They all knew it was a hundred to one that the Judge wouldn't show up; he simply *never could* remember such appointments. The entire company was astonished when, on the dot of four, the Judge drove up in front of the house to collect his wife.

Forty-five minutes later he drove up again, to the same house, rang the doorbell and then announced, "I've come to pick up my wife."

Dr. Wake said that there was an important difference between Judge Glenn's woolgathering and my own.

"Your case," he said, "is a simple one and should give you no concern because *you know* you're getting absent-minded. Judge Glenn doesn't. If you charged him with being absent-minded he'd deny it and probably get sore. If you know you're absent-minded, then you're okay; if you're so far gone in absent-mindedness that you don't know you're absent-minded, then you may be in trouble."

You can't imagine how that bucked me up. And there was more encouragement coming, much more. Dr. Wake was a walking textbook on the subject of absent-mindedness. He gave me examples of woolgathering by some of history's most brilliant men.

G. K. Chesterton, he said, often had to stop at a news stall and buy a copy of his own weekly magazine, G.K.'s, in order to find out where his office was. Chesterton once telegraphed his wife: "Am in Market Harborough. Where ought I to be?"

A similar tale concerned Dwight W. Morrow, once am-

bassador to Mexico and father-in-law to Charles Lindbergh. Mr. Morrow took a train into New York City and on arriving there telephoned his secretary back at his house in the suburbs. "I'm in New York," he said. "Why?" His secretary told him that he was en route to Princeton to deliver an address.

Dr. Wake said that Thomas A. Edison was standing in line one day to pay his taxes. When he arrived at the wicket he found that he had forgotten his own name. He turned to the man next in line and said, "Could you tell me who I am?" The man told him.

These anecdotes almost made me *proud* of my woolgathering. But even greater moral support was in the offing. We sat around for a while longer and then decided to run down to the village and get the afternoon papers. Dr. Wake went into the house to notify the women that we'd be gone ten or fifteen minutes.

In the car the doctor suddenly said:

"There's a lot of it going around."

"A lot of what?" I wanted to know.

"A lot of . . . a lot of . . . what was that we were talking about a while ago?"

"Oh," I said, "you mean woolgathering?"

"That's it," he said. "There's a lot of it going around."

We arrived in the center of town and got the papers and were about to start home when the doctor remembered something.

"She told me," he said, "to pick up . . . now, let me see . . . what the devil was it she wanted?" He stood there on the sidewalk rubbing his chin, concentrating. Finally his face brightened. "Got it!" he said. "Come on around the corner with me a minute."

We walked around to the hardware store and the doctor bought a can of Three-in-One oil. Then we returned to the car and drove back to the house.

Mrs. Wake was out by the fireplace, arranging the cooking tools. Her husband handed her the little paper bag containing the Three-in-One oil. "Here it is, dear," he said.

She opened the bag and looked in it and then glared at him through narrowed eyes.

"I told you," she said, "a quart of butter pecan ice cream."

Me . . . I've never felt better in my life.

＊

＊

＊

33. *A Shot of Adrenalin, Neat*

I RISE TO SPEAK in behalf of flaming, hackle-rousing, toe-curling anger. It is a blessing to humanity. It stimulates you physically by hurling gallons of homemade adrenalin through your body and making it easy for you to lift a horse over a hedge or whip Sonny Liston. Moreover, it is often beneficial in the way it affects your mental processes. Anger, said Francis Bacon, makes dull men witty. And we all know that a wild tantrum, properly timed, can be a good thing for democracy; in the American political credo it is well known that a man enraged at a butter-fingered shortstop is likely to forget all about that scheme he had for bombing the White House.

All this being so, it is pleasant to contemplate the vast number of things that have been put into the world for the purpose of provoking rage and wrath and cold fury in the human breast. And it is almost startling to note that in the area of anger, one man's poison is often another man's meat. A thing that is a luminous vexation to you may not bother me at all. I have a sister who is possessed of an even-tempered attitude toward life, who makes an effort to love all humankind, plus animals, also birds, maybe a worm or two. Yet there is one thing that will throw her into a high swivet. Let someone put milk on the table in the milk bottle, or carton, and she will shudder and clap a hand over her eyes and then maybe scream for someone to take the hateful object away. In passing I would like to say that this sister's normal serenity is not a family trait; I have heard others of the tribe holler like high C on a steam calliope at finding no drop of gin in the house. I myself, however, never grow unconscionably angry. Except perhaps when I hear some idiot remark that Mark Twain said so-and-so about the weather. He didn't say it. Never. Somebody else said it. Mark Twain didn't. He didn't say it. No. Yet I read that he *did* say it, or hear some TV jerk say that he said it, at least once every week of my life. *Goddamn it don't say he said it!* You some kind of an illiterate fink?

For years I have been accumulating little notes concerning the peculiar things that irritate and enrage individual men and women. In the days of the crusading journalists, some of the top columnists managed to stay angry a good part of the time because of some seemingly trivial situation or minor failing on the part of the populace. Franklin P. Adams (FPA) spent years crying out in pain because of certain inconsistencies in the system of numbering houses along the streets of New York. And Lucius Beebe waxed wildly wroth about once a month because of people who walk on the left-hand side of the sidewalk. Dorothy Kilgallen often got scratchy with people who thought W. C. Fields was a funny man; Miss Kilgallen considered his comedy to be "an utter drag." I have a theory that her dislike of Fields was atavistic, that the great comedian reminded her somehow of her own forefathers.

I have read somewhere that a lady named Rachel Peden always suffered deep irritation at the sound of someone eating an apple, but the thing that really gave her the revolving clammydamps was the sound of someone trying to eat an apple *quietly*. And it has been reported out of Seattle that a local fight manager named Deacon Jack Hurley goes into a wary sulk when he encounters a man smoking a pipe. Deacon Hurley has an instinctive dislike for all pipe-smokers and is on record as having said: "Never trust a guy who smokes a pipe. They sit around and look thoughtful but all

the time they're figuring out how they can steal a hot stove."

Unreasonable peevishness? Consider the case of a prominent New York book publisher who lies awake nights muttering curses because of the way English book publishers print the title on the spine of each volume. Whenever a title is printed lengthwise on a book's spine, the English have it begin at the bottom and read upward; in America it begins at the top and runs down. The English say a customer finds it easier, when facing a shelf of books, to cock his head to the left in order to read a title; Americans say poppycock, the human neck knuckles work smoother when the head is cocked to the right. This one publisher is so certain that he is right that he has come to hate almost all Englishmen because of the way they stand on head-cocking. I hear he is growing sickly because of it.

It is said that the late James Agee, a Southern writer of great talent and strong humanitarian instincts, harbored such a hatred of orchids that he had to be led out of their presence lest he flip his lid clean into the next parish. Arthur Godfrey loses his equilibrium and sometimes goes into shock when people, as they often do, mistake the Tahitian hula for the Hawaiian hula. James Street, who was a warm friend of mine for many years and who wrote distinguished historical novels, flew into a rage every time he saw an automobile with a low number or the owner's initials on the license plate. Mr. Street believed this to be the most ridiculous of all human conceits.

These several attitudes of course seem quite childish to my mind — I can't understand how people can let their tempers get out of hand over matters of such small consequence. I myself almost never lose control, although I must admit that I have had to quit going to the legitimate theater because of the rude and unmannerly people who surround me in the audience. They arrive late and walk on me and yammer and elbow me port and starboard and come back late after intermission and cough and hack and snort and snuffle and I would dearly love to rise up from my seat and punch them all in the snoot.

I know a businessman who has developed such a hatred for a certain baseball announcer on television that he, the businessman, has unwittingly lost interest in the fine points of the game itself. He tunes in the ball team that was once his passion and delight, but he spends all his time cursing the announcer, charging him with ignorance, stupidity, mopery and bum English. Because of this deep personal hostility, my friend never knows any longer who hit the key home run or which team won the game.

Most of us are subject to acrimony of this particular kind, and can be bitterly critical of public figures, such as politicians or television performers or authors or newspaper columnists. Yet Robert Ruark, a man with more than his share of violent opinions, reserves his harshest words for pigeons. He is overweeningly proud of the fact that he once kicked a pigeon on the sidewalk in front of St. Patrick's Cathedral in New York. It is difficult for me, with my own sweet disposition, to understand such conniptions, although I must confess that I grow furious whenever I hear people speak of "Somerset Mawn" — a stupidity that occurs more frequently (and in higher circles) than you might suppose. I heard it three times in one session of television's *Today* show.

Oh yes, there is one other detail in the art of living that gives me the frantics. All my adult life I have been bellowing against the cold fact that the strawberries on the bottom of the box are never as good as those on the top of the box. The finest compliment I ever got in my life came from another author who telephoned me one evening and said: "I now consider you to be *the* greatest living American writer, all on the basis of a single page in one of your books. I have reference to your forthright views on strawberries." When I get to going real good on this topic in company my wife will say, "Oh God, he's on strawberries again! He'll ruin the party!" I intend to fight against this hideous thing to my last breath, even though everyone else in the world accepts the fact that underneath those luscious ruby beauties are the rotten ones and the green ones and the runts.

There were many aspects of the national scene that were displeasing to that wise man James Thurber. He nurtured a violent distaste for the gobbledygook language of our politicians and advertising men, but he was also violently scornful of people who employ the indefinite "one" with sickening grammatical exactitude. What could be sillier, asked Mr. Thurber, than to write a lady: "One loves you, and one wonders if you love one." Question mark.

One never can tell just what innocent-seeming things will drive a person to the brink of distraction. There is the case of Dinah Shore, a model of serenity in the most difficult of situations. Miss Shore throws a cat-fit whenever one of the men in the orchestra fails to resolve his seventh. I have no idea what that entails, but it must be a frightful thing to do, or to *not* do. Once at a program rehearsal the music came to an end and I observed that Miss Shore grew suddenly rigid and she spoke a fairly dark oath through her clenched teeth. I asked the man sitting next to me what was bothering her. "Some fool in the orchestra," he said, "didn't resolve his seventh. It is the only thing that can kick her off her rocker."

There is a writer named Richard Wormser in New Mexico who makes a hobby of acquiring inferior novels (of which there is a greater surplus than wheat) and reading them and venting his spleen against all persons connected with their publication. There is nothing exclusive about this sort of conduct, of course, but what is unique in the case of Mr. Wormser is his critical technique. During the Hitler War he spent several years as a forest ranger in the flammable hills of Southern California. He learned to respect and even to revere trees, so much so that today he evaluates bad books in terms of board-feet of lumber wasted in making the pulp for the paper on which the books are printed. Whenever he reads one of these cruddy novels he explodes statistically, something like this: "You realize how many beautiful trees had to be cut down to print this horrible hogwash? I'll tell you. Let's see now. Hundred and twenty thousand hardcover copies . . . two paperback printings of fifty thousand each, two hundred and ninety-five pages, count in the jackets . . ." Here he begins working at a formula of his own devising to convert the literature back into lumber and the lumber back into forest. ". . . it comes to four thousand, eight hundred and ninety second-growth longleaf pine trees cut down so a rabble of fatheads can drool over this tripe. Eeee-gad!" If he is in the mood Mr. Wormser will go on from there, expanding his statistical survey to take in loss of wildlife, percentage of erosion, tons of topsoil sliding into the Colorado River, silt buildup at the mouth of the Mississippi, estimated value of berry bushes destroyed, and dead and wounded among the nation's heroic lumberjacks.

I know a young man in Michigan who closes his eyes tightly and grinds his teeth when he sees another man wearing the collar of his sports shirt outside his jacket. I know a young married matron in North Carolina who becomes furious when she gets a busy signal on the telephone; she considers this to be a personal affront, and blames the party she is calling, and spitefully refuses to try the number later. I know an attractive young woman who cannot bear to have a dance partner look her in the face, insisting that the proper posture is for him to avert his gaze and look beyond her shoulder. If he insists on staring into her face, she stamps on his foot and strikes him off her list.

Perhaps the most querulous person in this whole gallery is a man quite prominent in the entertainment world, a music lover all his life, who *hates the guts of the Budapest String Quartet*. He was formerly fond of the Quartet's music but today he cannot listen to it even on recordings. He believes that all four members of the famous group are hambones without equal anywhere in show business. "It has eaten its way right inside of me," he says. "One look at those four musicians at work and I feel like screaming. I begin clawing at my face and rolling my eyes back in my head. It's the way they wobble and wag and jerk their heads and their torsos. Wholly unnecessary! Uncalled for! Idiotic bobbings and weavings! I tell you, it's not only hammy — it's *cornball!*" He has asked that I not use his name, for fear that he will be waylaid and beaten up, four times in rapid succession.

These people all confuse and bewilder me; I say it again — it is not in my makeup to achieve a wrathful state of mind over such trivial irritants. My father grew livid about men's wrist watches as long as he lived. "A wrist watch," he said, "is for them queer fairies to wear." My wife cannot abide men who wear rings on their fingers, and distrusts them the same way Deacon Jack Hurley distrusts all pipe-smokers. I am not like that. Never. On the rare occasions when I do grow fretful, there is always sweet reason and pellucid logic behind it. In the summertime there are many roadside markets operating in my neighborhood, dealing in fresh fruits and vegetables and especially fresh-picked sweet corn. The women shoppers stand at the corn tables and boldly and wastefully rip open the ears, one after another, inspecting and then discarding. This infuriates me — it is an act of insolence, discourtesy, plain female villainy and gross selfishness. I have got into the habit of going to these roadside stands two or three times a week and buying corn, which I never tear open, just so that I can glare angrily at the women rippers. The dirty frumps! It has become a sort of compulsion with me, to stand and glare malevolently at them through slitted eyes, just to let them know that I consider them to be uncivilized and beastly. I can stand and glare for half an hour at a stretch, and it does something for my inner being. My wife says the women rippers actually pay no attention to me and that if they happen to notice me at all, they simply conclude that I am having stomach cramps. My wife also says that I am behaving in a most unreasonable manner. She has called my attention to the fact that during a courtroom drama on television recently, a woman got on the witness stand and was asked what business she was in, and she said she was a housewife. "Housewife hell!" I growled. "You're a – – – – corn-ripper." The consequence of my glaring campaign is that I buy much more sweet corn than I should; since I started doing my glaring on a steady schedule I have been eating more corn than an Illinois hog. Up twenty pounds.

In the matter of the corn-rippers I do not consider that I am in a class with the rather shortsighted people I have been telling about. I feel that I have been doing a public service. In minor situations I always manage to keep a checkrein on my emotions. Well, there may be one small exception. If someone puts a roll of paper on backwards (they do it in hotels and hospitals and the homes of the mighty) so that I have to reach under and behind to get hold of the end, I am likely to howl like an elephant with an impacted wisdom tusk and then rip the whole assembly off the wall. *Mercy! Is there no intelligence anywhere in this world?*

*

*

*

34. *The Habit Habit*

The American philosopher William James is often cited as one of the world's chief authorities on human habits. The plasticity of the living matter of our nervous systems, he said, is the reason we have habits and insofar as habit is concerned, the physiological study of mental conditions still remains on the whole the most powerful ally of hortatory ethics. I do not say that this is Neo-Pragmatic nugacity, but I do not say it ain't. I just want it on the record that I am not *in the habit* of being talked to in that tone of voice.

My own approach to habits involves not thinking, but transcendental eclecticism and crepe-soled shoes, and I have not permitted hortatory ethics to hinder my explorations one whit. As for a conclusion, the only one I've been able to reach is that human habit is closely related to absent-mindedness, invincible obstinance, and the behavior of milch cows and mule groups.

An old story tells of a grocer who was working on his income tax return one evening in his home. He was toiling away with pencil and paper, trying to cope with arithmetic that refused to come out right. Then a thought struck him and he called his young son. "Run down to the store," he said, "and get me half a dozen no. 14 paper bags." The boy did so and returned with the bags, and the grocer went to work at his figuring on those bags and soon had his tax return completed.

The man who delivers the mail on the rural route where

I live is Sidney Bush, an expatriate Nebraskan related in spirit to that grocer. He drives many miles each day sitting over toward the right-hand door of his car, because all the mailboxes are on the right-hand side of the road. He reaches across and steers the car with his left hand, operates footbrake and accelerator with his left foot, and all day long he never gets squarely behind the wheel. He has told me that after years of this unorthodox kind of driving, he finds it very clumsy and uncomfortable to sit in the driver's seat. When he goes off on long auto trips during vacation he sometimes stops the car and has his wife get into the back seat so he can shove over and drive in his accustomed manner. I asked him why he and other rural carriers don't get themselves English cars. Because, he said, sitting behind a steering wheel restricts and hampers his arm movements and his day consists of one arm movement right after another.

Day laborers and gardeners work around my place from time to time and I have always noted that they are shy about asking for drinking water. Every one of them prefers to drink from the garden hose. This practice always has disturbed me, possibly because of an old Midwestern folkyammer which held that it is dangerous to drink from a garden hose — you are likely to swallow a snake. Not a large snake, but one big enough to be unpleasant. In any case, I always try to entice the workmen away from the hose by fixing up pitchers of ice water, or jars and jugs of it, for them to take into the woods or the meadows. They will not drink from these vessels. They'll hide them behind a tree and when they get thirsty they'll head for the house and that sparkling, delectable hose water. When I recall that grocer with his paper bags, and Sidney Bush in his car, I sometimes visualize one of these workmen at home, having dinner with his family. Mom and the kids all have glasses of water beside their plates; but the master has a garden hose, running in through a window, and that is what he drinks from during his meal. I've even dreamed of this same workman becoming a wealthy contractor, sitting beside his kidney-shaped swimming pool, a straight rye in his right hand and, in his left, a garden hose for chasers.

The effect of habit on human behavior can often lead to acute embarrassment. Among the most famous legends of New York journalism is a story about a star reporter on one of the old Park Row newspapers, say the *World*. This reporter got into a quarrel with his boss and was fired. He was immediately taken on the staff of the rival *Herald* and told to report for work there on the morrow. On his way to his new job next day he ran into a terrific story, the greatest scoop of his life. When he had all his information he headed for his office. Out of habit, however, he went to his old paper, the *World*, made his way in deep thought to the desk he formerly used, and set to work. The editors and other wage-slaves in the city room quickly caught on to what was happening, and the suspenseful part of the story concerned their efforts to avoid disturbing the guy as he wrote sheet after sheet of his great scoop. I can't remember how the story ended, or even who wrote it; it was by Richard Harding Davis or William James or Truman Capote or somebody on that order.

Consider, too, the case of Bruce Edwards, who was a catcher for the old Brooklyn Dodgers. Mr. Edwards had been a fine catcher all his playing years, and then one day the Dodgers found themselves shy a third baseman. Mr. Edwards, a versatile athlete, was sent out to play third. On the first day of his new assignment, a high pop fly was lifted into the air just outside the third base line. Mr. Edwards, his eyes following the towering foul, instinctively grabbed at his face and almost tore his nose off — it had long been his habit, of course, to rip off his mask before going after such a pop-up. He was represented as being somewhat embarrassed.

An interesting aspect of the habit habit is sometimes observable in the manner by which people respond to a greeting that hasn't yet been spoken. I've done it myself. I encounter an old friend on the street and I sing out, "Fine!" before he has a chance to say, "How are you?" I remember a man who shouted, on December 24th, "Same to you!" before I could say "Merry Christmas!" And once I said, "So do you!" before a friend had a chance to greet me with, "You look wonderful!" I *knew* he was going to say it, and he did. That was the day when I looked wonderful.

These little things can be mildly embarrassing but nothing to the contretemps experienced by a young man not long ago in Ukiah, California. He took his best girl to a dance and they had a splendid time. Later he escorted her to his car and drove her to her home. After he had kissed her goodnight he was surprised that she made no move to get out of the car. Then it came back to him — he had been married to her for two weeks. It is my considered judgment that he may have had a short beer at that dance.

As in every other department of life, there is a negative aspect to habit. Recently I read that Tallulah Bankhead is unable to sleep unless a radio is going in her bedroom. If the radio suddenly stops, she wakes up. This puts me in mind of a sketch on the old Fred Allen radio show. A man and his wife lived in a New York tenement, their bedroom window looking out on the tracks of the Sixth Avenue El. It was their custom to hit the sack at midnight every night. The last train rumbled and clattered by at 1 A.M., no more than twenty feet from where they were sleeping. That last train never disturbed them, never woke them up. Then the Sixth Avenue El was discontinued and on the first night when its trains were no longer running, the man and his wife went to sleep at their usual time. Exactly at 1 o'clock, when nothing happened, the man leaped wildly awake and cried out: "WHAT WAS THAT?"

We all know about Pavlov's salivating dogs. Trailing along in Pavlov's footsteps I am able to show you that you should never be ashamed of strong habits — they are as integral a part of nature as the growth and spread of chickweed, buck-thorn and yarrow. Animals, in fact, are in the grip of habit to an even greater degree than people. I have three case histories to illustrate this.

MULES: In the desert town of Mojave, western terminus for the old-time twenty-mule-team borax wagons, it was a recognized fact of life that the mule skinners who drove the teams were unequaled anywhere on earth for the violence of their language. They habitually spoke to their mules in loud and firm tones, using words not even known to contemporary novelists. One day an itinerant evangelist came to Mojave and during his brief stay converted the most inflammatory of the cussers. The next day this subdued skinner mounted his wagon and stared out across the rumps of his mules and wondered what he should say to them as a signal for them to proceed. Finally he tried "Git ep!" The mules stood like statues. He said "Git ep!" again. Another long pause and then all twenty mules turned their heads in unison and looked back, to see if the end of the profane world were at hand.

COWS: O. P. Becker of Lake Worth, Florida, enjoys telling of a cow owned by his family when he was a boy. Mr. Becker's brother, Bill, was studying catechism at church and it was his custom to practice reciting the Creed and the Lord's Prayer while he was milking the cow each morning and again each evening. One day the boy got it all memorized and was accepted into church membership and there was no further need for rehearsal. That evening he began milking the cow in silence. She promptly went into cyclonic rebellion, leaping and kicking at him and refusing to yield up a drop of the old unpasteurized. It was necessary from then on for Bill to recite those prayers twice daily in order to achieve milk.

CHICKENS: Abe Lincoln used to tell about how his father was always looking for a better cabin a bit farther up the trail, and so the family was forever packing up and moving. The Lincoln chickens got so they could sense when moving

day had come round again. Those chickens would take note of certain activities in and around the cabin; then they'd all go over to the wagon, lie down on their backs and stick their legs up, ready to be tied.

Writers, of whom I am one of which, have always been famous for the strange habits they get into. The great Joseph Conrad, in conversation with his guests at dinner, had an unfortunate habit of rolling bread into little balls and then, using his thumb, flipping the pellets indiscriminately around the room. Mrs. Conrad wanted to break him of this mannerism and told him that whenever he began flipping bread she'd call his attention to it surreptitiously by saying, "Joseph, pass the molasses," or some such thing. At the next dinner Conrad began flipping pellets as if he were a Gatling bread-gun, and Mrs. Conrad called for the molasses, and the high-strung novelist cried out, "Get it yourself and quit interrupting me!" Joseph Conrad was more than a great writer; he was a great human being.

When engaged in their lonely work writers can sometimes appear to be quite daft. Gautier was unable to compose a sensible paragraph without a cat or two in his lap. Disraeli couldn't write a lick unless he was in full evening dress — he seemed to think his style influenced his style. Alfred de Musset, when he felt poetry coming on, had an elaborate supper for two served in his suite — the extra plate being

for Erato, the muse of passionate verse. Dumas the Elder, while writing, puffed at a cigar through his nostril. Before Coleridge started to write anything, he put all his money into his hat and then put his hat on his head. These are people out of my own profession, yet I don't seem to be afflicted with any special eccentricities during periods when I am writing, except that I cannot produce a line of intelligible prose unless I keep my thumb stuck in my right ear.

As a concluding example of the strong pull that habit can exert, let us consider the case of John Barta, New York City truck driver. He was on his way to a certain business address in Manhattan and on arriving at the street entrance, observed that it was marked one-way against him. He proceeded along one more block and circled around so he could come in from the other end. He *did* come in from the other end and was within a few yards of his destination when he suddenly realized that he was on foot.

That's habit. And what does it all signify? As old William James construed it, consciousness is essentially active, selective, interested and teleological. His devoted followers are not going to be happy about it, but in the light of all the foregoing evidence, I am simply unable to go along with him.

Essay completed. Thumb out.

*

*

*

35. *I Am a Hero . . . In Bed*

IN THE TIME OF MY BOYHOOD I can remember that people talked a lot about their dreams. Children and grownups alike told each other about their sleep-wrought fancies and usually their narratives were so weird and so cockeyed that they provoked gales of laughter. Then came Freud and a long period of silence on the subject. People quit discussing their dreams because they had heard there was something unwholesome about the business of dreaming. During all those years I personally dreamed some gassers, but I kept my mouth shut about them — I didn't want anybody *interpreting* them and finding out about my warped personality.

For some reason that I cannot fathom (we have either grown up or grown down) people are once again telling what happened in their sleep last night, and laughing about it. At a party the other evening I narrated a dream in which a strange thing happened to me at the Tomb of the Various Unknown Soldiers and when I had finished everybody laughed and nobody said anything about my tensions and anxieties and emotional conflicts and suppressed wantonness.

I'm glad the change has come because I have stored up a whole sequence of particular dreams that I have been keeping to myself for years. The job of holding them back, of never mentioning them to anybody, has been so nerve-wracking that at times I've felt I would crack under the strain. Now that I feel free to unload them, I'm certain that I'll be getting some kind of psychic relief without paying anybody for it. Then too substantial dreaming is a good thing for a writer. Not long ago I had a letter from a woman in Raleigh, North Carolina, who told me about a dream she had, a dream which clearly qualifies her for a career in literature. There were two scenes in her dream. The first was in a fashionable crematory where she was being reduced to ashes. (This is not the part that qualifies her for authorship.) Then came Scene Two: her husband was standing in the living room, letting her ashes slowly sift through his fingers, and saying in a sad tone of voice, "This is all that's left of all that beer she drank."

Among the classics of modern dream literature is a short story, or sketch, which can be read in four or five minutes. It is *The Secret Life of Walter Mitty* by James Thurber and already it has been reprinted in a score or more anthologies. I, for one, return to it again and again and always with great delight; yet whenever I reread it there is always just a slight feeling of disappointment.

The five heroic adventures in Walter Mitty's daydreams are these: (1) He is commander of a huge eight-engined Navy hydroplane heading fearlessly into a raging hurricane; (2) he is Dr. Mitty, the great surgeon, called in at a critical moment to operate on the millionaire banker, Wellington McMillan; (3) he is Walter Mitty, the world's greatest pistol shot, confronting a hostile District Attorney from the witness chair; (4) he is Captain Mitty, flying the big bomber alone to destroy the enemy ammunition dump; and (5) he is Walter Mitty, facing the firing squad with chin up, disdaining the handkerchief, flipping away his final cigarette with consummate contempt.

It is all quite beautiful, but there is something missing. I don't see how Walter Mitty could be considered a complete Walter Mitty without at least one venture into the world of sports. I say this because of my own vast experience in the area of twilight fancy. Some of my splendid athletic exploits take place in daydreams but most of them come to me when I'm in bed, just beginning to drowse off. I have scored more touchdowns against Notre Dame than all the people who ever played for Army. I play halfback for Defiance College against Notre Dame and we have never lost to the South Benders, largely owing to my brilliant running and passing. The reason I play with Defiance is that I lived in that town as a boy and sometimes watched the local college team play. They were not ept. But they are plenty ept when I am wearing their uniform.

I am five feet nine and weigh one hundred and sixty and am in my middle fifties, but I'm a phenomenal specimen for all that. Please remember, it's us little guys who furnish the real thrills in sports. I have pitched many a major league ball game although the managers, because of my age, often plead with me to be content with relief work. This is ridiculous, for I never fail and I never falter — except maybe as a ruse. During one period when I was a starting pitcher my contract specified that I was not to be bothered with signals, not even from my catcher. In one game I deliberately walked three men to get at Mantle and Maris and my manager, in the dugout, remarked somewhat nervously, "Well, I s'pose he knows what he's doin'." I did.

Usually, however, I'm celebrated for my hitting. They play me in right field and I'm not too handy at catching fly balls, but at the plate they can't get me out. I'm not a long-ball hitter. I have a knack of whacking them just over the heads of the infielders and I do it *every time I come to bat*. That is, unless they walk me. Sometimes they try a special Smith Shift, moving the infielders out and the outfielders in so that they are all congregated in the area where my hits usually fall. When they do that I smile contemptuously and rap one on the ground just out of reach of the pitcher — plenty good enough for a single, and there's always a man on third. I have never been at bat without a man on third and two out.

Once I won the Kentucky Derby. Not as a horse, but as a

jockey. I was, in fact, the dark jockey of the race. The owners of a horse named Gallant Rabbit called me in secretly
after announcing in the press that Eddie Arcaro would be
their rider. Nobody knew that I would be up on Gallant
Rabbit until the horses came on the track. Thirty thousand
gasps arose from the immense throng. "Who is it?" they
cried. "Who's that on th' Rabbit?" Then a sports writer of my
acquaintance recognized me and cried, "My God, it's H. Allen Smith! Have the Wheelers took leave of their senses?"
Little did he know! I let the Rabbit lay back in seventeenth
place, swung wide at the head of the stretch and then began
talking to him, using that marvelously resonant voice of
mine, the same voice I use on movie actresses, coaxing him
on, and we nipped the favorite at the wire. Paid $76.20 for a
two-dollar ticket, and while I was pleased with my performance, my thighs ached something awful, for I had never
ridden a horse before.

I well remember the night I broke the four-minute mile,
long before the time of Roger Bannister and the others. It
was in the Garden and I was a late entry, having got into
the thing on a dare flung at me by Rita Hayworth. The
crowd tittered when I came onto the track for my brief warm-
up. I suppose I looked rather awkward, being pigeon-toed. In
the early stages of that race there was nothing in my performance to suggest what was coming. I made my move in
the last quarter-mile and was actually sprinting in the final
lap, passing everything in sight. At the finish line, with other
runners throwing their heads back and flailing their arms
and collapsing all around me, I calmly extracted a cigarette
from my hip pocket, took a few puffs on it, inhaled deeply
defying carcinoma, and then did a brisk additional turn
around the track in order to get my pores closed. It was a
sensational evening — the first time in recorded history that
the four-minute mile had been broken. Frankie Sinatra's
Humility Corps carried me from the arena on their shoulders.

On another occasion I won the Memorial Day race at Indianapolis in a car which I built myself in my back yard. I covered the last two laps without a tire on the rear left wheel and with flames spurting out from around the dashboard clock. Don't try to tell me that racing cars never have dashboard clocks. Mine did.

In golf my specialty is putting. I drive accurately but my tee-shots are not as long as those of my opponents, such as Arnold Palmer and Jack Nicklaus and Stanley Halle. Yet I'm always on the green by three at the outside and I've never been known to miss a putt once I'm *in sight of the cup*. After I won the National Open at Augusta (Eisenhower applauded until his hands were raw) I got a wire from Bing Crosby and Bob Hope offering me two hundred thousand dollars if I'd come out to California and spend one week teaching them how to putt. Unhappily I had to reply: "Sorry fellas but money can't buy the kind of talent I got."

As far as I can remember I've only gone fishing once in my drowsy reveries. We were aboard a cabin cruiser in the Florida Keys. I didn't care a damn about fishing; I had gone along with these two fellows just for the laughs. My two friends were having no luck at all so I dropped a line into the water. Within five minutes I had hooked a one-hundred-and-thirty-six-pound sailfish and I fought him for seven and a half hours. My friends stood by, shouting advice at me until I finally told them: "Please! I'd rather do it *my* way!" After the big fish had been brought to guff, or goff, or whatever it is, I lit a cigarette nonchalantly in spite of the fact that I don't smoke and said, "Throw him back in. He has a right to life, the same as you and me." My two friends were so astonished by this display of compassion that Hemingway said he would autograph all of his books for me and there on the spot Godfrey elected me one of his friends.

What I consider my most thrilling exploit came as a consequence of an interesting wager. I was dining tête-à-tête with Eleanor Holm in a small intimate Manhattan restaurant. We talked chitchat for a while and then Eleanor said, "It's a shame that you've never gone in for aquatic sports."

"My dear," I said, lighting a cigarette, "how would you like to see me dive off the George Washington Bridge — two hundred and fifty feet above mean high water — with my shoes on?"

"Pshaw!" exclaimed Eleanor, using another word. "No person in his right mind would attempt such a thing. I'll bet you anything you can't do it — I'll bet you a month's alimony."

I gave her my world-weary smile and murmured, "Done and done." I took a deep drag on my cigarette, summoned the waiter and said in a soft untroubled voice. "Please have my lavender-colored T-bird convertible with air conditioning in it brought round."

At the bridge I mounted the rail, wearing only my glossy black nylon shorts given to me at Christmastide by Carol Burnett, and with my shoes and socks still on. Eleanor stood nearby, but by now alarm was written on her face, for she had been in love with me since 1929. She pleaded with me to forget about the wager. I pretended not to hear her and suddenly I leaped outward in a graceful arc and then shot downward through the darkling crepuscular void. About a hundred feet above the water I gave my body the secret Acapulco twist. It is a thing I perfected one evening at Acapulco when, to please Dolores Del Rio, I dove off the Quebrada cliffs at El Mirador. The twist starts my body spinning like a bullet fired from a rifle and I continue spinning until I cleave the water.

That was a good one, the dive for Eleanor. There have been many good ones — as good as any Walter Mitty ever experienced. I don't think I go too far. I must confess that I've done little in the way of boxing. In fact I've only been in the boxing ring once: the time I humiliated Dempsey in a special match in which he boxed and I used judo.

I want to emphasize the fact that in these adventures I am always sensible, always completely logical. Therefore I don't want any psychoanalysts examining these paragraphs and telling me that I need help. I warn them: I'm a swordsman without a peer in the land. I mean when I'm lying down.